INSIDERS' GUIDE®

OFF THE BEATEN PATH

D0005612

Off the
Beaten Path®

SEVENTH EDITION

massachusetts

A GUIDE TO UNIQUE PLACES

BARBARA RADCLIFFE ROGERS
AND STILLMAN ROGERS

with Pat Mandell
and Juliette Rogers

Comsewogue Public Library
170 Terryville Road
Port Jefferson Station, NY 11776

INSIDERS' GUIDE®

GUILFORD, CONNECTICUT
AN IMPRINT OF THE GLOBE PEQUOT PRESS

The prices, rates, and hours listed in this guidebook were confirmed at press time. We recommend, however, that you call establishments to obtain current information before traveling.

To buy books in quantity for corporate use or incentives, call **(800) 962–0973** or e-mail **premiums@GlobePequot.com**.

INSIDERS' GUIDE®

Copyright © 1992, 1996, 1999, 2001, 2003, 2005, 2007 Morris Book Publishing, LLC

All rights reserved. No part of this book may be reproduced or transmitted in any form by any means, electronic or mechanical, including photocopying and recording, or by any information storage and retrieval system, except as may be expressly permitted by the 1976 Copyright Act or by the publisher. Requests for permission should be made in writing to The Globe Pequot Press, P.O. Box 480, Guilford, Connecticut 06437.

Insiders' Guide and Off the Beaten Path are registered trademarks of Morris Book Publishing, LLC.

Text design by Linda R. Loiewski
Maps by Equator Graphics © Morris Book Publishing, LLC
Illustrations by Carole Drong
Spot photography throughout © Jon Arnold Images/Alamy

ISSN 1542-1775
ISBN 978-0-7627-4419-0

Manufactured in the United States of America
Seventh Edition/First Printing

For Tom and Joan Bross, good friends
and respected colleagues

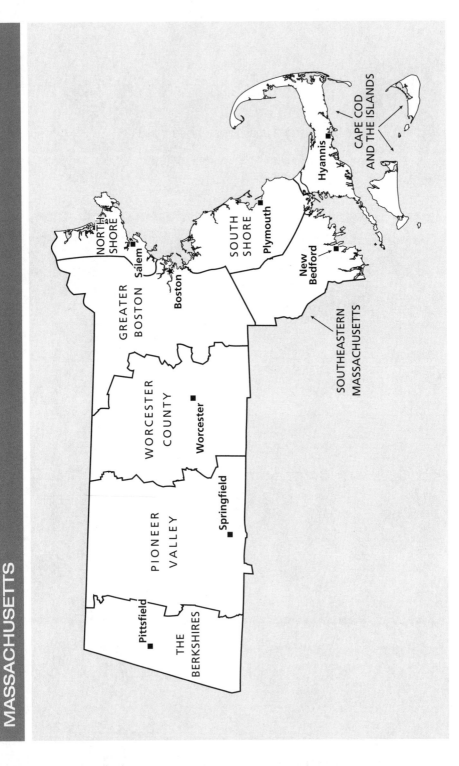

MASSACHUSETTS

Contents

Introduction

Almost the entire state of Massachusetts is off the beaten path, quietly waiting to be discovered. It's true that Massachusetts is New England's most populous state and its most densely settled one. And yes, Boston, Cape Cod, and the Berkshires are among New England's favorite tourist destinations.

But outside these tourist centers, the whole state is off the beaten path. If you've never visited the southern Berkshires, you'll discover a world of farmland and forests little touched by time. A wide swath of Massachusetts—Worcester County and the Pioneer Valley—is virtually unknown except to locals.

Even in downtown Boston, New England's largest city, there are little-known places where the tourists don't go. Stop to listen to the bells at the Church of the Advent, one of only fifteen places in America where you can hear change-ringing bells. Find out why you should visit Boston's tiny Chinatown. Walk along the nation's first Women's Heritage Trail, or visit Castle Island, where the discovery of a long-concealed murder inspired Edgar Allan Poe to write *The Cask of Amontillado*.

justthefacts, ma'am

Population: 6,398,743, U.S. Census Bureau 2005 estimate

Nickname: The Bay State

Capital: Boston, which is also New England's largest city

Area: 8,257 square miles

Highest elevation: Mt. Greylock (3,491 feet)

Miles of Atlantic coast: 192

Miles of shoreline: 1,519

Major airport: Logan International Airport (3 miles from downtown Boston)

And Boston is just the beginning of the journey. This book covers eight regions, from the Cape to the Berkshires, highlighting almost 200 attractions in detail. The choices were often arbitrary, because there are actually hundreds more. But making those choices was a lot of fun; you never can tell when straying down a back road will lead you to a Native American burial ground or the country's only museum devoted to plastic. In truth, this book barely scratches the surface of the off-the-beaten-path possibilities in this state. Think of it as a taste of the best.

Massachusetts's best includes unique scenic wonders, from glacial potholes big enough to swim in to a bridge that nature made out of marble. You can spend the night in a lighthouse on a windswept island off Cape Cod or visit a reservation where sixty-five varieties of holly grow. While we'd like to be able to tell you that the free map given out by the Commonwealth will show you the way to places in this book, it won't. First, the map's not very good, and second, a lot of places in this book are so off the beaten path that the roads aren't on most road maps. To really get into the back country of this state, we suggest The Massachusetts Atlas, published by DeLorme Mapping Company, P.O. Box 298, Freeport, ME 04032; (207) 865–4171; www.delorme.com. Easy to read, and marked to show the location of such things as boat launches, natural attractions, and covered bridges, these map books—there is one for each state—are invaluable. You can find them in bookstores or anywhere that maps are sold. We never travel without them.

what'sup?

Most newspapers run weekly entertainment guides or at least a weekly calendar of events. Many also print special summer activity supplements, which feature local activities and attractions. In Boston, look for the *Phoenix* for alternative and arts events, and to the daily newspapers, the *Boston Globe* and the *Boston Herald*. The *Martha's Vineyard Times,* the *Springfield Republican,* the *Cape Cod Times*, the *Worcester Telegram and Gazette,* and *The Berkshire Eagle* cover their respective areas.

This book will help you discover man-made wonders like the Bridge of Flowers, mansions of sea captains and Victorian eccentrics, and the longest wooden bridge on the East Coast. American history has its deepest roots in Massachusetts. You'll visit the homes of John Adams, Daniel Webster, and John Alden. You'll also meet some distinctly lesser-known historic personages, such as "the witch of Wall Street" and "the Copper King."

You will tour museums devoted to everything from the legendary Tom Thumb to dolls, shipbuilding, and Shakers. At farms and orchards, you'll sample Massachusetts's largesse: chèvre cheese, maple syrup, cider, and cranberry wine, to name just a few.

Revel in the quirky place and the oddball attraction, too: a house made entirely of newsprint and the country's only vintage plumbing museum.

Massachusetts is where you'll find the country's oldest continuously operating museum and its oldest continually operating church, the oldest art festival, and the longest-running carillon-concert series in North America.

This state's beaches and parks are some of its most interesting places. Follow the hidden barrier beach on Nantucket, reachable only by four-wheel drive, or visit the North Shore park that was once a wealthy estate and still has its carriage trails through rhododendron and laurel.

Some of Massachusetts's best-kept secrets are off-season delights, such as wintertime packages at a luxurious Berkshires inn, or visits to an Old Sturbridge Village clad in snow. Even its shops are an adventure: On Cape Cod there's an entire store for bird-watchers, and in Winchendon you can buy furniture direct from the factories.

When you're hungry, stop in at a nineteenth-century ice-cream parlor that still makes egg creams, a tearoom serving scones and cream, or a romantic alfresco dessert spot on the Cape.

For their generous help in researching this book, we would like to thank Lura Rogers, Eric Parks, Frank and Maria Sibley, Bob Bradford, Sue and Gordon Follansbee, Chris Lyons, Miriam Curran, Arsene Davignon, Kim Adams, Joan Jenkins, Tom Bross, Jessica Miller, Christopher Keiper, Tim Balcer, Jessica Marcus, Fran Folsom, and Pat Mandell (the original author of this book).

We need to say right up front that when we travel on Cape Cod, we choose our dining spots from those suggested by our year-round resident friends Bill DeSousa and Glenn Faria. From clam shacks to haute cuisine, they've never steered us wrong, and we can depend on them to know when chefs change or the service slips, as well as what great new place has opened. We rarely even think about a meal on Cape Cod without consulting them, and they are the source of most our culinary "discoveries" there. They also let us know when something else good opens on the Cape—a chic B&B, a homey inn, a scenic bike trail, a new adventure at sea—and we are most grateful to them for keeping us and our readers so well informed.

There's No Such Thing as Typical Weather

New England is renowned for its fast-changing, unpredictable climate. Summer temperatures can be in the low 70s or mid-90s, with humidity higher and breezes stronger near the coast. In the winter, expect coastal humidity and wind to make temperatures in the low 30s seem much colder. Winter snow cover is more likely as you move west, especially when you reach the Berkshires.

But it is the changeability that makes the weather "interesting." The warmest summer day may suddenly turn chilly, and the day that began with a downpour may be bathed in brilliant sunshine by noon. As a rule of thumb, be prepared for anything, and bring clothes for cool evenings even in midsummer. Weather changes so abruptly here that radio announcers joke that they need to go out and look at the sky before reading the weather report.

We are also grateful to Juliette Rogers, whose expertise on Boston restaurants keeps us well fed in the city, and whose passion for museums has led us to many we would have missed without her help. She has generously contributed her reviews of several of the restaurants in the book, as well as her copious travel notes.

Greater Boston

On any given day in downtown Boston, you'll see tourists rooted to a red line on the sidewalk, staring transfixedly at their maps. The ribbon of red paint or brick marks the Freedom Trail, and they are happy to follow it to the Old North Church, Faneuil Hall, and Paul Revere's House—in and out of town in one day. But in doing so they miss 95 percent of what's here.

Step off the Freedom Trail and you'll discover a world of neighborhoods so distinct that exploring them is like traveling from village to village—which these neighborhoods once were. You would never mistake the brownstones and wide Parisian boulevards of the Back Bay for the brick Federal-style houses and narrow nineteenth-century lanes of Beacon Hill. The old waterfront wharf buildings have been remade into condos and shops, surrounded by office towers and luxury hotels. Rather than clipper ships, today cruise boats and commuter ferries depart the quays.

The industrial landscape of South Boston also houses some unique museums and the city's fish piers and shipping terminals. Though almost no tourist knows where the South End is, it's the city's largest neighborhood. It was built on filled-in land—like the Back Bay, but long before it. The South End's Victorian brick townhouses bear a striking similarity to those of

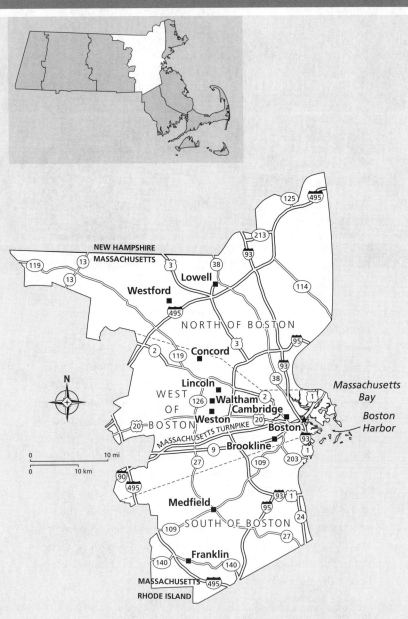

Back Bay. The midtown area wears a 1960s urban-renewal look but holds such nineteenth-century architectural masterpieces as Trinity Church and the Boston Public Library. The size of Boston's Chinatown doesn't rival New York's or San Francisco's, but its heart does.

Boston is a compact and walkable city—just don't try to drive here.

Downtown and Waterfront

The best way to get to know Boston's neighborhoods is by taking a tour. The **Historic Neighborhoods Foundation** focuses on one neighborhood at a time. In summer, weekly tours visit the waterfront and Chinatown. Tours of Beacon Hill and the Italian North End go off the Freedom Trail to find hidden courtyards and gardens and discover social history. Make Way for Ducklings tours for children follow the route of author Robert McCloskey's famous mallards through the Public Garden, where young tourists will find larger-than-life-size sculptures of the storybook ducks. HNF headquarters is at 99 Bedford Street; (617) 426–1885. **Boston by Foot** tours focus on architectural, engineering, and literary landmarks, in addition to more traditional neighborhood tours. An especially good tour for children ages six to ten is Boston by Little Feet; 77 North Washington Street; (617) 367–2345; www.bostonbyfoot .com). **Audissey Guides** lets you tour downtown and Beacon Hill at your own speed and gives commentary by experts in various fields, too. The tours use CD or MP3 players, taking you to sights many locals don't know, such as a back-alley route used by runaway slaves, a mirror used by Charles Dickens, and the table where then-Senator John Kennedy proposed to Jackie (www.Audissey Guides.com).

PhotoWalks offers camera-in-hand walking tours in Beacon Hill, the Public Garden, along Freedom Trail, and the Waterfront. Along with the usual historic and insider information, the guide, a professional photographer, shares secrets for composing artistic pictures and provides new perspectives for looking

AUTHORS' FAVORITES IN GREATER BOSTON

The North End and Market Tour	Boston Museum of Fine Arts
The Swan Boats	Isabella Stewart Gardner Museum
The Freedom Trail	Harvard University Museums

at Boston. The tour costs $25 for adults and $12 for children ages ten through seventeen, and includes the booklet *PhotoWalks Guide to Creative Photography;* (617) 851–2273; www.photowalks.com.

While they stroll the waterfront, many people don't look beyond the shops and offices. But a plaque here and there will tell you how much history is at hand. Look at the facades and you'll see that some of the old warehouses were designed to emulate Renaissance palazzi and Greek temples. John Hancock had his countinghouse on cobblestoned **Long Wharf.** Built in 1760, the countinghouse now houses a chain restaurant outlet, the **Chart House,** and still has Hancock's black iron safe embedded in the wall. Nathaniel Hawthorne served as a customs inspector at Long Wharf. Built in 1710, it is the granddaddy of all the wharves. The British marched ashore on Long Wharf when they occupied the city in 1768—and beat a hasty retreat back down it when the colonists routed them in 1776. In later years, Long Wharf bid adieu to missionaries, California-bound gold rushers, and clipper traders. One little jewel you should look for is **Waterfront Park** (immediately north of Long Wharf on Atlantic Avenue), a nicely landscaped pocket park with brick walkways and benches that offers a lovely harbor view along with respite.

With such a magnificent harbor—getting cleaner by the month—you would expect to find outdoor restaurants springing up all around the shoreline to take advantage of the almost five months of good weather that Boston has. But for outdoor dining along the waterfront, you have only one reliable choice: **Intrigue at Rowes Wharf** (617–856–7744). Luckily, the food is as good as the setting, with cafe tables overlooking the harbor boats. Located at the Boston

The Card to Carry

The Greater Boston Convention and Visitors Bureau issues the Boston USA Specials! Card that entitles bearers to a variety of discounts on Boston restaurants, hotels, sightseeing tours, museums, transportation (20 percent off some Amtrak Acela fares), shopping, and entertainment. More than one hundred businesses offer discounts from $5.00 off to as high as 20 percent off, all listed in a pocket-size directory. They also offer the family-friendly value pass, downloadable from their Web site and filled with discounts good for kids. Both passes are free. Ask for them at (888) 733–2678, or from the bureau's Web site at www.BostonUSA.com. You'll have to pay for the Boston Visitor Pass, which offers free transport on the T buses and subway and on inner-harbor ferries. These are available for one-, three- and seven-day periods, and can be ordered online at www.mbta.com. If you're arriving by plane, you can begin using it at the airport for transportation into the city.

ANNUAL EVENTS IN GREATER BOSTON

THIRD MONDAY OF APRIL

Battle Reenactment,
Lexington Green, Lexington, at dawn
each Patriot's Day (a legal holiday in
Massachusetts).

MID-MAY

Lilac Sunday,
Arnold Arboretum, Jamaica Plain,
features tours of North America's
second-largest collection of lilacs—
more than 400 varieties;
(617) 524–1718, ext. 176.

Annual Kite Festival,
Franklin Park, Boston, colors the sky
with thousands of kites;
(617) 635–4505.

MID-SEPTEMBER

Banjo and Fiddle Contest,
Boardinghouse Park, Lowell, where
performers from all over the East
Coast compete;
(978) 970–5000.

Harbor Hotel (617–439–7000), the cafe serves breakfast, lunch, and dinner from Memorial Day into October, weather permitting. You'll probably have to wait for a table at lunch, but you won't mind because the harbor is lovely and the mix of people getting on and off water taxis and excursion boats makes for an interesting diversion.

The **Boston Harbor Hotel** itself is one of Boston's finest works of modern architecture, and hotel guests can look out over the harbor from their rooms. Beautiful views greet you at the hotel's restaurant, **Meritage,** with a full glass wall offering the same harbor view. The platings, works of art, are always beautiful, sometimes amusing, but never contrived. The arrangement suits the ingredients, and the bottom line is always flavor. Fricassee of rabbit might be redolent of garden-fresh thyme, or a cocoa-dusted filet of ostrich might be roasted, then semi-sliced and served as a fan, with wild mushrooms in a chestnut puree. Vegetables too are paired inventively: Baby pumpkins may be filled with blue-corn polenta, for example. Living up to the restaurant's name, the wine list is extensive and well chosen, and served by a very well-informed (but not condescending) staff. Meritage is at 70 Rowes Wharf; (617) 439–3995; www.meritagetherestaurant.com. The hotel is at the same address; (617) 439–7000, (800) 752–7077; www.bhh.com.

Post Office Square Park, along Franklin and Milk Streets, is the new centerpiece of Boston's downtown. The city leveled an eyesore garage to build a wonderful green space with white latticework, brick walkways, fountains, beautiful flowers and plants, and trees from Harvard's Arnold Arboretum, all edged with low-lying granite walls. At all hours of every nice day, the park is full of people having coffee or lunch, chatting, and enjoying the sun and flowers. Children often play in the fountain at one end of the park, and a cafe at the other end serves snacks and drinks.

Serving French-inspired world cuisine in the heart of Boston's Financial District, **Radius** was an instant hit for its stylish environment, attentive and welcoming staff, and—most of all—its exceptional food. Begin with roasted golden beets and asparagus or with the foie gras, whose presentation changes nightly. While the meat entrees are excellent, we have sampled the various and changing seafood dishes often enough to know that this chef really outdoes himself with fish. Hold the prime rib and the perfectly roasted lamb, and bring us the sea bass, please. There is always a vegetarian plate on the menu. You'll find this place crowded after work, when the brokers and bankers head here for some of downtown's best cocktails and unique bar snacks—truffle-dusted fries, for example. 8 High Street; (617) 426–1234; www.radiusrestaurant.com.

Four centuries of notable Boston women have been recalled along the **Women's Heritage Trail,** believed to be the country's first. Four walking routes cover downtown, the North End, Beacon Hill, and the Chinatown/South Cove area, linking the stories of some fifty women. Among them are Phillis Wheatley, a slave who became the first publicly recognized African-American woman poet, and Abigail Adams, wife of President John Adams. Louisa May Alcott lived on Beacon Hill, and Fannie Merritt Farmer published her world-famous cookbook from Tremont Street. The National Park Service visitor information office at 15 State Street (617–242–5642) sells a guide booklet with a map. You can also order the book and download the neighborhood walks from the Women's Heritage Trail Web site at www.bwht.org. To learn the fascinating stories of some of the women you'll meet on this trail, including Abigail Adams, Fanny Farmer, Ellen Swallow Richards, Julia Ward Howe, and Elizabeth Peabody, read *More than Petticoats: Remarkable Massachusetts Women,* by Lura Seavey (The Globe Pequot Press).

Steps away from Government Center, the **Harrison Gray Otis House** conceals behind its Federal exterior one of the most opulent interiors in Boston. This three-story brick house, built in 1796, was the first of three that Charles Bulfinch designed for his friend Otis, a prominent lawyer and member of Congress. Everywhere you look are imported wallpapers and carpets, heavy swag curtains, and gilt-framed mirrors. High-relief dancing figures of maidens grace an Adam-style mantel in the drawing room. Neoclassical motifs frame every doorway and window; a dado depicts scenes of Pompeii. The Otis house, at 141 Cambridge Street, is headquarters for the Society for the Preservation of

New England Antiquities (617–227–3956). It's open Wednesday through Sunday for tours on the hour from 11:00 A.M. to 4:00 P.M. Admission is $8.00 per person, and $24.00 maximum for a family.

At 131 Cambridge Street, right next to the Harrison Gray Otis House, is the **Old West Church,** designed by an architect as famous in his day as Charles Bulfinch: Asher Benjamin. Benjamin wrote handbooks for builders and carpenters to guide them in working with his neoclassical style, thus influencing American architecture from the East Coast to the Midwest. Designed in 1805, Old West is a signature model of simplicity and symmetry. Three brick stories narrow to an Ionic cupola and a Doric third-story porch, with the gables of each story topped by graceful urns. The cupola has twelve columns flanking a clock garlanded in the Adam style.

Although few sightseers think to enter the **Verizon Building,** at 185 Franklin Street (formerly known as the New England Telephone Building), inside it is one of the most splendid murals in town. Called *Telephone Men and Women at Work,* the depiction circles the rotunda in a 197-foot oval, 12 feet high. The mural traces telephone history, starting with a mutton-chopped Alexander Graham Bell giving a telephone demonstration in Salem in 1877. Scenes of the 1880s are rich in period detail of top-hatted gents and long-skirted women. Also in the building is **Bell's Garret,** a re-creation of the attic laboratory where Bell worked to develop the telephone in 1875. Bell's Garret is open Monday through Friday, 8:00 A.M. to 6:00 P.M., and admission is free; (617) 743–4747.

Except for its restaurants, most guidebooks don't bother to list Boston's tiny **Chinatown,** located close to South Station. Chinatown fought for decades to push the old Combat Zone (the Red Light district) into a single alleyway and to claim the streets once walked by its seedier neighbors for its own. Now this larger Chinatown hosts other ethnic groups too, and a visit to the neighborhood will turn up Korean, Japanese, and Vietnamese businesses. The head of the main thoroughfare, Beach Street, is announced with dramatic green pagoda-topped gates—a theme echoed in the phone booths farther down the block. Don't be surprised if most signs and shop names are in a different writing system, let alone a different language; in many shops that cater to a local crowd, it may be difficult to find a clerk who speaks English too. Grocery stores are prime examples. **Cheng-Kwong Seafood Market,** at 73 Essex Street (617–423–3749), is one such place, a packed little store that, along with a fine selection of pantry goods, specializes in fresh seafoods, well-cared-for vegetables, and hard-to-find fruits like fresh lychee and durian.

For a better selection of Southeast Asian ingredients, **Thai Binh Market,** also marked "Pacific Supermarket," 3 Knapp Street at the corner of Beach, stocks Thai basil, fierce little peppers, and more kinds of rice vermicelli than you can eat in a year. Or swing in for a fantastic lunch for a pittance—$2.00 will buy you either of the two Vietnamese *banh mi* sandwiches they make to order at the small counter at the front of the store (grilled pork or cold cuts, served on a freshly heated roll with vegetables, cilantro, and sauces).

Pick up a duck or chicken, killed while you wait, at ***Eastern Live Poultry,*** 48 Beach Street (617–426–5960)—or just peek in the doorway for a look at the freshest meat in town. For sweets, ***Eldo Cake House*** has been at 36 Harrison Street (617–350–7977) for as long as we can recall, selling a wonderful selection of filled buns, sweet and savory, along with Asianized versions of Western cakes and rice sweets wrapped in banana leaves.

No cook's tour of Chinatown would be complete without checking out the right cookware and serving ware. ***Chin Enterprises*** at 33 Harrison Street (617–423–1725) stocks everything you need to outfit a restaurant, both kitchen and dining room. The family kitchen can benefit, too—choose from real steel woks that cook better than any nonstick pans, bamboo and steel steamers, pot racks to fit every size and shape pan, mesh skimmers from Lilliputian to industrial strength, and even bundles of prepackaged chopsticks by the hundred. The low prices put mall stores to shame and help you justify buying a set of Scorpion Bowl goblets just for the heck of it.

Amid the herbalists' shops, goldfish stores, car accessory shops, and kitschy gift emporia are scores of restaurants. The most varied options in one location are at the ***Chinatown Eatery,*** on the second floor at 44 Beach Street, a Pan-Asian food court with vendors of inexpensive edibles such as Vietnamese *pho* (soups), Chinese hotpots, and a juice bar with fruity milk shakes. If a more familiar restaurant setting suits you, the spare and attractive ***Shabu-Zen,*** 16 Tyler Street (617–292–8828; www.shabuzen.com), serves Japanese *shabu-shabu,* a simmering broth in which diners cook their own meats, vegetables, and seafood (the name *shabu-shabu* was given in mimicry of the sound of supper boiling). Seating is around a central U-shaped counter with individual pots or at booths with double pots for the broth. Choose a meat and seafood combo (the scallops are sashimi quality), served with shiitake mushrooms, tofu, and vegetables.

At the corner of Harrison Avenue and Oak Street, you'll see a building-size mural that depicts the history of the Chinese in Boston—the ***Unity/Community Chinatown Mural.*** Among its pigtailed Chinese figures are construction workers, a launderer, and women at sewing machines.

The annual ***Chinese Lantern Festival*** celebrating the Chinese New Year sets the streets glowing with lanterns and features a splendid costumed parade.

From Chinatown, it's just a few steps to **South Station,** whose curved, 1898 Beaux-Arts facade fronts on Summer Street and Atlantic Avenue. Once terribly dilapidated, South Station has been beautifully restored, its interior designed to resemble a European market square. The light-filled concourse sparkles with polished marble floors, brass railings, gleaming oak benches, and restaurants and shops within elegant dark-green kiosks. Travelers and nontravelers alike enjoy coming here. On sale are flowers, gourmet chocolates, foreign magazines, freshly baked croissants, frozen yogurt, and perfume.

Although it is technically in South Boston—that is, across the channel that marks the boundary—we include the next stop here because it is so close to South Station. When you cross the Congress Street Bridge, you'll see a giant white milk bottle—the **Hood Milk Bottle.** A landmark lunch-stand from the 1930s, it sells snacks today and signals the beginning of **Museum Wharf.** Especially if you have children, you won't want to miss **The Children's Museum,** one of the best in the country. It's also the country's second-oldest, founded in 1913. There are four floors of hands-on exhibits here, many creative and witty. Children can try out a giant bubble maker or star in their own show on Kid Stage. A complete Japanese home, brought from Boston's sister city of Kyoto, has been constructed inside the museum, and other cultures are explored in a Latin American supermarket and in a look at the life of New England Native Americans. In We're Still Here, children can handle real artifacts in the study area and learn about local tribes and their historic and contemporary culture.

Boats Afloat includes a replica of nearby Fort Point Channel in which kids can experiment with their own watercraft designs, while Construction Zone takes kids inside the Big Dig with tunnels, trucks, ramps, bridges, and even a chance to test their equilibrium on high steel, complete with safety equipment. On Friday afternoon from 3:00 until 5:00 P.M. and on weekend days from 2:00 to 4:00 P.M., Science Playground offers hands-on science experiments. The museum is at 300 Congress Street; (617) 426–8855; www.boston kids.org. Admission is $9.00 for adults, $7.00 for seniors and children ages two to fifteen, and $2.00 for one-year-olds. The museum is open from 10:00 A.M. to 5:00 P.M. daily and until 9:00 P.M. on Friday; Friday evening, admission is only $1.00 per person.

If you're looking for an off-the-beaten-path place to stay in Boston, try one of the bed-and-breakfast services. They might place you in a brick Federal home on Beacon Hill with fireplaces, four-posters, and a lovely hidden garden; a classic 1890 Back Bay brownstone with mahogany floors; or perhaps a South End Victorian townhouse. Contact Bed and Breakfast Associates Bay Colony, P.O. Box 57166 Babson Park Branch, Boston, MA 02157–0166; (888) 486–6018 or (781) 449–5302; www.bnbboston.com; doubles $75 to $300, most in the $75 to $150 range. Or try the Bed and Breakfast Agency of Boston, which specializes in the downtown area. It's at 47 Commercial Wharf, Boston, MA 02110; (617) 720–3540 or (800) 248–9262; www.boston-bnbagency.com; doubles $100 to $160.

Beacon Hill and Back Bay

One of the most photographed streets on Beacon Hill is tiny *Acorn Street,* a nineteenth-century byway only one lane wide and 1 block long. The antique charm of this street is undiminished. Acorn Street is so remarkably unchanged that it's easy to picture a horse and carriage rumbling down it. It's one of the few old cobblestoned streets left on Beacon Hill and one of the oldest-looking places in Boston. Coachmen and servants of the wealthy once lived on Acorn Street. Their Federal carriage houses and stables adjoined grand homes facing Chestnut Street, and are graced with black shutters and windowboxes, as well as black iron gaslights. Acorn Street is 1 block north of Chestnut Street, between West Cedar and Willow Streets.

Behind many Beacon Hill houses are lovely, walled gardens. Some are open to the public during the *Hidden Gardens of Beacon Hill Tour* the third Thursday in May. The self-guided tour reveals how artfully these tiny backyard spaces have been landscaped, with everything from flowering shrubs to herbs and some very old trees. Unusual accents might be a Japanese wind sculpture, stone cupids, antique French urns, or painted faux trellises. For tickets, which include refreshments, contact the Beacon Hill Garden Club, P.O. Box 302, Charles Street Station, Boston, MA 02114; (617) 227–4392; www.beaconhillgardenclub .org. Buy tickets in advance to ensure entry, as there is a limited capacity.

Charles Bulfinch won his greatest fame for designing the Massachusetts *New State House.* Its regal facade crowns the summit of Beacon Hill. Freedom Trail tourists dutifully regard the outside but often don't bother with the inside. There you'll see a patterned floor made of twenty-four kinds of marble, murals of the American Revolution, and hundreds of historic flags returned after duty in American wars. A stained-glass skylight depicts the seals of the original thirteen colonies. The black iron railings leading up the elegantly wide main staircase are a unique pattern of ironwork called "black lace." (The molds were broken after the railings were cast.) Don't miss the Sacred Cod in the House of Representatives chamber—a wooden fish hung there in 1784 to symbolize the importance of the fishing industry to Massachusetts. Free tours of the State House are given by reservation from 10:00 A.M. to 4:00 P.M. weekdays; call (617) 727–3676. There are also materials available for self-guided tours.

Just across Beacon Street from the State House is the beginning of the **Black Heritage Trail,** fourteen stops that follow the history of African-American life on Beacon Hill in the nineteenth century. The first stop is the **Robert Gould Shaw and 54th Regiment Memorial,** a bas-relief sculpture by Augustus Saint-Gaudens that pays tribute to the first black regiment recruited for the Civil War. The **African Meeting House** is the oldest standing black church in America, built in 1806. It was known in the abolitionist era as the Black Faneuil Hall, and Frederick Douglass and William Lloyd Garrison spoke here. The trail also takes you to one of the first schools for black children and to a house that served as an Underground Railway station and was visited by Harriet Beecher Stowe. Walking-tour maps are available at the Boston Common visitor information kiosk and at the **Museum of Afro-American History,** housed in the Meeting House at 46 Joy Street (617–725–0022; www.afroammuseum.org), a stop on the trail. It is open Labor Day through Memorial Day, Monday through Saturday from 10:00 A.M. until 4:00 P.M.; daily in the summer. Guided tours of the trail run daily in July and August at 10:00 A.M., noon, and 2:00 P.M.; (617) 724–5415.

The Boston Athenaeum, at 10½ Beacon Street (617–227–0270; www .bostonathenaeum.org), has occupied this building, with its dogwoods flanking the front door, since 1849, although the library was founded in 1807. There is no better place to go to find true New England personalities and sensibilities. A private library, the first two floors are open to the public after a stop at the door to sign in. The interior features high vaulted ceilings, pillared archways, and scores of marble busts. In addition to an extensive collection of books, the Athenaeum also has a collection of fine art, including works by Gilbert Stuart, John Singer Sargent, and Chester Harding. Fresh and lively flower arrangements are scattered throughout the reading rooms, which are furnished with solid wooden reading tables and red-leather, brass-studded armchairs. Be sure to visit the second-floor exhibit area, where quirky but always delightful thematic art exhibits are on display. The Athenaeum is open Tuesday through Friday from 9:00 A.M. until 5:30 P.M., Monday from 9:00 A.M. until 8:00 P.M., and Satur-day from 9:00 A.M. until 4:00 P.M., but is closed on Saturday during the summer. Free tours are given on Tuesday and Thursday at 3:00 P.M., by prior reservation. A weekly tea is offered on Wednesday, with advance reservations.

Almost directly opposite the Athenaeum is a smart new hotel retrofitted into a venerable old building. Rooms at the **XV Beacon** couldn't get much more twenty-first-century—or much more comfortable. Corner rooms overlook Beacon Street and the end of Boston Common, and each is decorated differ-ently. It may take a degree from the Massachusetts Institute of Technology to figure out the engineering of the elegant shower and bath faucets, but the bath-rooms are stunning, with towels so big and thick you could get lost in one.

Deep leather couches, state-of-the-art sound systems, gas fireplaces, a fully equipped desk (down to the paper clips), deliciously fine bed linens and a tray of chocolates at bedtime set this hotel apart. Rates, as well as the amenities and decor, place it firmly in the deluxe category. Located at 15 Beacon Street, Boston; (617) 670–1500, (877) 982–3226; www.xvbeacon.com.

There are so many haunts of the literati in Boston that a complete trail of places associated with well-known authors could fill an entire book. But the **Boston History Collaborative** has created a 20-mile trail that encompasses an impressive array of them and provides several interesting stops. It begins just down the street from the XV Beacon, at the venerable Omni Parker House (home of Parker House rolls) and home to the Parker House Bar, where the leading lights of Boston's literary heyday met regularly for the Saturday Club.

Boston has always placed a high value on ideas, and the members of the Saturday Club—Ralph Waldo Emerson, Henry Wadsworth Longfellow, Oliver Wendell Holmes, Nathaniel Hawthorne, Walt Whitman, James Russell Lowell, and others including Charles Dickens when he was in town—drew enormous inspiration from their mutual association. *Atlantic Monthly* was launched here, and Dickens first read *A Christmas Carol* to this group before its first public reading at the Tremont Temple next door.

Appropriately, **The Literary Trail** begins here, as do the guided tours of it the second Saturday of each month. Or, you can follow it on your own, with admission tickets to the three museums and a good book written especially for the project, describing the route and its literary history. Along with the sites in Boston and Cambridge, the trail continues on to Concord (see the West of Boston section of this chapter), where many of the luminaries lived. A guided tour costs $30 and leaves at 9:00 A.M. rain or shine. Reservations are required; (617) 621–4020; www.literarytrailofgreaterboston.org. The self-guided ticket costs $21, which is the admission price for the three museums; the book, *Literary Trail of Greater Boston Guidebook,* is a bonus (and well worth having). The History Collaborative also offers the **Innovation Odyssey,** a new tour that brings to life the inventive and technologically gifted part of Boston's past and future; for a schedule and tickets, contact Innovation Odyssey at (617) 350–0358; www.innovationodyssey.com.

On our own personal literary trail is the **Brattle Book Shop,** at 9 West Street, between Tremont and Washington Streets (617–542–0210, 800–447–9595; www.brattlebookshop.com). The building was once the site of Elizabeth Peabody's bookstore, publishing house, and literary salon—which drew the men of the Saturday Club as well as several female literary figures of the day who could not have gathered in a bar. Now it houses a rich source of second-hand books. We never leave without a small stack of new acquisitions. Those interested in Boston's history will find several hours of good browsing here. It's open Monday through Saturday from 9:00 A.M. to 5:30 P.M.

An offbeat way to see some of the less well-known sites of Boston history is on the **Ghosts and Gravestones Tour,** during the course of which you will see how some graves were filled more than once, visit the tomb of Benjamin Franklin's parents, and follow the trail of the Boston Strangler. The evening is spent walking through Boston's most historic cemeteries with actors who will put you in the right mood. Reserve your space with Historic Tours of America, (617) 269–3626; www.ghostsandgravestones.com.

When people say **Charles Street,** they almost always mean the Beacon Hill part, stretching from the corner of the Boston Common and Public Garden to the Charles River. Lining it are restaurants, neighborhood shops, and forty or so antiques stores offering everything from old New England lithographs to elegant English, French, and Chinese furnishings. Some shops, such as those selling linens and garden accessories, specialize in decorative arts, thereby adding to the feeling that you could supply an entire house from the goods offered here. The side streets also hold a few shops, so you may want to pick up an antiques map at one of the stores. The prices may be reasonable compared with regions of the country where antiques are less available, but don't expect flea market bargains.

Every Sunday morning, the bell ringers at the **Church of the Advent,** at the corner of Mount Vernon and Brimmer Streets, play concerts for the church-goers from about 10:30 A.M. until 11:00 A.M. services. Advent, built during the 1880s and 1890s, has a set of eight change-ringing bells. There are only fifteen sets of change-ringing bells in America, with more than half of them in Massachusetts. **Change bell ringing** is an English tradition in which hanging bells are worked by ropes according to mathematical patterns. The bell ringers, many associated with the Massachusetts Institute of Technology, personify the popular wisdom that mathematicians are musical. They ring the bells in different patterns so that no tune is ever repeated on a Sunday morning. As church services begin at Advent, they head over to Old North Church in the North End to give a concert for that neighborhood. The church interior is in the Italianate style, and its Sunday services (Episcopalian) feature an outstanding choir.

Among the most enduring symbols of Boston are the famous **Swan Boats** that ply the lagoon in the Public Garden. The Swan Boats were launched in 1877 by Robert Paget, who was inspired by the swan boat scene in Wagner's opera *Lohengrin.* They have been operated by the Paget family ever since. Many Bostonians walk past these boats every day and never ride them. The big surprise is that riding the Swan Boats is fun. These unique pedal-powered boats make a leisurely circuit of the lagoon, trailed by quacking ducks certain of a handout. The Swan Boats operate daily from mid-April to mid-June, 10:00 A.M. to 4:00 P.M., daily from mid-June to Labor Day 10:00 A.M. to 5:00 P.M., and after Labor Day noon to 4:00 P.M. weekdays and 10:00 A.M. to 4:00 P.M. on weekends. Tickets are $2.75 for adults, $2.00 for seniors, and $1.25 for children ages two to fifteen. Call (617) 522–1966, or see www.swanboats.com.

Another set of ducks in the Public Garden doesn't ask for handouts, but they get a lot of attention, especially from kids. These lifelike bronze ducklings were inspired by the ones in Robert McCloskey's perennial best-selling children's book, *Make Way for Ducklings,* about a family of ducks in the Public Garden. The sculpture, by Massachusetts sculptor Nancy Schon, is one of a number of her works that grace Boston. Her *Tortoise and Hare,* in nearby Copley Square, symbolizes the Boston Marathon.

Music lovers everywhere have heard of the Boston Symphony Orchestra, but few know that the city also has a newer orchestra with a growing reputation. This is the ***Boston Landmarks Orchestra,*** which first performed in 2001, presenting free outdoor concerts on the Common and in other venues in Greater Boston. Some of the other sites have included Franklin Park in Roxbury, Jamaica Pond in Jamaica Plain, and Chandler Pond Park in Brighton. Charles Ansbacher is the conductor for the series of concerts given annually in July and August. Concerts feature singers and instrumentalists from around the world and include a broad repertoire and commissioned works. More than thirty free concerts are presented each year, and the orchestra expects to offer even more in the future. For schedules and location information, contact Boston Landmarks Orchestra at (617) 520–2202 or www.LandmarksOrchestra.org.

With all the homage paid to colonial and Federal architecture in Boston, the Victorian age gets short shrift. But at the ***Gibson House,*** a Victorian house

Swan Boats, Boston Public Garden

museum, you can see the lifestyle of the Back Bay Victorians in all its full-blown opulence. This Italian Renaissance Revival home maintains its original 1859 interior of gold-embossed faux leather wallpaper and black walnut paneling. Family pieces include Turkish ottomans, eighteenth-century heirloom furniture, china, porcelain, and paintings and photographs. But history is more than veneer-deep; a recently begun restoration project is returning the home's electrical, plumbing, and heating systems to their mid-nineteenth-century status. Viewers will soon be able to see the antique underpinnings of the home as well as its decorative elements and rich appointments. The Gibson House, at 137 Beacon Street, is open Wednesday through Sunday. Tours are given at 1:00, 2:00, and 3:00 P.M. Admission is $5.00 for adults, $4.00 for students and seniors, and $2.00 for children. Call (617) 267–6338 for information on the house, or (617) 789–3927 to learn about the activities of the Victorian Society at the Gibson House Museum.

Commonwealth Avenue, a grand boulevard with a tree-filled park in its center, runs the length of Back Bay, an area that was literally a bay. The shoreline was at the foot of the Public Garden, where Commonwealth Avenue begins. The street is lined with stately brick and brownstone townhouses almost all the way to Kenmore Square.

On the way, it crosses busy Massachusetts Avenue (which you will meet later in Cambridge), and on the corner is Boston's venerable Eliot Hotel and the stylish restaurant *Clio.* We choose Clio especially for Sunday brunch. Boston takes on an entirely different persona on Sundays, and we like to begin ours in a leisurely way over a pot of real brewed tea and a plateful of caramelized exotic fruits and a mound of sugary beignets, or with poached eggs and sweet potato hash with ham. The dinner menu changes each day as the chef creates anew with the freshest and the best, and Uni, the newer sashimi bar, is proof of the freshness credo. In the dining room, you might begin with a salad of potatoes and wild mushrooms with a balsamic glaze or one of our favorites, a panroast of mussels with chanterelles and fennel. A vegetarian dish ($18 to $23) is available daily. Chef Ken Oringer's desserts may include a tart of fresh apricots with crème fraîche ice cream or a warm ricotta tart with thyme honey and strawberries. If you simply can't decide, or want to sample several dishes, choose the nightly tasting menu; (617) 536–7200.

A lot of restaurants of various stripes call themselves bistros, but few are, in the true French sense. *Petit Robert Bistro* really is, with a mix of the underused meats that bistros are famed for and other bistro classics, along with a few eclectic surprises. In short, French regional styles meet New England ingredients, and what a handshake it is. The trio of house-made pâtés with condiments is so outstanding that it almost outshines the perfectly seared foie gras. Or begin with the evergreen favorite, moules marinières. On the entree menu, tripe is offered Provençale style and calves liver is sautéed with caramelized onion and bacon. These, like the heavenly lamb cassoulet and the coq au vin are priced under $15, unheard of for a Boston hot spot. Also rare is the downstairs dessert bar, where you can sit and watch pastry chef Kristen Lawson work sweet wonders and sample the products. Adjourn there after dinner, or just drop in after the theater for coffee, a wedge of warm Tarte Tatin with crème fraiche or a fig-and-pistachio galette. Look for the little Eiffel Tower on Kenmore Square, at 468 Commonwealth Avenue; (617) 375–0699; www.petitrobert bistro.com.

Less than a block away, overlooking the Charles River and on a quiet street, is one of the rare B&Bs in the city. **The Gryphon House** is rare in several other ways, too. The gracious 1895 townhouse still has the original Zuber French scenic wallpaper in the foyer and along the stairs, in a pattern of tropical trees, flowers and birds. Rooms are decorated individually, and our favorite is the Riverview. Not only does it have views from the bay window overlooking the Charles River and Cambridge, but it is furnished and decorated in the arts and crafts style, with a mission-style bed, stained-glass sconces and several other period features. Each room and suite is quite different, but all have state-of-the-art bathrooms (most marble), refrigerators (one has cooking facilities), VCR/DVD (with a good free video library in the lobby), CD/tape player, two-line telephone, voice mail, and high-speed Internet. Rates begin at about $150. The inn is just off Storrow Drive at the Kenmore Square exit, at 9 Bay State Road; (617) 375–9003, toll-free (877) 375–9003, fax (617) 425–0716; www.inn boston.com.

The North End

Although Boston's Little Italy is no secret, and tourists head to Hanover Street to find local color and good food, few go farther than the line of trendy new cafes with glass-paneled fronts that open onto the street in fair weather. These recent additions are designed to look like what people think Italy looks like. But farther down Hanover, and in the streets adjacent to it, you'll find yourself in a neighborhood with rich traditions. Even though many Italian families have been replaced by young professionals, this is still the cultural heartland of Boston's Italian community. Those who have moved to the suburbs return often, on celebratory occasions and to renew their cultural and family ties. Even for many not born or raised in the North End, this is their return to the "old country" and to their roots.

On Salem Street people still shop for their daily groceries, and you won't find a supermarket in the entire area. Individual shops sell fish, vegetables, bread, meats cut to order, or cheese and pastas. Food is a way of life here, and the aromas emanating from the many restaurants are tantalizing. We can't possibly name them all—not even all the really great ones. But we can tell you that the hands-down choice for cannoli, which should *always* be filled fresh while you watch, is **Maria's Bakery,** at 46 Cross Street, where you can also find an array of breads, cookies, and sweets; (617) 523–1196.

The best way to learn about the North End and its food-rich heritage is on a **North End Market Tour,** with food expert Michele Topor. She knows everyone, so if a chef slips out of the kitchen for a minute, she'll stop and introduce you to him as he passes on the street. She wanders in and out of food shops and bakeries, tossing out cooking and buying hints—even recipes—in her wake and plucking up samples for you to try. You'll learn why real balsamic vinegar is so expensive (it's aged twelve years) and how to tell good dry pasta from mediocre. You'll taste seasonal fruits, sample grappa, nibble on cheeses and prosciutto, and learn about foods you never knew existed. And you'll leave with a list of food markets and shops. Three-hour tours begin at 10:00 A.M. and 2:00 P.M. each Saturday and Wednesday, 10:00 A.M. and 3:00 P.M. on Friday, and cost $50. Tickets must be purchased in advance; (617) 523–6032; www.north endmarkettours.com.

Michele also points out some of the best restaurants as you walk around the North End, giving you the latest inside information on who's serving what and how. You can't go wrong with her advice. Our own favorites in the North End? We could write a book. **Artu,** at 6 Prince Street, serves plain, unadorned, and wonderfully flavorful dishes from the Italian countryside. The food gets more attention than the atmosphere; (617) 742–4336.

At the upscale end, a place you'd choose for a very special occasion or a very special person is **Mama Maria's** on North Square. Don't expect the checkered tablecloths the name suggests; several intimate dining rooms are impeccably turned out in white linens and are newly and stylishly renovated. You'll hardly notice the pleasant views from large windows once the food arrives. Although the menu changes often to reflect the seasons, you are likely to find the baked goat cheese and smoked tomato tart leading the appetizers, since loyal patrons demand it, and for good reason. Other choices for starters might be a delicate ravioli of smoked sturgeon or a salad of a wide variety of baby greens with preserved pears and walnut-encrusted gorgonzola. From the entree menu, we've had pan-seared scallops skewered on rosemary branches and served over pearl-size couscous with cured tomatoes and lemon, or a perfectly cooked loin of tuna over squid-ink pasta with olives

Halifax's Annual Thank-You

The tall, perfectly shaped Christmas tree that stands each year at the Prudential Center is not just any tree. Each December since 1918, the city of Halifax, Nova Scotia, has sent the finest tree available as a gift to the people of Boston in appreciation for their outpouring of generosity after the explosion in Halifax Harbor during World War I that left 2,000 dead and most of the city in ruins. Help from Boston came quickly and continued until Halifax was rebuilt and the homeless were housed, fed, and clothed. Haligonians have never forgotten this bond that ties them to Bostonians.

and capers. All the pasta is hand-cut, made right in the restaurant. Entrees are $25 to $35 and the extensive wine list begins at $30. The maître d'hôtel is knowledgeable, and you can rely on him to choose the best wine in a price range. The restaurant is wheelchair-accessible (rare in the North End) and has valet parking, a blessing for out-of-town travelers. You will need reservations, since, although it's tucked into a corner far from Hanover Street, it's not a secret anymore; (617) 523–0077.

Italy's favorite dessert and snack, gelato, is available on a walk-up basis in Boston, as it is all over Italy. Owned by a major local chef and a Neopolitan *Maestro di Gelati,* **Gelateria,** at 272 Hanover Street, offers more than fifty flavors daily, including tiramisu, hazelnut, chocolate, zabaglione and pistachio, plus sorbetti in flavors such as piña colada and green tea. You can buy Italian soft drinks here, too.

Copley Square, Fenway, South End

When you're traveling, you might not think to stop at the library. But the **Boston Public Library** in Copley Square is worth a visit even if you never check out a book. Built in 1895 after the manner of an Italian Renaissance palace, the library has been recently restored so that its McKim, Mead, and White architecture, its Saint-Gaudens sculpture, and its Puvis de Chavannes murals glow as they did when Henry James walked through here one hundred years ago. Daniel Chester French did the elegant relief work on the massive bronze doors on Dartmouth Street. The grand entrance hall sweeps up an imposing marble staircase past twin stone lions. Siena marble arches and Corinthian columns frame frescoes of the muses. The landing overlooks a lovely central courtyard with a fountain and benches. Known as the Atrium, it is a favorite spot for workers in nearby office buildings, who bring their bag lunches here to read or just enjoy the gardens, which are maintained by the Back Bay Garden Club. A second-floor room is based on the library of the Doge's Palace in Venice. The library's main entrance is at 666 Boylston Street; call (617) 536–5400, extension 2216. The library offers guided art and architecture tours daily at set times; call them or visit www.bpl.org/guides/tours.htm for a current schedule.

Those with an interest in architecture will appreciate the distinguished pedigree of the other buildings that form the sides of Copley Square. Facing the library are the unmistakable Richardson Romanesque lines of *Trinity Church,* considered Henry Hobson Richardson's tour de force. The interior is the work of John La Farge. Tying those two together is the elegant facade of Henry Janeway Hardenburgh's 1912 *Fairmont Copley Plaza Hotel.* Each of these buildings is well worth a look inside. The lobby of the Copley Plaza is palatial without being formidable and its restaurant, The Oak Room, is classic Boston with rich paneling and a domed ceiling of ornate plaster work. In honor of its approaching centennial, the hotel has undergone a brilliant restoration that highlights its rich artistic heritage, as well as some discreetly blended modernizations. While rooms at the Fairmont Copley Plaza Hotel are not for every purse, a stay there is like turning back the calendar to The Belle Epoque. Marble bathrooms with big tubs, spacious rooms with big bay windows overlooking Copley Square, and a concierge who treats each guest as he would the queen make an overnight or weekend stay an event. Special weekend rates add pampering extra perks. Contact the hotel at (617) 267–5300, (888) 831–7077, or visit www.fairmont.com/copleyplaza.

The world's only stained-glass globe big enough to walk through is located at the First Church of Christ, Scientist. Thirty feet in diameter, the *Mapparium* represented the "global village" long before that concept was popular. Six hundred and eight glass panels make up the countries of 1931 and send visitors' voices echoing hollowly. A glass bridge spans the middle, where you can get a bird's-eye view of any country in the world—precisely the architect's intention. Although visitors once could see through the bridge underneath their feet to Antarctica, it so bothered people to be standing in the middle of nowhere that the church put a carpet down. Part of the world headquarters of the Christian Science Church, the Mapparium along with the Mary Baker Eddy Library and several other features reopened in the fall of 2002 after renovations. Open Tuesday through Sunday 10:00 A.M. to 5:00 P.M., until 9:00 P.M. on Thursday and Friday. Admission is $6.00 for adults and $4.00 for seniors, students, and children. The complex is at 200 Massachusetts Avenue; (617) 450–7000.

The *Museum of Fine Arts* is not only easy to find on Huntington Avenue, it also offers one of the best-known art collections in the country. But in addition to its knockout French impressionist paintings, its mummies, and its major traveling exhibitions, it has some corners visitors rarely reach. One is the series of period rooms featuring furnishings and decorative arts from a variety of times and places. Another is the small but well-chosen collection of medieval art, which includes an exceptionally fine stone-carved doorway. A Buddhist temple hides within the stunning Asian galleries, and outside is a Japanese garden, which you can enter without paying museum admission, although you cannot take your lunch there. Admission to the entire museum is free on Wednesday evenings, when it remains open until 9:45 P.M. The museum opens daily at 10:00 A.M. and closes at 4:45 P.M. Saturday through Tuesday. Special exhibitions in the West Wing are often open Thursday and Friday evenings until 9:45 P.M. as well. The MFA has guidebooks for families and free drop-in workshops for children ages six through twelve; (617) 267–9300 or www.mfa.org. Admission is $15; $13 for seniors and college students; and $6.50 for students seventeen and under until 3:00 P.M. on school days (their admission is free at other times).

During the growing season, one of the gems of Boston is the Fenway **Victory Gardens.** The gardens, under cultivation since World War II, have been expanded many times. The small plots hold mature fruit trees, vines and canes, perennial vegetables such as rhubarb and Jerusalem artichoke, and radishes, peas, and zinnias for cutting. Some of the gardeners are talented landscapers as well as vegetable growers. Their paths, retaining walls, and small shelters are labors of love and peacefulness. Many of these garden plots also reflect the ethnic diversity of the surrounding neighborhoods, most notably with Latin American, Chinese, and Southeast Asian gardens. Look for long, skinny gourds growing from trellises, snow peas, exotic melons, and lemongrass. These gardens don't waste any soil on landscape design; they are there to get the most food for the inch. The vegetation and the nearby Muddy River draw songbirds by the dozens.

Although a 1990 multimillion-dollar art heist focused international attention on the **Isabella Stewart Gardner Museum,** it still gets bypassed in favor of the Museum of Fine Arts. Hidden away behind a deceptively unprepossessing exterior is a fifteenth-century–style Venetian palazzo. Enter through a four-story courtyard with stone porticoes, arches, and columns; beautiful flowering plants; and Moorish-style windows. It's a suitably fabulous showcase for the personal art collection of Isabella Stewart (Mrs. Jack) Gardner, a wealthy Victorian matron whose independent spirit provoked Bostonians to label her an eccentric. "Mrs. Jack" liked to wear her two largest diamonds on gold wire springs over her head, among other unusual habits. Her collection, amassed over a lifetime of travel to Europe and opened to the public in 1903, spans an extraordinary range: Roman sarcophagi, Chinese porcelain, Flemish tapestries, Italian Renaissance paintings, American and British paintings, sculpture, furniture, and many prints and drawings. The museum also has a little lunchtime cafe and offers weekly chamber music concerts and Thursday afternoon tours. It's located at 280 The Fenway; call (617) 566–1401; www.gardnermuseum.org. Tickets cost $12.00 for adults, $7.00 for seniors, and $5.00 for students; children under age eighteen are admitted free in the company of an adult. The museum is open from 11:00 A.M. to 5:00 P.M. Tuesday through Sunday.

Boston's largest neighborhood, the South End, is listed on the National Register of Historic Places as the largest concentration of Victorian brick row houses in the country. Once the height of fashionable living, it was eclipsed by Back Bay and lapsed into decline. But in the 1960s, an influx of professionals renovated the dilapidated buildings and in their wake drew the chic boutiques, restaurants, and nightclubs that now line the main thoroughfares of Columbus Avenue and Tremont Street. South End artists exhibit regularly at the **Boston Center for the Arts's Mills Gallery** at 539 Tremont Street, open Wednesday and Thursday noon to 5:00 P.M., Friday and Saturday noon to 10:00 P.M., and Sunday noon to 5:00 P.M. (A call to 617–426–5000, or a visit to www.bcaonline.org, will fill you in on current and upcoming exhibits and programs.) In late October, house tours are given by the South End Historical Society, located at 532 Massachusetts Avenue (617–536–4445). The jewel of the South End is **Bay Village,** the few blocks just southeast of Arlington and Stuart Streets. This warren of narrow little streets looks more like Beacon Hill than Back Bay. Black shutters and iron grillwork doorways and window boxes accent its brick row houses—and wrought-iron gaslights line the sidewalks, just as they do on Beacon Hill. Bay Village is a neighborhood for good, fashionable dining and art galleries and is home to Boston's gay men's community.

Cambridge

Although it has its own rich share of the Hub's claim on history, Cambridge's ethnic neighborhoods and its colleges—Harvard, MIT, and others—give it a vibrant life in the here and now. Throughout the summer and fall some saint's day, some holiday, some festival, or just good weather brings people to the streets. Kids in costumes wave banners, men in suits carry heavy statues, and everybody eats street food, which we often suspect to be the real purpose of it all.

Some of these events stop traffic in busy Harvard Square itself, but many others are tucked away in neighborhoods, such as the **Feast of Cosmo and Damian** in the Italian enclave above Inman Square, which spreads over into

Somerville. Each September a parade of local bands, costumed kids, and women who wish they were wearing more-comfortable shoes follows the lines of men who carry the two saints, winding their way along a route lined by festively decorated houses whose porches and windows seem to be overflowing with people eating.

The parade doesn't move very fast—the statues are heavy—and it stops often, in front of houses where gifts of money are pinned to the robes of the little saints, until you can hardly see the statues for the bills. The grand finale is at Flowers by Sal, on Cambridge Street, where long rolls of ribbon with dollar bills pinned to their entire length are rolled from upper story windows and wrapped around the by-now nearly smothered statues. You can call Sal's for the exact date (617–354–7992).

Even before you get to Inman, Central, or Harvard Square, Cambridge offers a place to stay with sweeping views of Boston. The **Royal Sonesta Hotel** sits on the Cambridge side of the Charles River, a few minutes' walk from the Museum of Science and practically opposite the CambridgeSide Galleria Mall shopping center. Many of the rooms overlook the basin of the Charles River with its fleet of sailboats and views of Beacon Hill. Rooms are clean, bright, and attractively furnished in Euro-modern style, offering in-room data ports, laptop rentals, and high-speed Internet access. Guests also have access to the health club and pool. Runners and walkers choose this hotel for its access to the riverside promenade, one of the city's most scenic and pleasant routes. Rooms range from $169 and offer a good value for the convenient location and facilities. Located at 40 Edwin Land Boulevard, Cambridge; (866) STAY–RSB, (617) 806–4200; fax: (617) 806–4232; www.royalsonestaboston.com.

A few steps from Kendall Square, where there is a Red Line MBTA subway station, is the small **Hotel Kendall.** Smart, modern, and thoroughly comfortable, the hotel has a split personality. Rooms in the front are in a beautifully renovated old fire station—Engine 7 Firehouse—built in 1893 and in use as a fire station until 1993. Behind this oldest building in Kendall Square, the "tower" was purpose-built to house spacious modern guest rooms. Those in the renovated firehouse are more quirky in shape and configuration, but all are furnished in antiques and vintage pieces, skillfully blended with modern furnishings and accessories. Room 312, in the old building, is decorated with elegantly framed vintage wedding photos, and the large bathroom has a double whirlpool tub. For a convenient in-city location, rooms are surprisingly quiet; some have views across the Charles River to Beacon Hill and the State House dome. Thoughtful details abound, from free high-speed Internet access and local phone calls to high-end bathroom amenities and dreamy soft 100 percent cotton sheets. Rates begin at $109 for winter weekend nights and rise to just over $200 in the fall. Special packages include September "move-in" weekends for parents of college students: wine dinners, and combinations that offer tickets to special museum exhibits. You will need to reserve rooms for Harvard and MIT commencement weeks many months in advance. The Hotel Kendall is at 350 Main Street, Cambridge; (617) 577–1300, fax (617) 577–1377; www.kendallhotel.com.

In the same building is the **Black Sheep Café**, whose semi-enclosed terrace is a fine place for breakfast on summer mornings. Giant scones are fresh baked to order, the espresso is hot, and tea drinkers are pampered with a full-sized china pot and their choice of rare teas. A three-course dinner special with a choice of three entrees is $24; a la carte entrees run from $14 to $19. These range from wild salmon to fish and chips (the chef favors locally grown foods), but the style is familiar American cuisine. The Black Sheep serves three meals daily on weekdays, breakfast only on weekends, with light meals on Saturday evenings. For reservations, call (617) 577–1300.

Inman Square is the Portuguese heart of the Boston area. Although not as intensely so as New Bedford—it is mixed with Italian and other influences—it's still a recognizable piece of Portugal. Several restaurants are as genuine as the broa in the bakeries: At **Casa Portugal,** you can order *caldo verde*—a soup of kale and potatoes punctuated with slices of spicy sausage—then dive into a mélange of fresh shellfish or pork Alentejo, a delectable combination of pork and clams. Casa Portugal is at 1200 Cambridge Street; (617) 491–8880.

Irish pubs seem to thrive in the *auld sod* of Cambridge. These, unlike Boston's Irish bars, are the hangouts of those newly arrived from the land of green, and they ring with the poetic cadences of Dublin's Grafton Street. Here you will find a more widespread appreciation for a well-poured pint and a livelier *seisun* than in the downtown pubs. In Inman Square, look for **The Druid** at 1357 Cambridge Street, a Dublin-style pub with Friday night *seisun* and a dinner menu, where you'll sometimes hear poets, music, and an occasional Irish theatrical performance; (617) 497–0965.

Behind Porter Square, just over the line into Somerville, is Davis Square, where **The Burren** serves up Irish brew on tap and good rugged pub food, including traditional bangers and mash or the Guinness stew. The front room has live Irish music nightly and set dancing every Monday. The Burren is at 247 Elm Street; (617) 776–6896.

Harvard, which can rarely be accused of modesty, hides several fine museums within its historic walls, all within a short walk of Harvard Square. From ancient Chinese jades to dinosaur bones, these museums have it all. The **Harvard Museum of Natural History** is three museums in one, housing exhibits on botany, gems and minerals, and zoology. The spirit of nineteenth-century collectors who chased through jungles and mountains with butterfly nets and specimen boxes lingers here in the antique, glass-topped wooden display cases. The most celebrated exhibit in the ***Botanical Museum*** is the *Glass Flowers,* handmade glass replicas of 847 species of plants for teaching botany. The first time many people see them, they mistake them for real flowers, and marvel at how perfectly preserved they are. Strawberry and peach blossoms and palm leaves made of colored glass and wire rest gently in their cases. Whale skeletons hang from the ceiling of the ***Museum of Comparative Zoology,*** where rooms full of collected critters and stuffed beasties range from iridescent butterflies, giant beetles, and fish to a Mongolian tiger, 600 species of hummingbirds, and a wombat. The collection in the ***Mineralogical and Geological Museum*** dates back to 1784 and ranges from precious gems to meteorites. In the ***Peabody Museum of Archaeology and Ethnology,*** exhibits explore the lives and arts of cultures from prehistoric to the Native American peoples of today.

Artifacts are shown in well-conceived exhibits that interpret them as part of a living culture—even when that culture has vanished. This is a museum that takes its role seriously and, unlike others of its genre, has not morphed into an art museum in disguise. Here we learn about the issues that led to mounting tensions between the Native Americans and the European settlers and the ways in which the various groups reacted and learned to survive with their new neighbors. Some of the finest examples of Native American arts from many periods and cultures appear here, and visitors can see how these changed as Native Americans began to recognize the Europeans as a market for their goods. The differences among various European immigrants and their goals

Booklovers' Stop

Few bibliophiles can resist the lure of the family-owned *Harvard Book Store,* the very persona of Harvard Square. I worked there when I was in college, and my daughter was drawn to a job there by the same muse. Its young clerks know and love books, and several are writers themselves; all are readers. So engrossed was I late one evening, just before closing, in "shelving books" (a euphemism that thinly disguised reading in a secluded corner) that I didn't notice the time until the lights went off and I heard the big door at the top of the stairs close. Fortunately, it was winter, and another employee saw that my coat was still on the rack, so he came looking for me. To this day, although the store is larger and a door no longer separates the used book section in the basement, I won't browse down there at night.

—Barbara

here are also examined, as they relate to the ways in which native cultures survived, died out, or changed.

And for those who love the Victorian "Cabinet of Curiosities" feel of old traditional museums, the Pacific Islands balcony is like stepping back a century. The interpretive mission may not be so well served here, but this hidden corner is a little museum of Victorian interests, scholarship, and sensibilities—and we applaud its preservation. This entire complex of Harvard museums can be entered from 26 Oxford Street or from 11 Divinity Avenue, with wheelchair access through the basement on Oxford Street or the Tozer Library entrance on Divinity. All are open daily from 9:00 A.M. to 5:00 P.M. Admission is $9.00 for adults, $7.00 for seniors and students with ID, and $6.00 for visitors ages three through eighteen. The museums are free on Sunday mornings year-round and from 3:00 to 5:00 P.M. on Wednesdays, September through May. Call (617) 495–3045 for the Natural History Museum (www.hmnh.harvard.edu) or (617) 496–1027 for the Peabody Museum (www.peabody.harvard.edu).

Before heading back toward Harvard Yard to explore the art museums, you may want to make a short detour for lunch at the ***Oxford Spa***, 102 Oxford Street, between Sacramento and Garfield Streets; (617) 661–6988. This sandwich shop (the name *spa* here harks back to the days when New England lunch counters were often called spas) creates beautiful and bountiful sandwiches from premium meats and fresh vegetables. You can choose your own combinations (most at $5.00) or stretch your mouth over one of their creations. Our favorites are the So-LA, with Havarti, avocado, romaine, tomato, sprouts, and onion on thick-cut whole wheat, and the MooBah—roast beef and goat cheese with roasted red peppers, red onion, and balsamic vinaigrette on a French roll. They serve fresh scones, croissants, and bagels at breakfast and are open Monday through Saturday 7:30 A.M. to 8:00 P.M., and Sunday from 8:00 A.M. to 6:00 P.M.

Harvard has three art museums, all close together and largely unknown outside the Harvard community. The ***Busch-Reisinger Museum***, with its noted collections of Central and Northern European art, is the only such museum in the country and has recently been moved to a wing of the ***Fogg Art Museum***, at 32 Quincy Street. This museum holds master paintings by Fra Angelico, Rubens, van Gogh, Renoir, Homer, and Pollock. In a strikingly contemporary building opened in 1985, the ***Sackler Museum***, at 485 Broadway, displays ancient, Near Eastern, and Asian art, including an unparalleled collection of Chinese jade and cave reliefs. The art museums are open Monday through Saturday from 10:00 A.M. to 5:00 P.M. and Sunday 1:00 to 5:00 P.M. Admission is $7.50 for adults, $6.00 for seniors and college students. Visitors under eighteen are always free, and no admission fee is charged from 10:00 A.M. to noon on Saturday. Call (617) 495–9400.

OK, it's terribly trendy, but it's also terribly refreshing after a few hours on your feet in a museum, so we indulge ourselves in a stop at *Tealuxe,* at Zero Brattle Street, Cambridge; (617) 441–0077. We will tell you right here that one of our pet peeves (no, make that a full-fledged gripe) is asking for tea and being presented with a cup of tepid water in which is submerged a bag of ground tea leaf stems emitting an orange stain. Not here. In a genteel atmosphere, you can browse and sniff your way through more than one hundred bins of loose tea, but it probably won't take long to find one that suits your mood. Information on tea abounds, and if you are not familiar with the subtleties of the tea brewer's art, you will be when you leave. Take along an informative catalog to order tea varieties you won't find in your local grocery store.

Especially in the spring, there's no more beautiful place in Cambridge than *Mount Auburn Cemetery.* Acres of flowering plants and trees surround the graves in America's first garden cemetery, founded in 1831. Everywhere you look, trees towering over your head hang their soft petals in pink, white, lavender, and yellow over the ornate Victorian statuary and grave markers, gently obscuring the rough stone. A weeping willow leans soulfully into a pond. Many of the 2,500 trees in 380 species are rare—such as cedar of Lebanon, weeping flowering dogwood, and white Russian mulberry—but no less beautiful are the more common varieties: star magnolia, Corinthian dogwood, several types of cherry tree, and purple crabapple. The trees attract so many birds that birders come here regularly to spot them, and the cemetery is one of the best places to see the spring warbler migration. Other birds bring the number of species sighted in Mount Auburn to more than 235. And most of those famous Bostonians whose names you recognize are buried here—Henry Wadsworth Longfellow, Winslow Homer, Oliver Wendell Holmes, Charles Bulfinch, Amy Lowell, Julia Ward Howe, Henry Cabot Lodge, R. Buckminster Fuller, and Isabella Stewart Gardner, to name just a few. A map of the graves and an audiotape tour are available at the gatehouse. Burials take place regularly, and you cannot picnic, jog, play Frisbee, or otherwise disport yourself in a disrespectful manner. The main cemetery gates are at 580 Mount Auburn Street (Route 16). The gates are open daily, year-round, from 8:00 A.M. to 5:00 P.M. and until 7:00 P.M. May through September. Members of the Friends of Mount Auburn Cemetery (617–547–7105; www.mountauburn.org) lead seasonal walks and give lectures on the cemetery year-round. They also offer self-guided audio tours available at the gate and cemetary office weekdays 8:30 A.M. to 4:30 P.M., Saturday 8:30 A.M. to 4:00 P.M.

As you might expect, the Harvard Square area bursts at the seams with places to eat, many of them no more than just that. Hidden in a passageway behind Crate and Barrel, at 44 Brattle Street, **_Harvest_** opens into a garden courtyard filled with tables shaded by full-grown trees. Lunch is served Monday through Saturday from noon to 2:30 P.M., and Sunday brunch begins at 11:30 A.M. The main courses range from $25 to $35 at dinner, served every night starting at 5:30 P.M. Service is adroit and highly informed; (617) 868–2255.

L.A. Burdick Handmade Chocolates and Cafe is well known to people who know chocolate. The cafe, at 52D Brattle Street, is a place for a quiet getaway—and delectable chocolates. A small box from Burdick's is a flawlessly correct hostess gift. Open Sunday through Wednesday 8:00 A.M. to 9:00 P.M., Thursday through Saturday 8:00 A.M. to 10:00 P.M.; (617) 491–4340; www.burdickchocolate.com.

For very good, quick lunches or light suppers at most reasonable prices, Harvard Square foodies head for **_Campo di Fiori,_** in the Holyoke Center Arcade, 1350 Massachusetts Avenue, Cambridge; (617) 354–3805. Fresh-baked Roman flatbread is the base for the square's best sandwiches, which include fillings such as avocado, fresh mozzarella, grilled mushrooms, and prosciutto.

In a former parking-garage-turned-shopping-complex, you'll find an outstanding Vietnamese restaurant, **_Pho Pasteur._** Every time we have been there the place has been crowded, and there is a good reason. The food is well prepared and flavor combinations are enticing. Each dish is described on the menu, so you know what the ingredients and flavors will be. The extensive menu's entrees are almost all in the $5.00 to $10.00 range. It's a good place to dine with friends, so you can order several dishes and share. Pho Pasteur is at 35 Dunster Street, between Massachusetts Avenue and Mount Auburn Street, close to the Harvard Square MBTA station, Cambridge; (617) 864–4100. You'll also find Pho Pasteur at 123 Stuart Street and 119 Newbury Street in Boston and 137 Brighton Avenue in Allston.

Just because a restaurant is in the city doesn't mean it can't serve farm-fresh local fruits and vegetables—or at least that's the philosophy of chef Jody Adams of **_Rialto,_** 1 Bennett Street (in the Charles Hotel), Cambridge; (617) 661–5050. Mediterranean-inspired dishes change frequently to reflect the season. Look for heirloom tomato varieties in your summer salad, sweeter and tastier by far than the modern grown-to-be-shipped hybrids. Entrees range from $24 to $43.

Across Cambridge Common from Harvard Square, a block or two toward Fresh Pond, you'll find a pleasant little neighborhood where Concord Avenue meets Huron Street. **_Hi-Rise_** is a busy bakery at 208 Concord Avenue (617–876–8766), with a fine array of pastries and breads. Sunday they have cheddar pepper, walnut, and raisin pecan breads; Wednesday, olive bread; Thursday, Challah; Friday, cheddar pepper; and Saturday, olive bread. They also have a dinner menu of complete meals in oven-safe containers ready to be popped into your oven or microwave at the last minute. Coq au vin with mashed potatoes with scallions, asparagus, and fava beans is only $14, the same price as Portuguese pork loin with roasted new potatoes and vegetables. A different dish is featured daily. Open Monday through Friday 8:00 A.M. to 8:00 P.M., Saturday 8:00 A.M. to 5:00 P.M., and Sunday 8:00 A.M. to 3:00 P.M.

Trattoria Pulcinella is an attractive small Italian restaurant in a storefront in the same neighborhood. The Neapolitan-style entrees run from $17 to $22. *Primi piatti* might include curly fettuccine with porcini mushrooms; the entree menu might feature veal scaloppine with a sauce of almonds and dried figs. The cozy and rustic decor features Neapolitan stucco with plastic checked tablecloths and white cloth napkins. It's just off Concord Avenue at 147 Huron Avenue; (617) 491–6336. Open daily from 5:00 to 10:00 P.M. The Trattoria does not accept credit cards.

Just across the street is *European Country Antiques* at 146 Huron Avenue. They are direct importers of English, French, and Irish furniture—pricey, but fun to browse through. Open Tuesday through Saturday 11:00 A.M. to 6:00 P.M., Sunday noon to 5:00 P.M.; (617) 876–7485.

In an effort to keep a homey, neighborhood feel, and perhaps to avoid the crippling rents of Harvard Square, chef Tony Maws runs *Craigie Street Bistrot* from an innocuous basement location with unobtrusive decor. But who needs a flashy location when there is food worth making into a destination? Maws takes his inspiration from rural French fare—think checkered tablecloths, not white linen. There's a touch of the New American to the menu, though, that puts more vegetables on the plate than you might get at the typical neighborhood joint in Lyon. He upholds one driving principle true to both culinary styles: The quality of the ingredients determines the quality of the meal. The menu changes daily to reflect the availability of fresh, naturally grown ingredients that are sourced as locally as possible. As trendy as this might sound, his goals are really rather old-fashioned—people have been eating gizzards, tongue, and flank steak for millennia, not to mention carrots, lettuces, or kale grown without chemical intervention. The shame is that so many people have forgotten the simple pleasures and sophisticated tastes that these robust foods have to offer. Because of the local focus, don't expect strawberries in January, but those you order in June will be spectacular. An early fall menu might feature a white corn soup with ramps pickled by Maws back in the spring, and probably a choice or two featuring whatever delectable mushrooms the forager brought in that morning. In winter expect slow-roasted meats and root crops emerging from cellar hibernation into mellow, fragrant, warming sustenance.

On Wednesday and Sunday evening after 9:00 P.M., Chef's Whim, a four- or six-course meal, can be cooked specially for your table, for $39.99 or $55.00, respectively. Impromptu dishes that might not be on the regular menu show you the chef at his most creative and spontaneous; you can choose a meat/fish or vegetarian option. And on Wednesday, Thursday, Sunday and after 9:00 P.M. Friday and Saturday evenings, a three-course *prix fixe* Neighborhood Menu is $36. The bistro is at 5 Craigie Circle, Cambridge; (617) 497–5511; www.craigiestreet bistrot.com.

Between Harvard and Porter Squares, Massachusetts Avenue is dotted with restaurants. On the corner of Shepard Street, ***Chez Henri*** blends the flavors of France and Cuba in a pleasant fusion that treasures the nuances of individual ingredients. Look for the likes of grilled pork chops with an ancho chili glaze, saffron-infused conch chowder served with sweet potato biscuits, crab cakes with a jalapeño mango glaze, or curried coconut shrimp with black beans. The dessert chef is excellent, too. Entrees range from $24 to $35. The upscale dining room is not undiscovered, so make a reservation; (617) 354–8980.

Porter Square, two subway stops up Massachusetts Avenue from Harvard Square, is the center of the Japanese community, which congregates in the food courts in the ***Porter Exchange.*** This art deco building, which was once the main Sears store, has a Japanese grocery, restaurants, and a gift store specializing in ceramics. A row of small eateries in a food court serves big bowls of fat udon noodles, cooling plates of chilled soba in the summer, and steaming nabe pots in the winter. Cafe Mami makes a yummy green tea milk shake, and their Gyu-don lunch special is a steal: fried, thinly sliced beef with a sweet soy marinade, served over a bowl of rice with shredded pickled ginger. Next door, Sapporo Ramen serves hearty portions of noodles in glorious variety. We like the miso ramen, or the butter ramen when we're feeling self-indulgent. The faces, the voices, the aromas, and the tastes could make you believe you're in Osaka.

For another lunch or light dinner option, remember the Oxford Spa (see entry earlier in this chapter), just a block off Massachusetts Avenue.

One of the few bed-and-breakfasts that you can book independently in Cambridge is called ***A Cambridge House,*** an 1892 home listed on the National Register of Historic Places. It's nicely restored and richly furnished with floral print fabrics, patterned wallpapers, period antiques, and Oriental rugs. A number of rooms are available in an adjacent carriage house and another nearby property. Write A Cambridge House at 2218 Massachusetts Avenue, Cambridge, MA 02140; call (617) 491–6300 or (800) 232–9989; or visit www.acambridge house.com. Room rates (doubles $109 to $229) include fresh-baked cookies in the afternoon and an elaborate breakfast, which might feature chocolate waffles with fresh strawberries.

If you want to stay right in the Square, and in style, the **Charles Hotel** is convenient to all the action in Harvard Square, with upscale rooms and the **RegattaBar,** headquarters for haute-jazz in the Boston area. The likes of Wynton Marsalis and Dizzy Gillespie have played here. To reserve a room at the Charles, call (800) 882–1818. Like most city hotels, it has special summer weekend packages that could include gift certificates at local shops, valet parking, RegattaBar tickets, or privileges at a nearby fitness center.

South of Boston

If you're driving to Boston from the south, there's an unusual sight on Route 3. Heading north, look to your right at exit 13 and you'll see a white **Boston Gas Company tank** painted with huge swashes of bright colors in a spectrum of red, yellow, orange, blue, green, and purple. The rainbow-colored artwork gives a lift to a dreary urban landscape. It's signed simply "Corita." The artist was the late Corita Kent, a former Los Angeles nun who left her order and moved to Boston. She designed the popular love postage stamp and countless pop art silkscreen prints. Her gas tank design has been a Boston landmark since 1971 and is the world's largest copyrighted work of art. During the Vietnam War, many criticized the design, saying the blue stripe resembled the profile of North Vietnamese leader Ho Chi Minh. Corita denied it.

Incongruously neighbored by huge cranes and warehouses, **Castle Island** is a windswept green park with a long promenade perfect for strolling. The star-shaped Fort Independence, on the point, offers a great view of the harbor and islands on one side, and of the docks and container ships on the inland side. A small museum explains the pivotal role the fort played in the Revolution. This is the oldest continuously fortified site in North America. The fort, rebuilt several times, has stood here since 1634. The hilly lawns surrounding the high granite ramparts are a fine place to picnic. Edgar Allan Poe, who enlisted at Castle Island, based his story *The Cask of Amontillado* on an incident that took place here involving a young lieutenant who was killed in a duel and whose friends sealed up his killer in one of the fort's lowest dungeons. Weekend tours of the fort are offered in the summer. A beach just off the fort's parking lot, and another along the road to the fort, shows Boston at its summertime best. They are festive on weekends then, with band concerts, kiddie rides, and carts selling sausages, ice cream, and drinks. The park is at the end of William J. Day Boulevard in South Boston; call (617) 727–5290.

A short drive into "Southie" is the **L-Street Diner,** 108 L Street, South Boston; (617) 268–1155. It is at the corner of L and 5th Streets (5th is the street you come in on when you drive here from downtown), and is open Monday through Saturday 6:00 A.M. to 10:00 P.M., Sunday 7:00 A.M. to 9:00 P.M. It's not a diner architecturally, but a cozy restaurant with closely packed tables, table service, and a view over the counter of a burly owner flipping corned beef hash that our kids insist is as good as their mom's. Breakfast has the standards plus hash, hash omelets, Irish bacon, sausages, and good home fries. Lunch brings burgers, corned beef and tuna melts, grilled lemon-pepper chicken breast, and sides of Boston baked beans. Go on Fridays for the chowder. Dinner plates include grilled pork chops, meatloaf, knockwurst, and a roast turkey dinner with the traditional fixings. Nothing is ever over $10. South Boston is, to many people, the last true hideout of Real Boston, and it's worth a detour.

One of Boston's best-kept secrets is the **Boston Harbor Islands.** This group of some thirty islands scattered from Boston Harbor down the coast to Quincy and Hingham is accessible only by private boat or commercial ferry. Eight of them form a state park, with each island permeated by a unique flavor and character. The hub is Georges Island, where the ferry stops first and you can catch a free interisland water taxi during the summer. Exploring Civil War–era Fort Warren is the highlight of a trip to Georges Island, the most developed of the group. **Peddocks Island,** the largest, has a diverse terrain of woodlands, salt marsh, rocky beaches, and open fields. Tales of buried pirate treasure continue to surround Lovells Island, which also has a nice swimming beach. Berry pickers love Grape Island, where they can gather raspberries, blackberries, and wild rose hips, while watching the wide variety of birds the berries attract. Bumpkin Island is known for its beautiful wildflowers, Great Brewster for its profusion of wild roses. For information on visiting the islands and what they have to offer, contact Boston Harbor Islands Partnership at (617) 223–8666 or www.bostonislands.com.

To get to the islands, you can depart from Boston, Hingham, or Hull. The Boston-based Bay State Cruise Company, on Long Wharf (617–723–7800), sails daily in summer and on weekends through the spring and fall for guided sightseeing from on board only. To actually visit the islands, contact Harbor Islands Express; (617) 222–6999; www.fbhi.org. For complete and updated seasonal access information on harbor island ferries, call the Boston Harbor Islands National Park Area at (617) 223–8666.

West of Boston

The famed architect of Boston's Emerald Necklace (locals use this term to describe one of the oldest series of public parks and parkways in the country) lived and worked on a quiet, tree-lined street in a Brookline neighborhood. His former home and office are now the **Frederick Law Olmsted National His-**

toric Site, which holds photographs of Olmsted's work and a vault full of thousands of his landscape plans. The rustically paneled second floor served as offices, but Olmsted, ever a lover of the outdoors, often took his desk out to a shady hollow in the yard to work. The house, located at 99 Warren Street, is closed for renovations until the fall of 2007, so call ahead for times and status. Normally it's open from 10:00 A.M. to 4:30 P.M. Friday through Sunday and admission is free. Call (617) 566–1689 or visit nps.gov/frla.

Between Brookline and the Charles River is Brighton (follow Beacon Street out of Kenmore Square to get there), more down-to-earth than its upscale neighbors of Brookline and Newton. The Mexican restaurant *Zocalo* has been a winner from the start, offering something for everyone. Families appreciate its kid-friendly casual atmosphere and Mexican pizzas, but couples can find a romantic corner for a tête-à-tête here, too. The separate bar is lively (try it when a big Mexican soccer match is on the TV), and a cart dispenses fresh-made *ceviche*—chilled fresh fish rough-chopped and tossed with your choice of additions (such as cilantro leaves, onions, tomatoes), then topped with fresh-squeezed lime juice. The menu offers the old favorite Mexican (not Tex-Mex, but the real enchilada) favorites, and some rarely found north of the border. Fish tamales filled with red snapper are steamed in banana leaves, the chiles rellenos have just the right degree of heat, and the jumbo shrimps *mojo de ajo* sing with flavor. For those with allergies, twenty dairy-free or gluten-free options are offered, from chicken *pibil* to sauteed jumbo chipotle shrimp and creamed poblano-portobello enchiladas. Double-park in front while someone runs in and gets directions and a pass for the nearby parking. Zocalo is also right on the streetcar line, at 1414 Commonwealth Avenue, Brighton; (617) 277–5700.

As you drive on busy U.S. Route 20 in *Waltham,* you'd never know that just off it is a nineteenth-century country estate set in an oasis of green lawns and gardens.

On Lyman Street, just off U.S. Route 20, *The Vale* was begun in 1793, and although the Federal-style house itself is not open for individual visitors, its remarkable greenhouses are. These were built in 1804, are among the oldest in America, and are filled with a succession of blooms from bougainvillea in May to an entire greenhouse filled with camellias in late January and early February. During the summer you can buy plants here, including hard-to-find herbs such as lemongrass and patchouli. Other sales are scheduled throughout the year and include orchid plants in November. Admission to the greenhouses is $6.00, Monday through Saturday from 9:30 A.M. to 4:00 P.M., and you can tour the grounds and gardens as well; (781) 891–4882, extension 244.

Another of Waltham's great estates is also open to visitors, this one the collaborative effort of architect H. H. Richardson and landscape designer Frederick Law Olmstead (see previous entry). **Stoneburst** has the largest domestic interior designed by Richardson that is still in existence, and is considered the pinnacle of its style. The grand staircase that ascends from the great hall is a landmark of American architecture. The stone-and-shingle mansion was built in the 1880s, and both it and the surrounding 134-acre park have been carefully restored. Guided tours are given Thursday and Friday at 1:00, 2:00, and 3:00 P.M. and on the first Wednesday of each month at the same times. Admission is $7.00, $6.00 for seniors, and $4.00 for students; 100 Robert Treat Paine Drive, Waltham; (781) 314–3290; www.stonehurstwaltham.org.

Waltham made its name with watches and clocks. When we had railways connecting towns across the nation—and when they ran on time—they ran on Waltham watches. Some of America's best-known clock towers have Waltham works.

The Waltham Watch factory building is still there—and still handsome, with fine brickwork and good architectural lines—overlooking the Charles River, its original source of power. You can get a good view of it from the mile-long **Riverwalk,** which borders the opposite bank from the Moody Street Bridge to the Prospect Street Bridge, or you can float past it by boat, on the **M.V. Totem Pole II.** Leaving Cronin's Landing, at the Moody Street Bridge, four times a day on weekends (and for lunch cruises on Wednesday and Friday), this pleasant open boat with a shade canopy tours the quiet, tree-lined stretch of the Charles between Waltham and Newton. Along with the mills, it passes the sites of two of the Boston area's most famous ballrooms, Nuttings on the Charles and the Totem Pole, where all the greats performed—Frank Sinatra, Bing Crosby, and the "big bands"—and the island where John Philip Sousa and his band played to an audience of 5,000 people listening from canoes floating in the river. The cruise stops in Newton, where you can walk around in the riverbank park. You can board the boat from this end at the Newton Marriott's landing. The boat runs mid-May through mid-October. The cost is $8.00 for adults, $7.00 for seniors, and $5.00 for children; (781) 894–8604.

Along with ducks, geese, and swans, you'll see a lot of canoes in the river, and you can join them by renting a canoe or kayak at the half-timbered Newton Boathouse, opposite the Marriott in Newton, from **Charles River Canoe and Kayak;** (617) 965–5110; www.ski-paddle.com. This section of the river is known as the Lakes District because the river is so placid and the islands and coves seem more like lakes than a river. You can paddle alone or join a tour. The company also offers kayaking trips to Gloucester and other harbors and moonlight canoe trips on the Charles. Rentals start at $14 an hour or $56 a day.

Back in Waltham, in another set of old mill buildings, themselves a

And It All Ran like Clockwork

The Waltham factories did more than make the world's best timepieces and the first fiber-to-finished fabric; they were among the first to see the importance of taking care of workers. Many of these were young women who came from farms and rural communities and were not used to city life, so their company built them boardinghouses and made sure they had good food, safe and affordable lodgings, transportation to work, and even recreational facilities. Waltham Watch maintained a gymnasium and a fleet of canoes that its employees could paddle in the Charles River. The company sponsored concerts for them on an island where everyone arrived by canoe. In the winter it provided ice skates and kept the ice cleared so employees could skate on their lunch hour.

National Historic Landmark, is the newly renovated *Charles River Museum of Industry.* The Waltham mills are considered the fourth most important in America's Industrial Revolution, and this museum focuses not only on the whats and hows of manufacturing but also on the experience of the workers and how mills changed American life forever. Here you will see an early paper bag machine spitting out 600 bags per minute (and learn that the flat-bottomed bag was invented by Margaret Knight, who patented it in 1871). You'll also learn how the Industrial Revolution created the need for clocks, shoes, and lunchboxes. Admission is $5.00, $3.00 for students and seniors, and the museum is open Thursday through Saturday from 10:00 A.M. to 5:00 P.M.; 154 Moody Street; (781) 893–5410; www.crmi.org.

Aficionados of art deco architecture should look at the two facing buildings on Moody Street just south of the river. One is the Cronin Building and the other is the Watch City Brewing Company, each a classic of its type. Moody Street also offers restaurants, running the gamut of nationalities from Indian to Ecuadorian, with ample free public parking just a block or so away, near the river. As you stroll along, it will seem that every other entrance leads to food. *Tuscan Grill,* at number 361, is consistently rated among the best Italian restaurants in the Boston area, serving hearty dinners in an informal (and somewhat-cramped) setting; (781) 891–5486. A couple of doors up the street, we like *Lizzy's Homemade Ice Cream,* but not just for the ice cream. It's a cafe with sandwiches, soups, and light lunch dishes, and no table service; (781) 893–6677. At number 313, *Iguana Cantina* serves Mexican food; (781) 891–3039.

Just outside Waltham is *Weston,* where you'll find the *Spellman Museum of Stamps and Postal History,* one of only two such museums in the United

States. Based on the collections of the late Cardinal Spellman and the former National Philatelic Museum of Philadelphia, it also includes contributions from the collections of Jascha Heifitz, Theodore Steinway, Dwight Eisenhower, and Matthew Ridgeway, for a total collection of more than two million items. Special exhibits show world culture and events through postage stamps. It's a fascinating place where you can discover how much can be learned from stamps. The museum's shop has stamp-related supplies; there's even a contract post office, so you can buy any current U.S. postage stamp and the staff will help you find just the right stamp to use on your special mailing. Open Thursday through Sunday, noon to 5:00 P.M., admission is $5.00 for adults, $3.00 for seniors and students, and free for children younger than age sixteen. It's on the campus of Regis College, 235 Wellesley Street, Weston; (781) 768–8367; www.spellman.org.

Lincoln provides the rural setting for the **DeCordova Museum.** Set in a wooded, green, thirty-acre park that overlooks a lake, this peaceful and uncrowded art museum was founded in 1950. Its holdings in twentieth-century American art include paintings, sculpture, graphics, and photography. The outdoor jazz concerts in the summer are especially intimate gatherings. The museum also sponsors chamber music, ballet, modern dance, and rock music performances. The sculpture park (where leashed dogs are welcome) is open daylight hours, year-round. The DeCordova is located on Sandy Pond Road; (781) 259–8355; www.decordova.org. It's open from 10:00 A.M. to 5:00 P.M.

They Saw It Here First

The Boston Manufacturing Company, which opened in Waltham in 1814, in the building that now houses the Charles River Museum of Industry, had a long list of "firsts," including:

The first time in the world that spinning and weaving were combined in a single operation in the same building

The first power loom used in the United States

The first time silk was woven by machine

The first time young women were an important part of the paid workforce

The first brick textile mill

The first large successful manufacturing company in the United States (and the prototype for the modern corporation)

The first industrial labor strike in the United States—in 1821.

Tuesday through Sunday. Tickets to the museum cost $9.00 for adults, $6.00 for seniors and students; children younger than age six enter free. The museum's cafe is open noon to 3:00 P.M., Wednesday through Sunday, with slightly extended weekend hours.

Walter Gropius (1883–1969), founder of the Bauhaus school of art and architecture in Germany, designed and built his family home in the rolling green hills of Lincoln. *Gropius House* so perfectly embodied the Bauhaus principle of economy in design over ornamentation that it became much-visited by architects. Industrial-style materials typical of Bauhaus are seen in the glass-block wall dividing the study and dining room and in the welded tubular steel staircase railing. Much of the furniture was designed by Gropius's friend Marcel Breuer. And Gropius's artist friends, among them Henry Moore, contributed works of art. From June 1 to October 15, the Gropius House, at 68 Baker Bridge Road, is open for hourly tours beginning at 11:00 A.M., with the last tour beginning at 4:00 P.M., Wednesday through Sunday. From October 16 to May 31, the house is open weekends. Call (781) 259–8098. Admission is $10.00 for adults.

At the *Drumlin Farm Education Center and Wildlife Sanctuary,* 208 South Great Road (Route 117), Lincoln, you can visit injured animals and birds in their native habitat as you walk along the trails. Inside, in the Burrowing Animals Building, you see an underground exhibit with a cutaway of small animals in their tunnels. Special one-way glass lets you watch their activities without disturbing them. Call (781) 259–2200. They are open March through October Tuesday through Sunday, 9:00 A.M. to 5:00 P.M. and November through February Tuesday through Sunday, 9:00 A.M. to 4:00 P.M. Admission is $6.00, $4.00 for children and seniors.

Concord is on the literary and historical pilgrimage route, so it's hardly off the beaten path, but even it has its alleys. When you need a bite or two after visiting Concord Bridge and *The Minuteman* and paying your respects to Louisa May Alcott, try the *Main Street Market and Cafe,* down Anderson's Alley behind 42 Main Street. Informal and frequented by locals for breakfast and lunch, the cafe serves muffins, bagels, pastries, and breakfast sandwiches, as well as wraps and some fine-tasting grilled panini sandwiches. They also have regular sandwiches, burgers, fries, and fish & chips. Open Monday through Friday 7:00 A.M. to 5:00 P.M. and weekends 8:00 A.M. to 5:00 P.M.; (978) 369–9948.

Another lunch option is a picnic, provisioned at *The Cheese Shop,* at 29 Walden Street (508–369–5778; www.concordcheeseshop.com). The front of the shop is a cornucopia of fancy foods and fine wines, displayed without pretension, and their fine cheese counter. The staff are down-to-earth and quite knowledgeable and enthusiastic and are the perfect guides if you wish to push the boundaries of your cheese or wine knowledge. They sell excellent crusty

Together at Last

Nathaniel Hawthorne has been buried, along with other literary greats, in Sleepy Hollow cemetery since his death in 1864, but was not reunited with his wife until 2006, when Sophia Peabody Hawthorne was laid to rest alongside him. She and the children moved to England after his death, and Sophia and a daughter, Una, were buried in London's Kensal Green cemetery. There they stayed until a hawthorn tree planted above the graves fell on them. An order of nuns founded by one of the Hawthornes' daughters, who had looked after the graves all these years, took the fallen trees as a sign that it was time to reunite the Hawthornes, so Sophia's remains, and those of the daughter, were repatriated and driven through Concord in the same horse-drawn hearse that is believed to have carried her husband to Sleepy Hollow in 1864. Sophia Peabody was a painter (she illustrated some of Nathaniel's books) and a writer in her own right.

breads of several varieties, and house-made marinated olives. In the back is a prepared-foods counter if you hanker for more than a hunk of cheese with sourdough bread. They do have a few seats for eating in, if you must, but with the lovely scenic historic properties in walking distance, we recommend taking your local chèvre and crusty baguette to a more picturesque dining room under the pines.

North of Boston

More **snowy owls** congregate at Boston's Logan Airport than anywhere else in New England. From November to May, snowy owls migrate from their tundra habitats in Greenland, northern Canada, and Alaska to sit out the Arctic winter. To the owls, the vast landing fields of the airport look just like the tundra of home. As many as forty-seven snowy owls have been banded here in one winter by Norman Smith, director of the Trailside Museum in Milton and a lifelong raptor fan. You can rarely see the snowy owls out your airplane window, but you can see them at Plum Island on the North Shore. (See the next chapter.)

There are just six professional quilt museums in the United States, and one is in **Lowell**—the **New England Quilt Museum,** the only one in New England. The seventy or so quilts in its permanent collection date back more than a hundred years. Rotating exhibits also showcase antique, traditional, and contemporary quilts, and the Christmas quilt show is especially colorful. The museum is located at 18 Shattuck Street; call (978) 452–4207; www.nequiltmuseum.org. Admission is $5.00 for adults, $4.00 for seniors and children. Hours are from

10:00 A.M. to 4:00 P.M. Tuesday through Saturday and from noon to 4:00 P.M. on Sunday.

Butterfly Place at Papillon Park, in **Westford,** delights with hundreds of butterflies on view. Enclosed in a glass atrium, the mostly North American species feed on flowering plants set along brick pathways, where you can easily see them. The climate is kept warm and humid for the butterflies, and classical music playing in the background makes this a real escape for humans. You might see a kite-shaped butterfly with sky-blue-and-black-striped wings, a luna moth, and plenty of monarchs. An observation area shows a video about butterflies and displays larvae and caterpillars, and a naturalist answers questions in the atrium. Butterfly Place is open from 10:00 A.M. to 5:00 P.M. daily from March 1 through Columbus Day, closing at 4:00 P.M. in March. Admission is $8.50 for adults, $6.00 for children ages three through twelve, and $6.50 for those over age sixty-five; children younger than age three are free. At exit 34 from US 3, take Westford Road for half a mile and bear left onto Swan Road, which becomes Tyngsboro Road; the park is a mile down on the right. Call (978) 392–0955.

Bucolic Route 113 meanders westward through farmlands, never far from New Hampshire and passing through the attractive town of Pepperill before joining Route 119 in Townsend. Here, in the tiny settlement called Townsend Harbor, the Historical Society maintains the **Reed Homestead,** an 1809 home with a pleasant garden and a small museum shop, usually open 9:00 A.M. to 2:00 P.M., but call ahead, to be sure, at (978) 597–2106. Next to it, at South and Main Streets, *The Cooperage* stands above the falls that once powered its wood-shaping equipment. Now the mill houses a shop selling herbs, dried flowers, wool, and antiques, and the owner invites you to picnic in the herb garden overlooking the old mill pond and dam, and even provides a table. An early gristmill faces The Cooperage from across South Street, completing a nice ensemble of historic buildings.

Beyond, Route 119 goes through **Willard Brook State Forest,** a deep, bosky terrain of stone walls and bridges cut by hiking and bicycle trails and bridle paths. In the winter it is popular with cross-country skiers and snowmobilers. The park headquarters, at the Ashby town line, has trail maps. A lovely wooded campground with twenty-one well-spaced campsites is 1 mile west of the headquarters; (978) 597–8802.

More Places to Stay in Greater Boston

Hotel Buckminster,
645 Beacon Street,
at Kenmore Square,
Boston;
(617) 236–7050 or
(800) 727–2825.
Newly renovated, this hotel often has rooms available when chain hotels are full and offers bargain rates and continental breakfast.

Midtown Hotel,
220 Huntington Avenue,
Boston;
(617) 262–1000 or
(800) 343–1177.
Near Copley Square, with clean basic rooms at attractive prices; free parking and a pool.

Fairmont Copley Plaza Hotel,
138 St. James Avenue,
Boston;
(617) 267–5300 or
(800) 527–4727,
fax (617) 375–9648;
www.fairmont.com
With generations of tradition as one of Boston's leading hotels, the Fairmont is known for its extra-mile service, accommodating staff, sumptuous decor, and location, forming one side of Copley Square.

Hotel Marlowe,
24 Edwin Land Boulevard,
Cambridge;
(617) 868–8000 or
(800) 825–7040;
www.hotelmarlowe.com
On the Charles River near the Science Museum, the Marlowe, manages to make a 236-room hotel feel like a boutique hotel, with stylish and well-equipped rooms and personal service.

Seaport Hotel,
1 Seaport Lane,
Boston;
(617) 385–4000 or
877–SEAPORT,
fax (617) 385–4001;
www.SeaportBoston.com
The new star on the waterfront, adjacent to the New England Trade Center and with beautiful views of the harbor and skyline, with spacious rooms, fine dining at Aura, and a full fitness center with an indoor pool.

Mary Prentiss Inn,
6 Prentiss Street,
Cambridge;
(617) 661–2929;
www.maryprentissinn.com
A modest but comfortable lodging a block off Massachusetts Avenue between Porter and Harvard Squares; inexpensive for the city.

Irving House,
24 Irving Street,
Cambridge;
(617) 547–4600 or
(877) 547–4600;
www.irvinghouse.com
A pleasant inn with nicely decorated rooms (starting under $100) and off-street parking near Harvard Square.

More Places to Eat in Greater Boston

Betty's Wok and Noodle Diner,
250 Huntington Avenue,
Boston;
(617) 424–1950.
Asian-Latino diner near Symphony Hall and the Huntington Theatre, offering noodle and rice dishes with do-it-yourself toppings, at moderate prices.

Bricco,
241 Hanover Street
(North End), Boston;
(617) 248–6800;
www.depasqualeventures
.com
Smart Italian restaurant serving *cucina nuova:* roasted veal chop with honey-tangerine jus, served with a fava bean, pea, and kashi risotto, for example.

Mare,
135 Richmond Street
(North End), Boston;
(617) 723–MARE.
Italian seafood using 98 percent organic produce, deep-water fish, cultivated shellfish, and organic wines. Look for entrees such as skate Milanese with organic arugula, baby tomatoes, and lemon-caper aioli. Entrees are from $18.

Pomodoro,
319 Hanover Street
(North End), Boston;
(617) 367–4348.
Although chefs change often here, the quality doesn't, nor does the familiar air, where everyone seems to know the owner. Entrees are under $20.

Sandrine's Bistro,
8 Holyoke Street,
Cambridge;
(617) 497–5300.
Just off Harvard Square, serving Alsatian dishes, which combine French and German influences; the

choucroute Alsacienne, a blend of sausages, meats, and sauerkraut, would feed an army on the march; prices are below the norm for fine dining in the Square.

Portugalia,
723 Cambridge Street,
Cambridge;
(617) 491–5373.
Near Inman Square, serves reasonably priced Portuguese favorites in a traditional old-country atmosphere.

Redbones,
55 Chester Street,
Somerville;
(617) 628–2200.
A very casual, laid-back place whose good ribs, catfish, wood-grilled chicken, and moderate prices make it very popular with grad students. Be prepared for the wait, but it's worth it.

Umbria Ristorante,
295 Franklin Street
(North End), Boston;
(617) 338–1000.
Updated Italian specialties. Try the Raffiche di Calamari—thin gnocchi with baby squid and scallops—and end with the espresso semifredo for dessert.

TO LEARN MORE ABOUT GREATER BOSTON

Greater Boston Convention and Visitors Bureau,
Two Copley Place, Suite 105,
Boston 02116;
(617) 536–4100,
(888) SEE–BOSTON (888–733–2678);
www.BostonUSA.com

For the best current information on what's happening in the Boston area, check the web page of Frank Avruch, *"Boston's Man About Town"* and well-known authority on classic movies and the arts in general:
www.bostonman.com

WORTH SEEING IN GREATER BOSTON

**John F. Kennedy Library
and Museum,**
Columbia Point,
Boston 02125;
(617) 514–1600;
www.jfklibrary.org
Admission $10.00 adults, less for
students and seniors; open daily
9:00 A.M. to 5:00 P.M..

Museum of Science, Science Park,
Boston 02114;
(617) 723–2500;
www.mos.org
One of the finest, with an OMNI
theater and state-of-the-art displays.

New England Aquarium,
Central Wharf,
Boston 02110;
(617) 973–5200;
www.neaq.org
Sea creatures of all types in realistic
environments.

Paul Revere House,
North Square (North End),
Boston 02113;
(617) 523–2338;
www.paulreverehouse.org
The only building left in Boston from
the 1600s.

USS *Constitution,* "Old Ironsides,"
Charlestown Navy Yard,
Boston 02129;
(617) 426–1812;
www.ussconstitution.navy.mil
One of the major experiences of a trip
to New England.

North Shore

It's ironic that most people's introduction to the North Shore of Boston comes by way of whizzing U.S. Route 1, arcadelike in its density of fast-food shops and gas stations and the famous fiberglass cows outside Saugus's Hilltop Steakhouse, for just beyond this urban surrealism lies some of the territory most prized by blue bloods, exclusive and expensive residential areas for Boston commuters. Three-hundred-year-old colonial towns with quaint seventeenth-century houses. Farmland and horse country, including a polo club in Hamilton where spectators throw champagne tailgate picnics and Princess Anne has been known to show her face.

Lining the coast all the way up to the Merrimac River and New Hampshire are seaports and fishing and boatbuilding capitals that became famous all over the world in the nineteenth century: Salem, Essex, Gloucester, and Newburyport. Serious yachters around the globe know of chichi Marblehead, which has a long tradition of maritime prowess—it was Marblehead men who ferried George Washington across the Delaware.

Magnificent white sand beaches stretch along miles of open ocean in Ipswich, Newbury, and Nahant. Cape Ann is known not only for fishing and boatbuilding but also for its artists' colonies, one of which is the oldest in the country.

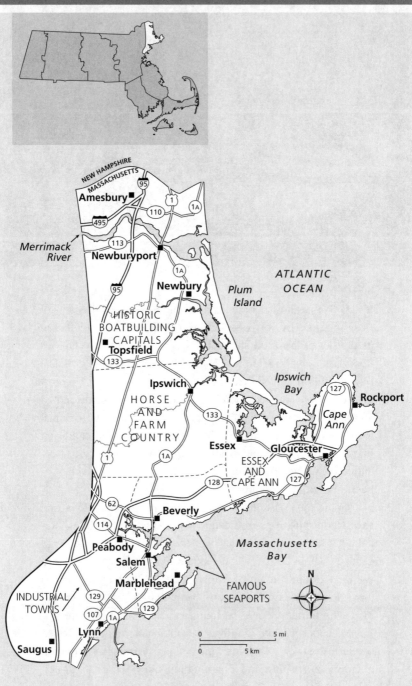

But back to US 1. Despite the fact that this is not the most attractive stretch you'll see in Massachusetts, it brings you to some interesting towns with industrial histories, among them Saugus, site of a Puritan ironworks, and Lynn, once known as "Shoe City." And you won't have to stand in line in these towns.

Industrial Towns

Tucked away in **Saugus** is an unusual piece of history: the **Saugus Iron Works National Historic Site.** Here the Puritans built an ironworks in 1650 to supply the growing colony with nails and wrought iron, previously shipped at great cost from England. The buildings have been faithfully reconstructed. Guided tours lead you from the two-story blast furnace, with its 18-foot bellows, to the forge, with its giant hammer and anvil, to the rolling-and-slitting mill, where iron was flattened and cut for various products. The guide sets the waterwheel to turning, powering the blast furnace bellows. In the casting shed down below, it smells all dank and iron-y.

The site is so peaceful today that it's hard to imagine the hellish noise and heat the men worked in back then. Now it looks like a green park. You might even see a snapping turtle laying its eggs on the slag heap, or a field of yellow coreopsis in bloom. A nature trail winds along the Saugus River, once mighty enough to power seven waterwheels, now a tidal marsh. A museum holds artifacts found on the site and exhibits on the ironworks' history. There's also a tour of the seventeenth-century ironworks house. To get to the 244 Central Street site, follow signs from either exit 43 off Interstate 95 or the Main Street exit off US 1. It's open from 9:00 A.M. to 5:00 P.M. daily April through October, and 9:00 A.M. to 4:00 P.M. in winter. Admission is free. Call (781) 233–0050 or visit www.nps.gov/sair.

The city of **Lynn** became a shoemaking center in the eighteenth century and was nationally known by the end of the 1800s. Shoemaking exhibits are displayed at the **Lynn Historical Society** in a small yellow house on a quiet side street. Hanging on the wall is a large medallion under glass, almost 5 feet

AUTHORS' FAVORITES ON THE NORTH SHORE

Saugus Iron Works	Beauport
Peabody Essex Museum	Essex River Cruise
Hammond Castle Museum	

in diameter and made entirely of tiny shoe soles in concentric rings. The 234 soles, each unique to the maker, represented all the Lynn shoe manufacturers and dealers of the day at the 1893 Chicago Exposition. Ladies' turned shoes were Lynn's specialty; they were turned inside out to make the stitching fashionably invisible. Other exhibits are shoemakers' tools, antique clothes, postcards, and an 1896 telephone switchboard. Lynn's 1860 shoemakers' strike made national news. A walking-tour brochure of some of the old shoe factories is available at the museum, at 590 Washington Street. It's open from noon to 4:00 P.M. daily. Admission is $5.00. Call (781) 581–6200 or visit www.lynn museum.org for details.

You've never seen a magic show like *Le Grand David and His Own Spectacular Magic Company* in Beverly. The show is held in the Cabot Street Cinema Theatre, a beautifully restored art deco movie palace built in 1920, all frescoed and gold-leafed. In the red plush lobby, a top-hatted accordion player, a juggling jester, a puppet show, and popcorn and candy for sale amuse children before the two-hour show and during intermission. "Spectacular" doesn't do justice to the grand, belle epoque, elaborately painted silk

ANNUAL EVENTS ON THE NORTH SHORE

LATE JUNE

St. Peter's Fiesta,
Gloucester, with parades, Italian food, and the highlight, a greased-pole contest at sea;
(978) 281–8865;
www.stpetersfiesta.org

MID-AUGUST

Salem Maritime Festival,
Salem, includes historic tours, a craft show, and demonstrations;
(978) 744–1660.

MID-SEPTEMBER

Essex Clamfest,
Memorial Park, Essex, the town where fried clams were invented;
(978) 283–1601.

MID- TO LATE OCTOBER

Haunted Happenings,
Salem, brings creepy doings throughout town;
(978) 744–3663;
www.hauntedhappenings.org

EARLY DECEMBER

Christmas Boat Cavalcade,
Gloucester, when thirty pleasure boats decorated for the holidays go up Plum River and around the harbor;
(978) 283–1601.

Christmas Celebrations,
Newburyport (see entry under Historic Boatbuilding Capitals);
(978) 462–6680.

backdrops, lavish costumes out of the *Arabian Nights,* and the music of *Scheherazade.* The stars of the show, Le Grand David and Marco the Magi, perform feats of prestidigitation, Houdini-like escapes, and levitation, as well as present classic magic acts such as sawing people in boxes and making doves and ducks disappear. Many in the large, three-generation cast have performed together for almost twenty years, and it now includes David's two young nieces, veteran performers since the ages of seven and nine. Performances are given at 3:00 P.M. Sundays from mid-September through July. Tickets cost $15 for adults and $10 for children under twelve; call (978) 927–3677. The Cabot Street Cinema Theatre is located at 286 Cabot Street, off Route 1A south, in Beverly.

Famous Seaports

The harbor at **Marblehead** is one of the most beautiful in New England. The fine shops and restaurants here, as well as three centuries of architecture that wind up and down the climbing narrow streets of its Old Town, draw big summer resort crowds. Still, there's no disputing the beauty of a drive out to **Marblehead Neck** (take Pleasant Street to Ocean Avenue to reach the connecting causeway). The winding road passes a pretty beach and fantastic mansions, and then a stone castle. A sign on the right marks **Castle Rock,** where a short path leads to the rock, which you can climb for a lovely view of the coast. The road ends at **Chandler Hovey Park,** a pocket park high up that's a vantage point for stirring ocean views, and the Marblehead Light.

At a quiet remove from downtown is a splendid old English Tudor mansion cresting a seaside cliff, **Spray Cliff on the Ocean Bed and Breakfast.** Guests can enjoy the ocean views from three terraces, one reached via a cliffside stairway, and from a private beach. The living room is light-filled, airy, and spacious. Seven guest rooms, each with private bath, are decorated in a casual California-country style, with whimsically painted furniture. Breakfast offers bounteous choices of quiches and muffins. Spray Cliff is located at 25 Spray Avenue, Marblehead (doubles $200 to $250). For reservations, call (781) 631–6789 or (800) 626–1530; www.spraycliff.com.

Salem, which is connected to Boston year-round by the commuter-rail system, is so filled with maritime wonders that you could easily spend a couple of days here. Boosted by its maritime trade, Salem was once the nation's sixth-largest city. By 1800, so many Salem ships filled Asian ports that some traders thought Salem was a country. You can see a great wealth of this history at the **Peabody Essex Museum,** a complex of several buildings in downtown Salem on the Essex Street Mall. The museum has engulfed the former East India Marine Society, founded in 1799 by sea captains who knew they were bringing home rare oddities. Their "museum of natural and artificial curiosities" is annexed to the rest of the museum, whose mission seems to be changing from historical and ethnographic to art. That's a shame, because the Marine Society's collections, shown in their original context, made it the most treasure-filled maritime museum in all of New England. Now maritime artifacts, Asian export art, and collections in ethnology, natural history, and archaeology are mixed and interpreted more as art and artifact instead of offering a glimpse of the world as the Salem sea captains found it. Ships' figureheads and paintings of Salem ships and Chinese ports are still exhibited, however, among exotic treasures from Bombay to Zanzibar. Asian export art made just for trade with the West includes engraved silver teapots, a secretary made entirely of carved ivory, and a Chinese "moon bed" whose oval-shaped, dark wood canopy is inlaid with ivory and cut out with hundreds of infinitesimally small designs of people, pagodas, and boats. Whatever its emphasis, it is still among the finest museums in the Northeast and well worth savoring at a leisurely pace. Docent-led tours are especially interesting.

Diagonally across the Essex Street Mall are a gallery and three historic houses that span three centuries of architecture: the 1684 *John Ward House,* the 1727 Georgian *Crowninshield-Bentley House,* and the 1804 *Gardner-Pingree House,* considered the Federal masterpiece of famed Salem architect Samuel McIntire. The Gardner-Pingree House has many elaborate details: door and window corners with carved sheaves of wheat (symbols of prosperity), painted floorcloths, and Adam-style marble mantelpieces. The museum's main building has just undergone extensive construction and renovation. The striking modern entry, intended to evoke a ship's hull in concrete and glass, may be incongruous along the old brick buildings nestled around the neighborhood, but it does fill the museum with light. A major part of the museum's renovation was the inclusion of a centuries-old Chinese house, imported and reassembled in a garden at the museum. You'll need to sign up for the $4.00 tour in advance because it has a limited capacity, or take your chances. The older parts of the museum still house the majority of the New England decorative arts collections, as well as Asian export wares, including the historic gallery with white Corinthian columns and vaulted ceiling that features oil portraits of such leading figures as Nathaniel Hawthorne and Daniel Webster, as well as period silver pieces. Also among the collections are hundreds of pieces of eighteenth- and nineteenth-century European porcelain and glassware.

The museum complex is open daily from 10:00 A.M. to 5:00 P.M. Tickets cost $13.00 for adults, $11.00 for seniors, and $9.00 for students; admission is free for youth sixteen and younger and Salem residents. Admission to the historic house tours is included in the ticket price; (978) 745–9500, (866) 745–1876; www.pem.org.

Magnificent sea captains' houses line the entire length of quiet, tree-shaded **Chestnut Street,** just west of the Essex Street Mall. Federal-style temples to wealth stand in neat rows, painted in pastels of creamy yellow, white, or taupe. Wonderful period details stand out: a gold eagle medallion over a door, urn-topped fence posts, fanlight windows, white pillared porticoes, and tidy black shutters.

Among these stately homes stands the **Stephen Phillips Trust House** at 34 Chestnut Street. This house, now a museum, has an interesting history—part of it was moved here from neighboring Danvers by oxcart. Along with its furniture, the house contains porcelains, Persian rugs, intricately carved wooden weaponry from the Pacific Islands, and a good collection of Native American pottery. The carriage house displays horse-drawn vehicles and rare vintage automobiles. The fascinating thing about this relatively new house museum (newly opened as a museum, that is) is that its curator has chosen to show the house as exactly what it is—the collections of generations as last lived in by a family in the early twentieth century. Through its collections and exhibits, it interprets one of Salem's historically significant families throughout the city's history. We also like the inclusion of the kitchen, pantry, laundry, and other areas that illustrate life for the staff in a household of these eras. Ask about the occasional special theme tours, focusing on topics from family life to art in the collections. The house, easy to spot by the Hawaiian flag that flies in front, is open late May through October, Monday through Saturday 10:00 A.M. to 4:00 P.M., when the last tour begins. Admission is free; (978) 744–0440; www.phillipsmuseum.org.

Down near the waterfront, **The Grapevine,** at 26 Congress Street (978–745–9335), offers an Italian-inspired seafood and pasta menu, rounded out with *pizzettas* and wood-fire grilled meats cooked to specification. An enchanting alfresco patio evokes Florence. The restaurant is open for dinner, with entrees from $18 to $30.

Salem Willows Amusement Park (Fort Avenue, Salem; (978) 745–0251; www.salemwillows.com) may sound all very grandiose, but banish from your mind images of Six Flags and $20 to $30 admission fees. The Willows is a public park on a point into Salem Sound, filled all summer with family picnics, impromptu folk ensembles, and couples out for a promenade. The site was home to an old smallpox convalescence home, and plaques tell you the history of the park and the islands in sight. The park bandstand continues to welcome jazz performers in the summer, as it did in the 1920s when Duke Ellington played here.

The amusement park is housed in a row of low buildings facing the park, chock full of all the corny goodness of the boardwalk in a small scale. Rides are all meant for small children, and include an old carousel that grown-ups are welcome to ride on. An arcade is filled with video games and pinball, and a second one with myriad games we all grew up playing (whack-a-gopher, ski-ball, and dozens more). Many of the games are as fun for three-year-olds as adults. Naturally, you win tickets redeemable for prizes (and you get a token ticket or two just for playing, which makes kids very proud of themselves). Several food vendors have stalls along the street, offering all the summertime favorites—hot dogs in grilled buns, burgers, homemeade ice cream, saltwater taffy (made daily at 11:00 A.M.), caramel corn, slushies, fried clams, and more substantial meals. Best of all, there is no charge for parking or to wander around and enjoy the day there, and the fees for games, rides, and food are very reasonable.

Horse and Farm Country

A genteel atmosphere of yesteryear still lingers at the **Wenham Tea House,** which opened in 1910 as a fund-raising arm of the Wenham Village Improvement Society. Ladies brought their daughters for birthdays and bridal showers to the tearoom, with its painted yellow chairs and flowered curtains. Dainty and traditional lunches include creamed chicken on toast, lobster roll, and cottage cheese with fruit. Lunch is served Monday through Saturday from 11:30 A.M. to 2:30 P.M. Tea, served from 3:15 to 4:30 P.M. daily (starting at 2:00 P.M. on Sunday), is an elegant affair of scones with whipped cream and raspberry jam, cinnamon sticks, and tea bread. A really nice gift shop sells jams, teas, cookies, and candies; a profusion of books on gardening, cooking, birds, and travel; and such handcrafts and housewares as Waterford crystal, silver, handbags, and painted ceramics. The teahouse is located on Route 1A in the center of Wenham, two houses left of the church. It is best to call ahead to reserve a seat, especially for lunch; (978) 468–1398.

The **Wenham Museum** looks at how New Englanders lived, dressed, and played—especially played. The collections of toys and dolls, and especially the model-train room, give a wonderful picture of childhood pleasures throughout several centuries. But the doll collections of the former owner of the Claflin-Richards House, part of the museum, is particularly significant, as the oldest continuously held doll collection in the world. The exceptional assemblage of more than 5,000 dolls dates as far back as ancient Egypt, with an Egyptian funerary figure from about 1500 B.C. School programs and a busy schedule of lectures and activities keep the museum a busy place. It's open Tuesday through Sunday 10:00 A.M. to 4:00 P.M., and admission is $5.00 for adults, $4.00

for seniors, and $3.00 for children; 132 Main Street, Wenham; (978) 468–2377; www.wenhammuseum.org.

The **Ipswich River Wildlife Sanctuary** is the Massachusetts Audubon Society's largest. The property is remote and wild: 2,000 acres of meadow, swamp, ponds, drumlins, kettles, and eskers surrounding the Ipswich River. Highlights are an unusual rockery, waterfowl ponds, and an observation tower overlooking swamp and meadowland. One of the buildings has a long and narrow bird-viewing window high up from which you can see many birds at a profusion of feeders in the backyard. Programs include guided river float trips, maple sugaring, canoe rentals, cabin rental and camping on Perkins Island, and many nature programs for children. The sanctuary is located on Perkins Row in **Topsfield,** just off Route 97 east of US 1. It's closed Monday. There's a trail fee of $4.00 for adults and $3.00 for seniors and children ages three through twelve. Admission is free to members of the Massachusetts Audubon Society. Call (978) 887–9264.

The 1677 **Whipple House** in **Ipswich** is one of the oldest continuously operating historical house museums in America and also one of our country's oldest standing structures. In excellent condition, authentically restored, and expertly interpreted, it's maintained by the Ipswich Historical Society, which also owns the Early-Republic-style **Heard House,** built in the 1790s for a major player in the China trade. The Heard House features a magnificent carved staircase and interior mouldings and decoration, Palladian windows, pocket shutters, and false-grained doors, nearly all untouched originals. Collections shown in the house include Chinese porcelain and artifacts, textiles, and works by the nineteenth-century Ipswich Painters. Especially interesting is the collection of lace made by local women in the late eighteenth century. Black Ipswich lace was made in the late 1700s by women in about 600 Ipswich households. This was the only town in America that made bobbin lace commercially.

The Whipple House features crease-molded boards, painted in bright colors, which surprise those who believe the myth that the early settlers always used dark, dull colors. The kitchen fireplace has a walk-in cooking hearth, and the "housewife's garden" is one of the finest examples of seventeenth-century gardens. Also exhibited is a portion of the largest collection of works by Arthur Wesley Dow. Besides Dow's oil and watercolor paintings, woodblock prints, and early black-and-white photographs, Whipple House also houses a collection of works by the Ipswich Painters, a group that gathered in Ipswich in the late nineteenth and early twentieth centuries. The Heard House is open Wednesday to Saturday, 10 A.M. to 4:00 P.M., and Sunday, 1:00 to 4:00 P.M. It's at 54 South Main Street, Ipswich; (978) 356–2811; www.ipswichmuseum.net.

One of the most splendid estates in all of Massachusetts is also in Ipswich on Argilla Road. This fifty-nine-room seaside mansion was built by Chicago industrialist Richard T. Crane Jr., whose father made a fortune in plumbing valves and fittings. Crane succeeded his father as president in 1914 and made the company famous for elegant bathroom fixtures in the 1920s, partly by advertising them in *National Geographic*. Built in 1927, **Castle Hill** was a summer home for Crane and his wife. Touring the mansion is like touring one of the great castles of Europe. A long drive winds up and up through the landscaped grounds, past the stone walls and balusters of a sunken Italian garden and a rose garden. The mansion's long, symmetrical lines reflect great seventeenth-century English houses of the Stuart period. Inside, you find yourself staring up at 16-foot ceilings and elaborately carved ceiling moldings, marveling at serpentine marble fireplaces and crystal and brass chandeliers, and noticing such exquisite details as delft tiling, parquet floors, and sterling-silver bathroom fixtures. Bay windows in many rooms offer sweeping views of the barrier beach and the ocean down below and of the green lawns of the grounds. A particularly striking view is of the Grand Allée, which slopes down a wide path straight to the sea. Lined with spruce trees and stone garden statuary, the allée was the site of a casino used for summer parties and of a saltwater swimming pool, now filled in. One terraced lawn was formerly a bowling lawn; another held a classically designed boxwood maze.

Inside, the entrance rotunda offers an unusual example of circular architecture. Its round surfaces are covered with canvas painted with murals of Roman emperors, Corinthian columns, and the Crane children, Florence and Cornelius. You can see most of the house on the tour, from the 63-foot-long gallery to the dining room, kitchens, and guest and family bedrooms and bathrooms. The library was taken entirely from an English estate in Hertfordshire. Warm and rich wood paneling culminates in ornately carved fruits and flowers framing a doorway and several paintings, the work of famed seventeenth-century English craftsman Grinling Gibbons. Surrounding the bathtub in daughter Florence's bathroom is a striking mosaic of reverse-painted glass tiles in a black clipper-ship motif framed in silver. Mrs. Crane's bathroom was done entirely in green-and-white serpentine marble and *faux marbre*. The green marble was designed to make the bathwater look like seawater.

The house is open for public tours from 10:00 A.M. to 4:00 P.M. on Wednesday, Thursday, and Friday from 9:00 A.M. to noon June through October. Tickets cost $10.00 for adults and $8.00 for seniors and children ages six through twelve. Appointments can also be made for groups. Call (978) 356–4351 for information. Castle Hill also hosts summer concerts and other special programs on its beautiful grounds, events that sometimes include preliminary house tours. Picnicking on the Grand Allée before a summer concert is a popular activity.

Visitors are welcome to stroll through the lovely grounds anytime there is not a private function.

Just below Castle Hill, at the foot of Argilla Road, is one of the North Shore's most magnificent beaches: *Crane Beach,* once part of the Crane estate. A white sandy beach stretches more than 4 miles, reaching down from a scenic sweep of dunes and marsh grasses and a view of the Ipswich River. There are bathhouses and a snack bar as well as lifeguards from Memorial Day weekend through Labor Day. Parking fees are $22 on weekends and $15 to $17 during the week, depending on the season; $2.00 per bicycle and for those who arrive by foot. The beach is open daily from 8:00 A.M. until sunset, and vehicle parking is half price after 3:00 P.M. For information call (978) 356-4354.

On your way back from the beach, be sure to stop at *Russell Orchards* on the left, at 123 Argilla Road (978-356-5366). This is a great old-fashioned barn of a place, famous for its homemade cider doughnuts. Come fall, you can wash down the doughnuts with cider, stocked in three antique white refrigerators. The barn rambles back forever, and its rafters are piled high with old wooden bushel baskets. It smells perennially of good things: homemade fruit pies, newly harvested berries, jams and jellies, stick candy, vegetables, and cut flowers. Children love the place for the hayrides and farm animals—the pig, goats, geese, ducks, chickens, and horses, and adults love the range of pick-your-own fruits and wines made from the farm's productions. The orchards are open daily from 9:00 A.M. to 6:00 P.M. May through Thanksgiving.

Essex and Cape Ann

At the entrance to Cape Ann, the town of *Essex* is well known as an antiques capital. What is typically overlooked here is the *Essex Shipbuilding Museum,* even though it is in the thick of the antiques shops, right on Main Street (Route 133). Into this small but fascinating museum are crammed a great number of artifacts and photos illustrating Essex's 300-year shipbuilding history, during which more than 4,000 ships were built. Essex became famous for its Chebacco Dogbody boat, a two-masted fishing boat designed to be built quickly to help replace New England's fishing fleet after it was destroyed by the British. There are models of schooners with beautiful linen sails, as well as many half-models of Essex-built fishing schooners from the Smithsonian collection in Washington, D.C. Half-models were used in boat design, their lines judged for speed and seaworthiness. Near a workbench with antique tools is an 1890s trunnel lathe, used to make trunnels (wooden pegs also called treenails). The appealing smells of oakum (tarred hemp) and pine pitch permeate the caulking exhibit. Everything for Essex ships was made in town: windlasses, blocks, pumps, sparks, cordage, anchors, sails, and riggings. Many Essex ships were built at the A.D. Story Shipyard, a five-minute walk from the museum. Museum hours are 10:00 A.M. to 5:00 P.M., Wednesday through Sunday from June to October, and weekends only the rest of the year. Tickets cost $7.00 for adults, $6.00 for seniors, and $5.00 for kids ages seven and up. Call (978) 768–7541.

Leaving from Essex, ***Essex River Cruises*** (800–748–3706) pass by all the harbor islands and along the back of the Plum Island wildlife reserve. ***Hog Island*** is where the movie *The Crucible* was filmed, and you can see one building from the set as you sail past. To see the islands up close and learn the story of "Hollywood Meets the Trustees of Reservations" (the island's owner), take the boat-and-hay-wagon tour offered by the trustees: ***Hog Island Tours,*** Trustees of Reservations; (508) 365–4351. Or take a guided tour with ***ERBA Sea Kayaking*** at the Essex Shipbuilding Museum and paddle there yourself; (978) 768–3722, (800) KAYAK–04 (800–529–2504). You can explore the island on foot, but you must stay in the tracks so as not to disturb the wildlife. From its top, you can see all the way to the Maine coast on a clear day.

In ***Gloucester,*** looking just like a real castle, is the ***Hammond Castle Museum.*** Its stone battlements and towers, built right on the rocky shores of the Atlantic Ocean, house one of the most unusual private homes in America. The castle is a fitting monument to the man who built it, Dr. John Hays Hammond Jr., America's second-greatest inventor, next to Thomas Edison. When he died in 1965, Hammond held 465 patents on more than 800 inventions. He collected monuments all through Europe, items such as Roman tombstones, Renaissance furniture, and a medieval fireplace. To house it all, he built his castle in the 1920s.

Tours begin in the thirteenth-century–style Great Hall, whose 60-foot ceiling complements an 8,200-pipe organ, the largest organ in the world installed in a private home. You can hear a recording of the organ music. The walls surrounding the courtyard and pool are made of half-timbered shop facades from a fourteenth-century French village: a bakeshop, wine merchant, and butcher, complete with symbols for the illiterate. A church front holds Hammond's collection of Roman tombstones set into the wall. There's also a Renaissance dining room, along with Gothic and early American bedrooms. The lobby contains a list of Hammond's patents and exhibits some of his patent models. An "inventor's inventor," Hammond pioneered in radio, television, radar, and remote-control radio. He and his wife entertained Serge Koussevitzky, Helen Hayes, George Gershwin, Cole Porter, John D. Rockefeller, and Noël Coward, as well as Ethel and Lionel Barrymore, who staged readings of Shakespeare in the Great Hall. The museum is open summer 10:00 A.M. to 5:00 P.M. Monday through Thursday, and 10:00 A.M. to 3:00 P.M. Friday through Sunday. It's also open 10:00 A.M. to 3:00 P.M. on weekends mid-May through mid-June. It is wise to call ahead for weekend hours, because this is a popular spot for weddings. Special programs and tours are available. Admission is $8.50 for adults, $6.50 for seniors, and $5.50 for children ages four through twelve. Hammond Castle is located at 80 Hesperus Avenue, Gloucester; call (978) 283–7673 or (800) 649–1930 (in Massachusetts); www.hammondcastle.org.

The marine heart and soul of Gloucester show at the **Cape Ann Historical Association,** starting with the nation's largest collection of paintings and drawings by Fitz Hugh Lane. A Gloucester native, Lane was the first American marine painter to gain national stature. His scenes of Gloucester Harbor and other shores in New England are full of light and sky. Decorative-arts exhibits include Queen Anne and Hepplewhite furniture. Upstairs are fisheries exhibits. Long oars, painted in bright colors and carried in the annual St. Peter's Fiesta (see Annual Events at beginning of this chapter), hang on the wall. A flake yard shows how fish was salted and dried years ago. Connected to the museum and part of the tour is an 1804 Federal-style sea captain's house, the **Captain Elias Davis House.** The museum is located at 27 Pleasant Street; call (978) 283–0455. Hours are 10:00 A.M. to 5:00 P.M. Tuesday through Saturday. Admission is $6.50 for adults, $6.00 for seniors, $4.50 for students. Children younger than age six are admitted free. For tours of the house, call ahead.

In Gloucester's fishing heyday, thousands of schooners fished the outer banks for cod and haddock. The nation's last active dory-fishing schooner was the **Adventure,** a two-masted knockabout built of sturdy oak and pine in 1926. On board this 121-foot ship, it's easy to picture yourself alongside Spencer Tracy in a scene from *Captains Courageous.* Topside, you can learn how the gaff-rigged sails are set and handle some lines. Take your turn at the large spoked wheel and feel the hollows in the deck worn by the feet of helmsmen over the years. Down below, you'll see the galley, with its old-fashioned black iron stove and pump, the fo'c'sle, and the former fish holds, where the catch was kept on ice. The ship is open to the public on Saturday mornings and by arrangement, but sometime in 2007 its restoration should be complete and hours will be expanded. Visitors should call to verify hours and location after than time; (978) 281–8079. Admission is $5.00 for adults and $3.00 for children. The schooner is berthed on the Harbor Loop off Main Street in Gloucester, next to a white building with a sign that says GLOUCESTER MARINE RAILWAYS CORP.

The Rudder, at 73 Rocky Neck Avenue (978–283–7967), is a real institution, Gloucester's oldest restaurant. It's situated out on Rocky Neck, America's oldest art colony, and dinner or drinks here is a nice way to cap a day spent gallery hopping. Housed in a 175-year-old former fish-packing shed right on the water, the dining room is all dark wood and brass lanterns. An oceanfront porch opens up for summertime dining. The chief attraction is not so much the food, although the variety of seafood is well prepared, as is the "spontaneous entertainment" provided by its theatrically minded family owners. They are likely to flit about the dining room or accompany themselves in an impromptu number on the piano every night. A "celebrity wall" holds photos of famous guests: Liv Ullmann, Anthony Newley, and Judy Garland. The ceiling is plastered with menus from restaurants around the world, collected by the owners' many globe-trotting friends.

Out on Gloucester's exclusive Eastern Point is one of the most intriguing houses you'll ever see: ***Beauport.*** This rambling shingled-and-turreted house was built in 1907 by the daring interior designer Henry Davis Sleeper, who numbered among his clients Henry Francis du Pont, Joan Crawford, and Fredric March. Sleeper collected pieces of decorative art and then ran out of room to display them in his three-room house. He began adding on, and kept adding on, for more than twenty-six years, until his death in 1934. The final fantastic product has twenty-two roof levels and more than forty rooms. Without a guide, you could get lost wandering these cramped and dark little rooms that honeycomb throughout the house, occasionally opening on only a peek of a view of Gloucester Harbor. Sleeper built secret staircases, fake windows, and doors to nowhere. He indulged his every fancy. He built shrines to the American colonial past, honoring George Washington and Benjamin Franklin. The China Trade Room started as a medieval hall until Sleeper acquired some hand-painted eighteenth-century Chinese wallpaper. The wallpaper's large murals show village scenes in China. The Chinese theme is completed with a Chinese pagoda–shaped ceiling and a Buddha in the fireplace. The Octagon Room has eight sides and contains a collection of eight-sided antiques. A guest room called the Strawberry Hill Room is done with a strawberry theme, vaulted ceiling, and red-and-black lacquered wallpaper of elephants and camels. Beauport is at 75 Eastern Point Boulevard. (This is a private road but open to visitors to Beauport.) Admission for adults is $10.00, $5.00 for children six through twelve. The house is open from 10:00 A.M. to 4:00 P.M. weekdays June through mid-September; daily mid-September through mid-October. Tours depart hourly from 10:00 A.M. to 4:00 P.M. Call (978) 283–0800 for information.

When you arrive in ***Rockport*** at the tip of Cape Ann, you'll find dozens of restaurants—but you can't get any more genuine than the ***Lobster Pool.*** You place your own order, serve yourself, and bus your own picnic table. Set right on the ocean's edge, the restaurant has many tables outside, for smashing views of lobster boats putting in, the rocky coast, and the pounding surf. Specialties are fresh, excellent lobster in the rough and fried and broiled seafoods, but there are also hamburgers and french fries. Save room for homemade desserts: strawberry shortcake, peach cobbler, and blueberry and apple pie. Open April through October from 11:30 A.M. to 8:30 P.M., the Lobster Pool is on Route 127, just south of downtown Rockport; call (978) 546–7808.

Many galleries cluster around the **Rockport Art Association** (12 Main Street; 978–546–6604), itself a gallery, and the length of Bearskin Neck. The **Village Silversmith,** on the Neck, offers original jewelry that spotlights the natural beauty of semiprecious stones in elegant frames. In nearby shops, other artists work in glass, ceramics, and two-dimensional media. If shopping makes you peckish for something smaller and softer on the wallet than seafood, **Top Dog,** out on the Neck, is man's best friend. You'll have lots of choices here for high-quality steamed or grilled dogs; from combos named after breeds (the Chihuahua: jalapeños, cheese, and salsa; the German shepherd: sauerkraut; the Boston terrier: baked beans) to a smorgasbord of self-service toppings (ten kinds of mustard!), to a staggering selection of fried potato treats. And though Top Dog doesn't have many tables, you can walk your dogs to the waterfront and soak in the briny sea air. Open midday daily (into evening on weekends) at 2 Doyles Cove Road; (978) 546–0006.

Ellen's Restaurant is the sort of unassuming place beloved of locals. Its lunch and dinner menus offer classic, down-to-earth foods that are well prepared and modestly priced. Locals rave about the chowder, which has repeatedly won the town's competition, and it has a classic seafood selection as well as a big pit–BBQ menu. A new liquor license means Ellen's offers local microbrews, along with wine. The unassuming dining room faces onto the harbor on two sides, so most tables come with a view. Open daily for lunch and dinner in season, at 1 T Wharf, (978) 546–2512. For dessert, swing by **Sundays** ice-cream shop (3 South Road, 978–546–2490), or **Tuck's Candy,** made while you watch through the workshop's big glass windows. Our friend Tim babbles giddily about their creamy fudge, and, as is right and proper, they make scrumptious saltwater taffy (15 Main Street; 978–546–6352).

We all have our curiosities. Elis Stenman of Rockport wanted to see how far you could push newspapers without destroying the print. Accordingly, he built a house out of them, starting in 1922, and the structure is still standing today—the **Paper House.** The two-room house has walls made of 215 thicknesses of newsprint and contains furniture made of rolled-up newspapers. You can still read the print under the shellac. A desk gives an account of Charles Lindbergh's historic flight. A grandfather clock made in 1932 contains papers from the capital cities of forty-eight states. The mantel is made of Sunday rotogravure sections. Stenman and his wife used the house and its furniture for four summers. The house is located at 52 Pigeon Hill Street. Take Route 127 north to Curtis Street; then follow signs to the Paper House. It's open daily from 10:00 A.M. to 5:00 P.M. April through October and can be seen by appointment in spring; call (978) 546–2629. Admission is $1.50 for adults and $1.00 for children.

At the northernmost tip of Cape Ann is an old quarry site that is now **Halibut Point State Park,** a small but fascinating park. A film at the visitor center tells the story of how granite was king here for almost a hundred years. Paving blocks went to Boston, Philadelphia, New York, and Havana. Halibut Point granite blocks were used in Boston's Custom House tower, the Brooklyn Bridge, and the Holland Tunnel. A self-guided trail passes by the vestiges of quarrying and emerges on a stunning vantage point overlooking a quarry pool high up over the Atlantic Ocean. This is also a great place for bird-watching; hundreds of species have been sighted. The reservation is open 8:00 A.M. to 8:00 P.M. from Memorial Day to Labor Day; dawn to dusk the rest of the year. From late May to Columbus Day there are weekend tours, with a Saturday morning bonus of granite-cutting demonstrations (a $2.00 parking fee is charged during these months). The visitor center is usually open in season from noon to 4:00 P.M., but call before you go (978–546–2997).

If you'd like to stay at a place that's handy to Halibut Point, try the **Old Farm Inn,** right next door. A rambling old red farmhouse set way back behind a stone wall, the Old Farm Inn is a real farmhouse that dates to about 1799 and once housed granite workers from the Halibut Point quarry. At a distance from Rockport Center, it's a restful alternative to the crowds and noise of downtown Rockport. The country decor includes original gun-stock beams, handmade quilts, and braided rugs. Breakfast is served in a glassed-in sunroom overlooking the landscaped grounds. For reservations, write the inn at 291 Granite Street, Rockport, MA 01966, or call (978) 546–3237 or (800) 233–6828; www.oldfarminn.com (doubles $75 to $110 off-season, $90 to $140 at peak and shoulder seasons).

Another welcoming Cape Ann home port is the **Yankee Clipper Inn,** where we choose a second-floor room overlooking the village of Rockport, which can be seen across an expanse of waves breaking onto the granite ledges that line the shore. Whether or not you're lucky enough to get a room at the Clipper, you can enjoy its sophisticated dinner menu and the sea view from the dining room. The Yankee Clipper Inn has rooms beginning at around $200 in high season, including a splendid breakfast. It is at 96 Granite Street, Rockport; (978) 546–3407 or (800) 545–3699.

Within a five-minute walk of shops and harbor is the **Peg Leg Inn,** on Beach Street, whose public rooms are decorated with a fine collection of paintings by Tom Nicholas, a well-known artist who now lives in Rockport. Guest rooms are well decorated, and the chef has a winning way with seafood. A sec-

Annisquam Footbridge

ond building across the street has guest rooms overlooking the water. Rates are between $145 and $180; (978) 546–2352, (800) 346–2352.

If you keep following Route 127 around the back side of Cape Ann, it goes to *Annisquam,* a remote village that was a fishing and boatbuilding center for more than two and a half centuries. Annisquam is tiny, with just a few narrow streets hemming the ocean, winding uphill and down. The people who live here have stately ocean views from their attractive Victorian shingled and wooden saltbox houses. The *Annisquam Yacht Club* is unusual, built out on the water on stilts. And the *old wooden footbridge* crossing Lobster Cove is a nice place to stroll and admire the cove.

Historic Boatbuilding Capitals

Plum Island, which juts south more than 6 miles into the Atlantic, is the site of one of the best birding spots on the East Coast, the *Parker River National Wildlife Refuge,* one of the last undeveloped barrier beaches. More than 300 species have been sighted here. The spectacular scenery encompasses 5,000 acres of wide sandy beaches, dunes, bogs, freshwater pools, and tidal marshes reaching into river and ocean. Boardwalks lead to the beach, and there are several nature trails, observation towers, and camera blinds. Because this is a very popular place, the best time to come is off-season. Another good reason to come off-season is that the beach is closed to people from April until July or August, to allow the endangered piping plover to nest and fledge its young undisturbed. The rest of the refuge is open for birding, biking, hiking, and nonbeach recreation. You'll find something happening and something to see every month. In November and December, you can watch migrating Canada and snow geese;

January brings snowy owls; and you can pick wild beach plums and cranberries in September and October (within limits). Call (978) 465–5753 for information. Admission is $5.00 per car and $2.00 per pedestrian or bicyclist. Annual passes are $12.00. Park headquarters is at the northern end of the island and is open from 8:00 A.M. to 4:30 P.M. weekdays. To get there, follow signs from Route 1A.

The city of **Newburyport** is one of the most attractive on the coast. Along High Street (Route 1A) stand dozens of sea captains' houses, ranging from Greek Revival and Federal to Georgian and Victorian, some with cupolas and widow's walks. Downtown, nineteenth-century brick commercial buildings in Market Square have been made into a handsome shopping and dining complex, gracefully accented with cobblestone sidewalks, black iron, street lamps, and lots of trees and potted geraniums.

A hop, skip, and a jump away, at 25 Water Street, is the **Custom House Maritime Museum,** whose collections are beautifully set off in the classic 1835 Greek Revival granite structure. Its small rooms still have their original vaulted ceilings, brick floors, marble windowsills, and tall, wide windows. A cantilevered granite stairway leads to the second floor. Newburyport is the birthplace of the U.S. Coast Guard, and the first revenue cutters were built here by Newburyport shipwrights. The office of the collector of customs holds chests of Ceylon tea, barrels of rum, and lacquered boxes. There are antiques and oil portraits memorializing shipping families, as well as many other maritime memorabilia. The museum is open April through December, Tuesday through Saturday from 10:00 A.M. to 4:00 P.M. and Sunday from noon to 4:00 P.M. Tickets cost $5.00 for adults, $4.00 for seniors and children twelve and older; entrance is free for children younger than twelve. Call (978) 462–8681.

The **Cushing House Museum** is the home of the Newburyport Historical Society, a National Historic Landmark, at 98 High Street. This fine Federal home belonged to the Cushing family, whose ships sailed under three generations of owners during Newburyport's golden era of shipping. Along with the furnished rooms, the house displays several outstanding collections, including fans and toys. The period gardens beside the house are in the process of being restored by local volunteers. The museum is open Tuesday through Friday 10:00 A.M. to 4:00 P.M. (last tour begins at 3:00 P.M.) and Saturday noon to 4:00 P.M., May through October. Admission is $5.00 for adults, $2.00 for children; (978) 462–2681.

The downtown streets seem lined by restaurants. **Scandia Restaurant,** at 25 State Street, serves lunch and dinner with entrees such as salmon with lobster, artichokes, and brie. Prices run from $14 to $26. Sunday brunch is a treat, featuring such tony dishes as orange-brandy French toast; (978) 462–6271. **Kathy Ann's Bakery,** at 350 Merrimack Street, is where locals head for breakfast; (978) 462–7415.

For a retro moment, stop at **Fowles Coffee House,** just down the street, to sit at its old-fashioned marble soda fountain or in one of the original booths. Breakfast is served from 6:00 A.M. (6:30 on Sunday). Those who once wanted to run away to sea should continue downhill to browse in one of the several antique shops specializing in nautical goods.

Newburyport goes all out for the holidays, beginning with Santa's arrival by Coast Guard boat and the lighting of the giant **Christmas tree in Market Square.** For weekends in December, the downtown and waterfront area is alive with music, street performers, bells, gleaming candles, and bright decorations. Shopkeepers welcome visitors with warming drinks and goodies, historic homes are open for tours, and sailors in costume sing rollicking sea chanteys on street corners. Munch on hot roasted chestnuts, ride in a carriage, shop at craft shows and bazaars, listen to choral concerts and Christmas carols, or bring the kids to meet Santa's elves. The final event is First Night on December 31. For a complete schedule, visit Newburyport's Web site at www.newburyport chamber.org.

Hidden away from downtown Newburyport is **Maudslay State Park,** acquired in 1985. Once the private estate of a wealthy family, the property retains its beautifully landscaped grounds, carriage roads, and trails. Enormous rhododendrons rise over your head along the paths, as do centuries-old stands of laurel, one of New England's largest natural stands. Although the mansions are gone, there are still an allée of red oak, the stone foundations of greenhouses, and the foundations of a formal Italian garden and a rose garden. A walk through the woods brings you to a large clearing on a rise, offering a stunning view of the Merrimac River. Lots of special programs and arts performances take place in the park, including autumn hayrides and children's outdoor theater. In winter, cross-country skiing here is pleasant. The park is on Curzon's Mill Road. From Route 113 east, take a left onto Noble Street and follow the signs. There is a $2.00 fee for parking. Call (978) 465–7223.

High Street (Route 1A) continues south to the historic town of **Newbury,** where the first settlers landed in 1635. They are buried in the **old cemetery,** about a quarter of a mile north of the Lower Green. A small sign on the roadside marks the spot, but when you step through the lilac hedge, you feel miles from busy Route 1A. Small stones without inscriptions mark early graves, but you will find dates from the 1600s and winged cherub stones from the time of the Revolution. You're also likely to see rabbits, as well as a herd of deer browsing in the field beyond.

Behind the cemetery, off Newman Road, is **Old Town Hill Reservation,** which includes a glacial drumlin rising 170 feet above the coastal marshes that was used as a mariner's landmark. Climb the trail, and from the top you can see Plum Island and Newburyport. You can also be eaten alive by voracious mosquitoes, so wear a good insect repellent. The first settlers spent the winter of their arrival in shelters they dug into the sides of this hill, with the open sides enclosed by saplings covered in thatch to protect them from the wind. Trails through the reservation cross Newman Road at several points, where you can access the marsh, meadows, and Little River, a tidal estuary. This and the little waterways through the marshes offer good canoeing. On the opposite side of Route 1A at the Lower Green, follow signs to the landing place of the first settlers, where there is a stone marker and a good boat put-in on the Little River.

Sleepy little **Amesbury** is so far off the beaten path that few people come here. But they're missing **Lowell's Boat Shop,** which dates to 1793 and is still making handmade wooden boats on the original site, making it the oldest boat shop in America. Although few others know it is here, wooden-boat fanatics from around the world seek it out. Now a National Historic Landmark, the shop was founded by the Lowell family, who owned and ran it for seven generations, until 1976. In 1793 Simeon Lowell found boats unseaworthy for the three-knot current at the mouth of the Merrimac River. He designed himself a boat that would not capsize and that would be rowable in the heavy surf: a double-ended lapstrake skiff with a raked transom. The world-famous design was called the Amesbury skiff, or dory. Thousands were made for Grand Banks schooners, the U.S. Life Saving Service (forerunner of the Coast Guard), the U.S. Army and Navy in World War II, and early nineteenth-century pleasure boaters.

The shop still looks the way it did more than 200 years ago, sitting right on the banks of the Merrimac River. Only a woodstove heats the wooden building, which smells of sawdust and spar varnish. Downstairs in the paint shop, the paint drippings of centuries are so thick—some 7 inches deep—that the floor looks paved. Amesbury skiffs are still handmade exactly the way they were in 1793, of hand-cut white oak, mahogany, and pine. It takes almost two months to build a boat, and orders come from as far as California, Florida, and Africa. The shop holds classes in antique boatbuilding, woodworking, tool care, and making Windsor chairs. You can visit the shop during business hours—usually Wednesday through Saturday 8:00 A.M. to 5:00 P.M.—but you should call ahead to ask permission. Lowell's Boat Shop, owned by the Newburyport Maritime Society, is at 459 Main Street; (978) 388–0162; www.themaritimesociety.org.

John Greenleaf Whittier lived in Amesbury for fifty-six years, until his death in 1892. The **Whittier Home** is entirely furnished with this Quaker poet and abolitionist's belongings and books. A white frame house with a picket fence, it has small, cozy rooms done in simple country style. Whittier, who never married, lived here with the female triumvirate of his mother, sister, and aunt. Memorabilia include the desk where he wrote his famous poem *Snow-Bound* and his newspaper-lined traveling case. The Garden Room, where Whittier did most of his writing, has his woodstove and divan in place, and the room's walls are full of pictures of his favorite writers. His boots stand on the floor, and his shawl and hat are draped on the rocker. The home, at 86 Friend Street, is open from 10:00 A.M. until the last tour at 3:15 P.M. Tuesday through Saturday, May 1 to October 31. Fees are $3.50 for adults and $1.00 for children. Call (978) 388 1337.

More Places to Stay on the North Shore

Addison Choate Inn,
49 Broadway,
Rockport;
(978) 546–7543 or
(800) 245–7543;
www.addisonchoateinn.com
Beautifully furnished rooms in a historic bed-and-breakfast, close to downtown and the harbor. Rooms from $110, $140 in summer and fall.

Pleasant Street Inn,
17 Pleasant Street,
Rockport;
(978) 546–3915 or
(800) 541–3915;
www.pleasantstreetinn.net
A hilltop Victorian close to the center of town. Rates are $100 to $140.

The Clark Currier Inn,
45 Green Street,
Newburyport;
(978) 465–8363.
The elegant Federal home of a Newburyport shipbuilder, with antique features and furnishings, continental breakfast, afternoon tea, and central location. Rooms from $95 to $185.

The Salem Inn,
7 Summer Street,
Salem;
(978) 741–0680.
Three historic buildings centering in the West House, a row of Federal-period townhouses, a few steps from Salem's prime attractions. Peak-season rooms range from $129 to $189 for suites with kitchenettes.

WORTH SEEING ON THE NORTH SHORE

Whale watching off Cape Ann with Cape Ann Whale Watch,
out of Gloucester,
(800) 877–5110; or
Captain Bill's Whale Watch,
also from Gloucester,
(800) 33–WHALE
(800–339–4253).

Fishing, whale watches, or harbor tours and sunset cruises
leave from docks near Newburyport's Waterfront Park;
Newburyport Whale Watch,
(978) 499–0832 or (800) 848–1111;
Captain's Fishing Parties,
(978) 462–3141, (800) 427–1333;
(full- and half-day deep-sea fishing excursions).

More Places to Eat on the North Shore

David's,
11 Brown Square,
Newburyport;
(978) 462–8077.
Eclectic "New American" dishes, with child care provided while you dine. Why didn't somebody come up with this idea before?

Finz Seafood & Grill,
76 Wharf Street,
Salem;
(978) 744–8485;
www.hipfinz.com
Expertly prepared seafood, within sight of the sea.

Stripers Grille,
175 Bridge Road,
Salisbury;
(978) 499–0400.
Known for its low prices and large quantities.

TO LEARN MORE ABOUT THE NORTH SHORE

Cape Ann Visitors Center,
Gloucester;
(800) 649–6839;
www.seecapeann.com

Newburyport Chamber of Commerce,
29 State Street,
Newburyport 01950;
(978) 462–6680;
www.newburyportchamber.com

North of Boston Convention and Visitors Bureau,
17 Peabody Square,
Peabody 01960;
(800) 742–5306 or (978) 977–7760;
www.northofboston.org

South Shore

It sometimes seems as though the South Shore has been left off most tourist maps of Massachusetts. People tend to just drive through it on their way to Cape Cod. But that's a mistake. Snubbed as the least preferred of the three bedroom regions of greater Boston, the South Shore is a truly undiscovered area—except Plymouth, of course. Most of the colonial shipbuilding and fishing villages that stretch all along the coast from Hingham to Plymouth still have the traditional look of a New England village, with their pretty saltbox and shingled houses. Small-town life is remarkably well preserved in the distinctive downtowns of Cohasset, Duxbury, Scituate, and Hingham.

The beaches and coastline are so appealing that much of the South Shore became a resort area in the nineteenth century. Vacationers came by steamer to grand hotels in Hull. Wealthy Boston Irish politicos, including Mayor James Michael Curley, took to summering in Scituate, hence its nickname, "the Irish Riviera." The inland countryside of the South Shore offers scenic vistas of pine forest, farmland, and the banks of the North River. Most of Massachusetts's cranberry crop grows on the South Shore, spreading its low-lying russet leaves across the landscape for miles in Carver, Middleborough, and Plymouth.

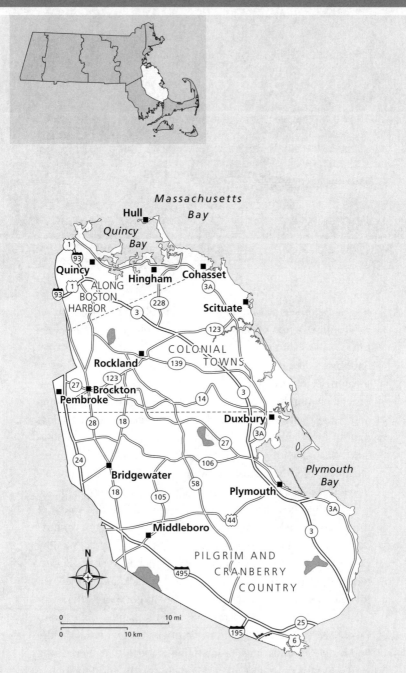

Massachusetts
Bay

Hull

Quincy
Bay

Quincy

Hingham   Cohasset

ALONG
BOSTON
HARBOR

Scituate

COLONIAL
TOWNS

Rockland

Brockton
Pembroke

Duxbury

Bridgewater

Plymouth
Bay

Plymouth

Middleboro

PILGRIM AND
CRANBERRY
COUNTRY

N

0   10 mi
0   10 km

Along Boston Harbor

Though tourists usually bypass **Quincy,** it's the only American city that was home to two U.S. presidents: John Adams and John Quincy Adams. You can see the family home of four generations of Adamses at the **Adams National Historic Site.** It's hard to picture this stately gray house surrounded by farmland, gardens, and orchards, as it was when John and his wife, Abigail, moved in, in 1788. While John pursued his duties in Washington, Abigail busied herself managing the farm and adding a new wing to the house. Family possessions give a deep sense of how loved and used the house was as a family seat. A good-luck horseshoe hangs over the door where Abigail placed it. The wing chair that John Adams died in is still there. Waterford crystal bowls in a china closet are cracked because John Adams sprouted seeds in them. The lovely landscaped grounds hold formal gardens, lilacs with waist-thick trunks, and climbing wisteria. The site, at 135 Adams Street, is open daily from 9:00 A.M. to 5:00 P.M. April 19 to November 10, and Tuesday through Friday 10:00 A.M. to 4:00 P.M. the rest of the year, with more limited access and no tours. Call (617) 770–1175. Your $3.00 ticket also admits you to the nearby **Adams Birthplaces** on Franklin Street, where John Adams and John Quincy Adams were born.

The city of Quincy was one of the country's preeminent builders of navy ships for more than sixty years. The Fore River Shipyard opened at the turn of the century and operated until 1986. It lay dormant for nine years, but in 1995 the city opened the **U.S. Naval and Shipbuilding Museum** in the former yard, just south of downtown Quincy. The museum's centerpiece is a 700-foot heavy cruiser that served as the Sixth Fleet's flagship in the Mediterranean, the USS *Salem.* Visitors can tour the machine shops, hospital, and crew's quarters, as well as the bridge and the command center. The museum grounds house the military archives for Massachusetts from the Revolutionary War up to the present day. Open daily from 10:00 A.M. to 4:00 P.M., the museum charges $5.00 for visitors ages four and up. Call (617) 479–7900 for more information. The museum is off Wharf Avenue; to get there, from Route 3A south, bear right at the rotary just before the Fore River Bridge.

AUTHORS' FAVORITES ON THE SOUTH SHORE

Adams National Historic Site	Cranberry harvest
U.S. Naval and Shipbuilding Museum	

Just barely over the line from Quincy into North Braintree on Route 53, you'll have to look hard to spot the discreet sign for *Spazio* in a tiny strip of shops at 200 Quincy Avenue. You'd never expect a restaurant of this caliber in such an unlikely setting, but it's here, and enough people have found it to make reservations advisable. Begin with grilled quail stuffed with sausage and fresh thyme, served on a bed of caramelized vegetables and drizzled with a blend of port and plums. The last time we ate here, the daily special was a filet of salmon encrusted in potatoes and grilled, served over a ragout of fall vegetables, but each day brings new takes on the freshest locally caught seafood. Dessert might be a "simple" McIntosh apple tart or an espresso cheesecake in chocolate graham crust topped with mocha. Inspiring chef/owner Michael Richardi are the influences of Greek, Spanish, and North African foods found in the cuisine of southern Italy, where he returns twice a year to "cook with friends." The restaurant is open Monday through Saturday from 5:00 to 10:00 P.M. Entrees are reasonably priced at $13 to $19; (781) 849–1577.

Route 3A takes you the whole length of coastal South Shore. The first stop is *Hingham,* a colonial town whose *Main Street* (Route 228) Eleanor Roosevelt called "the most beautiful Main Street in America." This wide, tree-lined boulevard is an oasis of restored homes spanning three centuries. Downtown Hingham has a wealth of historic sights. Unique among them is the *Old Ship Church,* at 90 Main Street (781–749–1679), America's oldest continuously operating church, since 1681. It's one of the few Tudor-style structures left in New England, and like many other early churches, was built by ships' carpenters. Following its liberal tradition, the church's denomination is Unitarian Universalist.

Just beyond Hingham Square, at 21 Lincoln Street, you'll find the *Old Ordinary,* once a seventeenth-century hostelry and now a museum of Hingham history. As a tavern, the Ordinary served an "ordinary meal of the day" to travelers. The taproom looks just as it did three centuries ago, with bar and wooden grille, wooden kegs, and copper tankards. An eighteenth-century parlor, kitchen, dining room, toolroom, and small library are furnished with period antiques. Upstairs, bedrooms display memorabilia of local families and rare silk mourning samplers, an embroidered scene that memorializes a national figure or a family member. The museum is open Tuesday through Saturday from 1:30 to 4:30 P.M. mid-June to Labor Day. Admission is $3.00 for adults and $1.00 for children. For information on special tours on other days, call (781) 749–0013, or visit www.hinghamhistorical.org.

Across the street from the Old Ordinary is a small, green park with a *statue of Abraham Lincoln,* whose ancestor Samuel Lincoln hailed from Hingham. In the summer, ferries run from Hingham (board at the same dock where the Boston shuttle ferry departs) to Georges Island, the launch point for ferries to other islands. Call Boston Harbor Cruises (617–227–4321) or the Harbor Island information line (617–223–8666) for current schedules and fares.

Also in Hingham is one of the South Shore's nicest parks, **World's End.** Planned as a housing subdivision in the nineteenth century, World's End has wide allées designed by Frederick Law Olmsted. The paths sweep uphill to stunning views of the Boston skyline, especially at sunset. To get there, go straight through the rotary on Route 3A south onto Summer Street and turn left onto Martin's Lane. Call (781) 740–6665 or (781) 784–0567 for information. The park is open 8:00 A.M. to sunset year-round, daily. Admission is $4.50 per adult; children age twelve and younger are admitted for free.

At the turn of the century, the town of **Hull** was a stylish resort, complete with grand hotels and an amusement park with a roller coaster. Bathing-costumed vacationers sought summer relief on the miles of white sand and surf at Nantasket Beach, one of the largest beaches on the South Shore. In later decades, Hull deteriorated into a more honky-tonk atmosphere. But the town is once again metamorphosing into a sparkling place, spurred by its arts community.

One vestige of the amusement park that still charms is the vintage 1928 **Carousel under the Clock,** also known as Paragon Carousel, across the street from the beach in a wooden pavilion under an antique clock tower. A ride on the carousel is magical in summer. Infectious antique-pipe-organ music pumps away, the lights shine, and a breeze from the beach sweeps in through the open doors. Brightly painted horses and mermaid-bedecked chariots ferry you around in season. Call (781) 925–0472 for information.

ANNUAL EVENTS ON THE SOUTH SHORE

MID-AUGUST

Marshfield Fair,
the oldest in Massachusetts (it's been held for more than 130 years); (781) 834–6629; www.marshfieldfair.org

LATE SEPTEMBER

Chowda-Fest,
Nantasket Beach, Hull, with plenty of chowder to sample; (781) 925–9980.

EARLY OCTOBER

Massachusetts Cranberry Harvest Festival,
Edaville Cranberry Bogs, off Route 58 in South Carver, has crafts, hayrides, and country music; (508) 866–8190.

LATE OCTOBER

Halloween Tours,
Plymouth, weave ghostly stories into a tour of town, with each participant carrying a lantern; (508) 747–4161 for reservations.

Nantasket Avenue, Hull's main street, takes you out to the ***Hull Lifesaving Museum,*** an engaging place that re-creates the days of valiant surfmen and tragic shipwrecks. The bare wood walls of the station show the spartan surroundings the surfmen lived in one hundred years ago. They drilled every day, simulating capsizing accidents, practicing with the breeches buoy, and working on boat launchings and resuscitation techniques. You can tour the galley, an equipment room, and the bedroom of Joshua James, the station's first captain. Dedicating his life to rescues at sea after his mother and baby sister drowned, James became the nation's most decorated lifesaver, rescuing more than 540 people from eighty-six wrecks. When this station opened in 1889, it was the first official lifesaving service in America. There are lots of memorabilia and photos to look at, as well as a breeches buoy (pants attached to a ring buoy to aid rescue) and faking box (a box on the ship's deck in which a rope is faked or coiled). In the boathouse you can admire a hundred-year-old surfboat with 16-foot pulling oars. A ladder climbs up to the lookout tower. The museum, at 1117 Nantasket Avenue, is open 10:00 A.M. to 4:00 P.M. Wednesday through Sunday, with extended hours for holidays and school vacation weeks. Admission is $2.00 for adults and $1.50 for seniors; children are admitted free. Call (781) 925–5433, or visit www.lifesavingmuseum.org.

Up behind the Hull Lifesaving Museum, you can climb ***Telegraph Hill,*** the highest point on the South Shore, for a splendid view of Hull Harbor and the Atlantic Ocean. Work is underway to clean the graffiti from the stone, Revolutionary War–era ***Fort Revere,*** which was once fired on by the British, and make it into a waterfront park.

Hull Lifesaving Museum

If you'd like to stay in a place where you can admire the views in Hull, choose the **Allerton House,** once a turn-of-the-twentieth-century home, on Allerton Hill. From the top of this hill, you can see Boston Light, America's oldest lighthouse. The Victorian house has wonderful ocean views and a large wraparound porch for enjoying the breeze. Rooms are decorated with hand-painted furniture from the innkeeper's gift shop and watercolors by a local artist. The large living room features a massive fieldstone fireplace. Breakfast of fruit and French pastries is served either on the wide porch or in the dining room. It's just a two-minute walk down the hill from the inn to the beach. Doubles with private baths are $120, with shared bath $100. The inn is at 15 Tierney Avenue, Hull; (781) 925–4569, or, during the day, (781) 383–6317.

An unusual restaurant find in this beach town is **Saporito's Florence Club Cafe,** at 11 Rockland Circle—a gourmet Italian restaurant where the food is so good that it lets the South Shore turn up its nose at Boston's North End. Well disguised inside a beat-up, 1940 Italian club is a gardeny Florentine retreat done up in turquoise and peach. The mouthwatering food includes such intriguing appetizers as grilled *pizzettas*—perhaps topped with lamb, veal, sausage, red and yellow peppers, and feta—and swordfish Involtini with lemon, sesame, capers, and marinated white beans. Entrees of seafood, meats, and pastas in original sauces include black-olive pasta ragout with roasted peppers, red onions, and baked goat cheese; and a veal chop with grappa, capers, anchovies, and cream. Saporito's is open for dinner only and is closed Monday and Tuesday; call (781) 925–3023.

Colonial Towns

Newport has Ocean Drive. **Cohasset,** east of Hingham, has **Jerusalem Road.** This scenic drive winds between Route 228 and North Main Street along rocky coast and secluded beaches, past million-dollar houses perched perilously close to the sea. Offshore, the tall granite spire is **Minot's Light,** whose famous signal flashes (1–4–3), which has been traditionally interpreted as I–LOVE–YOU. To learn more about this historic light, whose predecessor was washed away in a terrible storm, go to the **Maritime and Irish Mossing Museum** maintained by the Scituate Historical Society, on the Driftway. Its collections and photographs give a clear view of Scituate in the glory days of sail and shipbuilding and a new exhibit by National Oceanic and Atmospheric Administration on the discovery of the *Portland,* wrecked in 1898. A gallery is dedicated to the process of gathering Irish moss for commercial use. This is one of three small museum buildings belonging to the society, each of which is worth a visit. The museum is open Saturday and Sunday 1:00 to 4:00 P.M. Memorial Day through Labor Day and Sunday only in the spring and fall. Admission is $4.00 for adults, $3.00 for seniors, and $2.00 for children older than age six. Call (781) 545–1083.

Downtown Cohasset has a classic town green with a duck pond and white-steepled church. At the other end stands a tall granite church, Saint Stephen's. This church is home to the oldest running **carillon concert series** in North America, begun in 1924. Its fifty-seven-bell carillon, cast in England, is the largest in New England. Concerts by famous carillonneurs from all over the world are given Sunday at 6:00 P.M. from late June through August. Hearing a concert is a delightful way to spend a summer evening, perhaps also picnicking on the green lawn of Cohasset Common. Call (781) 383–1083 for a schedule.

A hop, skip, and a jump from Cohasset Common is a really nice take-out restaurant, **Henry's Rootbeer Stand,** at 2 Pleasant Street (781–383–9681). A green lawn with flower gardens holds a scattering of picnic tables where you can take your homemade rootbeer and burger or dog. Follow up with an ice-cream float. Around the corner is an excellent gallery—the **South Shore Art Center,** at 119 Ripley Road (781–383–2787)—that features the work of local artists. Founded in 1955, the South Shore Art Center sponsors the longest continuously operating art festival in the country, held each summer on Cohasset Common.

When you drive through downtown **Scituate,** you may be startled to see a fifteenth-century, Roman-style tower standing in the middle of a green near the library. It's the **Lawson Tower,** built at huge expense by Thomas Lawson, "the Copper King" of Wall Street. Lawson made a fortune in copper, only to be ruined in later life. The water tower stood on his large estate here, called Dreamwold, which had its own railroad and post office. He wanted to cloak the tower's utilitarian purpose. Now, Dreamwold has been converted to condos; however, in 1902 Lawson gave the water tower to the town, and it now plays carillon concerts in summer. At 153 feet tall, the tower is a landmark for ships at sea and offers a clear vista of the South Shore when you climb its steps. To see the tower, take a left off Route 3A south onto First Parish Road and drive up behind the First Parish Church. The tower is open for tours during the summer and by appointment through the Scituate Historical Society (781–545–1083 or 781–545–0474), as are several other sites.

One is the 1811 granite **Scituate Lighthouse,** out on Lighthouse Point at Lighthouse and Rebecca Roads. In the War of 1812, the keeper's quick-witted teenage daughters prevented the British from sacking the town. Seeing two barges approach in the harbor, they grabbed up a fife and drum and played with all their might, hiding behind some cedars. The British, thinking an entire Yankee regiment awaited, beat a hasty retreat. For this feat, the girls went down in history as "the Army of Two."

Front Street in Scituate bustles with interesting little shops, galleries, and restaurants; a working fishing fleet anchors at its northern end. At the **Quarterdeck,** 206 Front Street, you'll find a blend of wares so eclectic that they also caught the eye of Hollywood scouts choosing locations for *The Witches of Eastwick.* This little shop with windows on Scituate Harbor is crammed with antiques, imports, nautical items, and an impressive collection of historic postcards of local scenes.

The stretch of Route 3A from Scituate south to Marshfield is one of the prettiest drives on the South Shore. The tidal marshes of the **North River** reach out for miles on both sides. The play of sunlight is an artist's dream and makes this road a joy to drive. In a reversal from industrial wasteland back to pristine wilderness, the dozens of shipyards and factories that once lined the river's banks are now gone. More than a thousand ships were built here, including the brig *Beaver,* of Boston Tea Party fame, and the ship *Columbia,* the first to carry the Stars and Stripes around the world.

Just over the little bridge at the town line of **Marshfield,** you'll see **Mary's Boat Livery** (781–837–2322) on the right. You can rent a boat here for either a day or a half-day and take it up the North River, an ideal way to take in its scenic meanderings. Half-day rentals (under five hours) are $45, full-day $70, including oars, gas, and life vests.

In its day, the 1699 **Winslow House** was a mansion, as befit its owner, Judge Isaac Winslow, grandson of Plymouth Colony Governor Edward Winslow, the Pilgrim founder of Marshfield. The leading men of Plymouth Colony were entertained here, at formal teas and dinners. Although the house looks plain by our standards, its Jacobean staircase with acorn finials was a standout in its time. Behind the Georgian paneling in the drawing room is a secret chamber where Tories reportedly hid. Daniel Webster had an estate in Marshfield for twenty years, and his law office was moved here; the office has letters and photos of Webster's. Also on the property are a blacksmith shop and a one-room schoolhouse. The Winslow House, at 634 Careswell Street, is open June to mid-October, Wednesday through Sunday 10:00 A.M. to 4:00 P.M., with hour-long guided tours. Admission is $5.00 for adults, $3.00 for seniors, and $1.00 for children. Call (781) 837–5753, or visit www.marshfield.net/winslow.

No matter what the season, it always smells like Thanksgiving at **Gerard Farm,** a family business for fifty years. The smell of roasting turkey and chicken fills the air at this wonderful shop, which sells many kinds of homemade foods, with freshly roasted turkey its specialty. Where else—if it's not the day after Thanksgiving—can you get a thick turkey sandwich made with two kinds of bread, cranberry sauce, stuffing, and mayonnaise? Freezers stock frozen turkey pies ("all dark meat" and "all white meat"), turkey croquettes, roast turkeys, and turkey soup. The shop is at 1331 Ocean Street (Route 139). Call (781) 834–7682.

Each spring thousands of herring fight their way 16 miles from the ocean up the North River to spawn in freshwater ponds, as they have for centuries. The herring, also called alewives, were a vital source of food for the Pilgrims and the Indians. Colonists regulated fishing rights strictly, appointing a "herring superintendent" to oversee the harvesting and distribution of fish. Widows, spinsters, and other needy persons were given bushel baskets of fish. There are half a dozen points on the South Shore where you can watch the herring run. A good spot is *Herring Run Park* on Route 14 in *Pembroke,* which celebrates the herring run with an annual fish fry in late April or early May. Formerly, attendees could catch their own with nets or bare hands. However, a herring ban is in place through 2009 to help replenish the dwindling numbers of the fish, which used to be known as "poor man's salmon." The fish fry goes on though, with good old-fashioned cod cakes substituted for the herring. Watching the increasing numbers of these fish in the spawning run will have to be its own reward for the time being. For the date and other information, call the Plymouth County Development Council at (800) 231–1620 or (781) 293–9083.

beforeNPR

The world's first radio program was broadcast from Blackman's Point in Marshfield on Christmas Eve in 1906. This historic broadcast was a weather report to ships at sea. Radio communication has improved since then; however, weather forecasting in New England remains a challenge.

Pilgrim and Cranberry Country

The town of *Duxbury* was settled as early as 1625, by Pilgrims from the nearby Plymouth Colony. Among them were colonists with names that ring through history: Alden, Standish, Brewster. Although there is no evidence that John Alden had to win his wife, Priscilla, away from Myles Standish as Longfellow's famous poem recounts, the couple are known to have lived out their later years in a tiny house built in 1653. The *John Alden House* is cramped and dark and looks none too comfortable. Its low, rough plaster ceilings were made of crushed clam and oyster shells, and even the formal parlor has a stark look to it. Other features of the house are the cambered panels in the "best room" and the gun-stock beams in the bedchambers. The house, located at 105 Alden Street, off Route 3A, is open from noon to 4:00 P.M. Monday through Saturday, from mid-May through early October. Admission is $5.00 for adults, $4.00 for seniors and students, $3.00 for children younger than age six. Call (781) 934–9092 for information.

Down the street from the Alden House is a much brighter, contemporary place: the **Art Complex Museum.** This small but intriguing museum was founded by Carl Weyerhaeuser—grandson of the founder of the lumber company of the same name—and his wife, Edith, as a home for their private collection. Much of it is Asian art, as well as Shaker and American works. There are semiannual showings of contemporary New England artists. A unique feature of the museum is an authentic Japanese teahouse designed in Kyoto; traditional Japanese tea ceremonies are conducted in the summer months. The museum, open from 1:00 to 4:00 P.M. Wednesday through Sunday, offers free admission. It's located at 189 Alden Street, which you can reach from Route 3A. Call (781) 934–6634.

For dessert (or a luxurious breakfast), you can't beat **French Memories Bakery.** This bakery was founded by natives of France, who bake real French croissants and baguettes on the premises. They also create mouthwatering pastries that are colorful works of art: kiwi, strawberry, and apple tarts; chocolate mousse; brioches; and opera cake. The shop is at 459 Washington Street, next to Sweetser's General Store; call (781) 934–9020.

The town of Duxbury once had sixteen shipbuilders. The wealthiest of them, Ezra Weston and his son, Ezra Weston II, grew so rich that they both came to be called "King Caesar." In 1808, the son built a gorgeous, Federal-style mansion overlooking his wharves. The light-filled **King Caesar House** shows off exquisite woodwork and fanlight windows, as well as sweeping ocean views. One room displays treasures of the China Trade, such as Chinese writing implements and beautifully hand-painted fans. The two front parlors display rare French mural wallpapers. The many fine furnishings include a thirteen-light cabinet symbolic of the thirteen colonies, a 1795 girandole mirror, and Sandwich and cable glass. (Cable glass was made in a cable-shaped pattern to commemorate the laying of the first transatlantic cable from France to Duxbury in 1869.) The house, on King Caesar Road, is open from 1:00 to 4:00 P.M. Wednesday through Sunday from early June through Labor Day and on Friday and Saturday in September. Admission is $5.00 for adults and $2.00 for children. Call (781) 934–6106.

If you follow King Caesar Road out to **Duxbury Beach,** you'll pass over the **Powder Point Bridge,** the longest wooden bridge on the eastern seaboard (some say the longest in the nation). About 2,200 feet long, it was first built in 1892 and was then rebuilt after it burned in 1985. Cars are welcome to cross this wide span, which offers a pretty view of a little inlet just before Duxbury Beach. The bridge is favored by fishermen, the inlet by sailboarders. Duxbury

Beach is a grand stretch of sand 6 miles long that faces the open Atlantic. It's one of the few South Shore beaches open to the public.

NEW ENGLAND'S LARGEST BREAKFAST MENU trumpets the sign at **Persy's Place** in **Kingston.** Indeed, you might spend all morning perusing the offerings: sixteen egg dishes; twelve kinds of omelets, including lobster, *chourico,* and "build-your-own"; and almost everything else your breakfast fancy might desire, from asparagus to rainbow trout, from finnan haddie to SOS (uh, chipped beef on toast). Persy's hews to Yankee traditions with fish cakes, corned beef hash, Boston baked beans, and grilled corn bread (outstanding). Four generations of the Heston family (the youngest is "growing as fast as she can") serve breakfast all day long. The small dining rooms with wooden booths are so homey that they feel like your own kitchen. An outdoor deck opens in nice weather. Next door, the owners run a small country store that sells hand-painted wooden decorations. Persy's Place is at 117 Main Street (Route 3A), just south of exit 9 from Route 3. Call (781) 585–5464.

Plymouth is a small town with a big story, and a mecca for people seeking the roots of the United States. In a place so permeated with history, they don't expect to find the almost genteel, unhurried atmosphere that the town exudes. Distances are short, and it is a great walking city. Begin at the waterfront, where you'll find the **Waterfront Tourist Information Office** in a house near Memorial Drive; (800) USA–1620, www.visit-plymouth.com. **Mayflower II,** itself now a respectable fifty years old, is an authentic reproduction of the original that started a nation. *Mayflower II* floats at dock at State Pier, where you can board it and explore it, after reading the informative display on Pilgrim life, on the dock. Be sure to explore the tight confines of its below-decks interior. Just beyond it you'll see the classical columns of the **Plymouth Rock Memorial.**

Backtrack a bit to Memorial Drive and head uphill to the **Pilgrim Hall Museum,** a reliquary of thousands of items left behind by the original settlers and the Native Americans that helped them, Collections include letters, furniture, personal pieces, and even a fragment of the ship *Sparrow-Hawk* dating from the seventeenth century. It's open daily from 9:30 A.M. to 4:30 P.M. from February through December. Admission is $6.00, $5.00 for seniors, and $3.00 for ages five through seventeen; 75 Court Street; (508) 746–1620; www.pilgrimhall.org.

At the other end of Main Street (Court turns into Main) find Leyden Street and follow it past the 1749 Court House and the First Parish Church to the path into the cemetery on **Burial Hill.** Here you'll find the graves of the earliest settlers, including Governor Bradford, whose wise counsel guided them to survival. At the south end of the cemetery, a stair descends to a path that leads to Summer Street and the **Sparrow House,** the oldest surviving building from the early era. Its sparse interior is a reminder of the harshness of life in the first years. Open April 1 to December 24 Thursday through Tuesday, 10:00 A.M. to 5:00 P.M., and January through March by appointment.

Around the corner on Spring Lane, the *Jenney Grist Mill* is a reconstruction of a grain-grinding mill that stood on the site from 1637 until 1847. It is authentic, and visitors can watch grain being milled by the gregarious miller. Its gift shop is a good place to look for souvenirs and ice cream to eat outside beside the huge waterwheel; (508) 747–4544. Tours cost $6.00 for adults, $3.00 for children. Guided walking tours of town are also available.

A path runs along along Town Brook back down to the waterfront. On its way it passes through *Brewster Gardens,* an attractive grassy place to rest. This park was the site of the original settlement, so try to picture the small crude houses nestled together here. Look for the Pilgrim Maiden Memorial and the stunning modern Immigrant Memorial. On the uphill side of Water Street is the sarcophagus containing the bones of original settlers, the famed *Massasoit* statue, and the Pilgrim Mother Memorial, snuggled into its own little park.

Plimoth Plantation re-creates that original settlement. The visitor center has well-planned exhibits to introduce you to the story, before you wander out into the real world of seventeenth-century America. You'll feel the fragility of their sapling houses, watch meals being cooked, see cloth being spun and woven, and chores being performed. Around you the docents speak authentic period English, a taste of the old, old world. In a separate area Wampanoag Indians build wetu houses and tell tales in the communal hall. The men may be burning out a dugout canoe and women stripping bark for lashing material and cooking traditional meals. Open March 25 to November 26 daily, 9:30 A.M. to 5:00 P.M. Find the plantation on Warren Avenue; (508) 746–1622; www.plimoth.org.

There are several options for lodging in town. *Governor Bradford on the Harbour* is inexpensive, motel-like, and close to everything; 98 Water Street; (800) 332–1620, (508) 746–6200; www.governorbradford.com. But we like the elegant comfort and warm greeting at the *Jesse Harlow House,* a small B&B close by at 3 North Green Street; (508) 746–6877; www.jesseharlow house.com. Rooms are impeccably furnished and decorated, all with private bath, and the enjoyable hosts Jay and Tom Blue may even invite you for a glass of wine on the deck overlooking the city. The rates include an outstanding three-course breakfast.

For family-style dining on the wharf, *Wood's Seafood* is right down on Town Dock. Food is ordered at a window and brought to a table where you might sit next to a local (they like it here) or even a foreign visitor. Get there early or expect to wait; (508) 746–0261. *The Vine,* at 18 Main Street Extension, just above Brewster Garden, is small and intimate, with a nice collection of fine wines by the glass. On weekends they usually have music performed by talented local people; (508) 830–1942.

If you're on Pilgrim overload, you might try a whale watch. As big as the whale-watching business has grown in Gloucester and Provincetown, few people know you can sail from Plymouth. Head over to Town Wharf, where you'll find **Capt. John Boats,** which from April through October runs four-hour whale-watching cruises to Stellwagen Bank, the whales' feeding ground. These boats have a high success rate and have spotted finback, humpback, right, and minke whales, among other kinds. Cruises cost $34 for adults, $30 for seniors over age sixty-two, and $22 for children under age twelve. Call (508) 746–2643 or (800) 242–AHOY in Massachusetts, or look them up at www.captjohn.com. Capt. John Boats also runs harbor tours, cruises to Provincetown, and deep-sea fishing charters.

Massachusetts grows roughly half the country's cranberries right here on the South Shore. In the fall, the landscape blazes with bogs in crimson. Locals routinely see the **cranberry harvest** in progress as they drive along the country roads of Plymouth, Carver, Middleborough, and Wareham. The harvest is big business and is well promoted—bus tours arrive en masse. Still, watching the colorful harvest is a great way to spend a crisp, sunny fall day, and one that will prompt you to reach for the camera. The wet-harvesting method first floods bogs and then uses water reels like giant eggbeaters to loosen the berries from the vines so that they float to the surface. The huge sea of red berries contrasts vibrantly with the deep blue of the water. Enriching the tones of this picture, workers wearing yellow hip-waders corral the berries. Then a hose vacuums them up into a truck. Harvesting goes on from about Labor Day to late October or early November. You'll pass several bogs on Route 44 west through Plymouth, down Seven Hills Road, and out to Federal Furnace Road, or drive out Routes 106 or 58.

You might want to sample some cranberry wine on your tour. If so, turn in to the **Plymouth Colony Winery** (508–747–3334), on Pinewood Road in Plymouth, a left off Route 44 west. Housed in an 1890 cranberry-screening house, the winery also makes blueberry, raspberry, peach, and grape wines. They are open April through December, Monday through Saturday 10:00 A.M. to 5:00 P.M., and Sunday noon to 5:00 P.M.; and February and March, Saturday 10:00 A.M. to 4:00 P.M., and Sunday noon to 4:00 P.M.

To learn all there is to know about cranberries, stop in at the **Cranberry World Visitors Center,** on the waterfront in Plymouth—the country's only museum devoted to cranberries. Exhibits illustrate cranberry history and trace harvesting methods and tools, from antique wooden scoops to modern ways. The cranberry bouncer, designed years ago, is still used to test ripeness by how high berries bounce. The low entry charge for the museum is more than worth the free samples of juice and the product coupons they send you home with. The museum, on Water Street, is open May 1 to November 30, from 9:30 A.M. to 5:00 P.M. daily. Call (508) 747–2350.

There's a lot to see at the ***Middleboro Historical Museum.*** You might start with the collection of Tom Thumb memorabilia, collected from General and Mrs. Tom Thumb's Middleboro house, built to their miniature size. The pair, who toured with P. T. Barnum, received gifts from queens, emperors, and kings. Also among the memorabilia are Tom's pipe and smoking stand, along with miniature clothing. The museum also has eighteenth- and nineteenth-century museum houses (historic homes that may be toured), antique vehicles, a blacksmith shop, and many period vignettes, such as a country store, an old-time print shop, and a straw-hat works. Nineteenth-century wedding gowns, antique children's toys, and Indian artifacts are on exhibit as well. The museum is located on Jackson Street, off Route 105, behind the police station. Hours are from 1:00 to 4:00 P.M. Wednesday and Saturday, June through October, and by appointment. Admission is $5.00 for adults and $2.00 for students. Call (508) 947–1969.

Middleboro is a pleasant town convenient to all parts of the South Shore but without the overcrowding of the waterfront towns. Two B&Bs here make it a particularly good place to settle in. In the center of town, next to the impressive domed town hall, is the 1831 ***Zachariah Eddy House***, a well-restored Victorian home with unusual architectural details. The upstairs bath, for instance, with the stained-glass window set in an alcove, was once the private chapel of the original builders. Rooms are very nicely furnished; we especially like the Copperbeech Room, which has a window seat and a half-domed ceiling. One small room is decorated with vintage hats. Plan to arrive in time to enjoy the large porch set in a shaded yard, with a view of the town hall through the trees. On warm mornings your breakfast table will be set up out here. Rates begin at less than $100. The B&B is at 51 South Main Street, Middleboro; (508) 946–0016.

In contrast to this historic downtown setting, ***On Cranberry Pond Bed and Breakfast*** is in the open countryside and occupies a beautiful new home, built especially to welcome overnight guests. The setting overlooks a cranberry bog and a pond, with birds to watch, walking trails, and bicycles, and a skating pond in the winter. Guest rooms are large and nicely decorated, with thoughtful touches such as plenty of closet shelves and good-quality soaps.

Elmwood Post Office

Breakfast is likely to include baked cranberry French toast, in keeping with the setting. Several comfortable parlors provide places to read or sit, and a flower-surrounded deck is a great place to sit and watch the cranberries grow. Although the setting is peaceful and quiet, On Cranberry Pond is easy to find, about a mile off Route 44 and close to Interstate 495. Rates begin at $95 and range upward for the suite with private living room and whirlpool bath. On Cranberry Pond is at 43 Fuller Street, Middleboro; (508) 946–0768.

Middleboro is just south of ***Bridgewater,*** a town thick with interesting stops. Route 18 north all the way to East Bridgewater is lined with antiques shops—small stores in old houses filled with an agreeable clutter of furniture and collectibles. Look particularly for ***Antiques at Forge Pond.***

Where Route 18 meets Route 106 west, you'll find a post office that has stood its ground since 1861. The ***Elmwood Post Office*** was commissioned by Abraham Lincoln. The Elmwood section of Bridgewater was the birthplace of the shoe industry, and a tannery was built here as early as 1650. Lincoln ordered the post office so that the village could ship badly needed shoes to the Union army. The post office stands in a small, white-columned building, taking up only a tiny corner for its ancient black window grille and old-fashioned metal mailboxes with brass combination dials. Behind the grille is an old, slant-topped wooden desk, and hanging above the desk is a framed picture of Lincoln. The post office shares its floor space with an antiques shop.

More Places to Stay on the South Shore

Pilgrim Sands Motel,
150 Warren Avenue
(Route 3A),
Plymouth;
(508) 747–0900 or
(800) 729–SAND;
www.pilgrimsands.com
Rooms from $84 off-season,
$155 in summer, with a private beach for guests.

White Swan B&B,
146 Manomet Point Road,
Plymouth;
(508) 224–3759,
fax (508) 224–1948;
www.whiteswan.com
This 200-year-old farmhouse
has been an inn for more
than a century and is a two-
minute walk from the beach.
Rooms are $115 to $165.

More Places to Eat on the South Shore

The Barker Tavern,
21 Barker Road,
Scituate;
(781) 545–6533.
The tavern was built in 1634,
and it seems to shine most
brightly with classic dishes
like the swordfish, which
melts in your mouth. Open
for dinner Tuesday through
Sunday. Entrees around $25.

The Mayflower Restaurant,
14 Union Street,
Plymouth;
(508) 747–4503.
Outside the maddening
crowds of Pilgrim-town, this
oasis serves stylish entrees
($10 to $20) in a nice setting
overlooking the water.

Hearth 'n Kettle,
25 Summer Street
(at The John Carver Inn),
Plymouth;
(508) 746–7100 or
(800) 274–1620.
Specializes in fresh seafood
and hearty portions, in an
informal atmosphere. Prices
are family friendly and portions generous.

TO LEARN MORE ABOUT THE SOUTH SHORE

**Plymouth County Convention
and Visitors Bureau,**
170 Water Street, Suite 24,
Plymouth 02360;
(508) 747–0100;
www.seeplymouth.com

Cape Cod and the Islands

We know that about eleven million people visit Cape Cod each year. And we know that on a summer Saturday, traffic on U.S. Route 6 looks as though they had all come at once. But there must be something here to see or there would be no lines of people waiting to see it.

Miles of tacky strip development, traffic jams, and some overcrowded beaches notwithstanding, there's a lot to enjoy on the Cape and even in midsummer you'll find uncrowded, peaceful corners. So drive past the T-shirt shops and the fast-food havens, and stick to the North Shore as much as you can, abandoning US 6 for the leafy roadsides of Route 6A.

Here you will travel through villages that look as though they had just awakened from the nineteenth century, and you'll be near the long, white beaches of Cape Cod Bay. Forty more miles of windswept dunes and beaches are protected as part of the Cape Cod National Seashore, an area that Henry David Thoreau or Eugene O'Neill would still recognize, unchanged from the times when each walked the sands.

The Cape is a dream world for photographers and artists, with its lighthouses, cranberry bogs, windmills, beach roses, dunes, and weathered-shingle houses. Elegant homes of long-

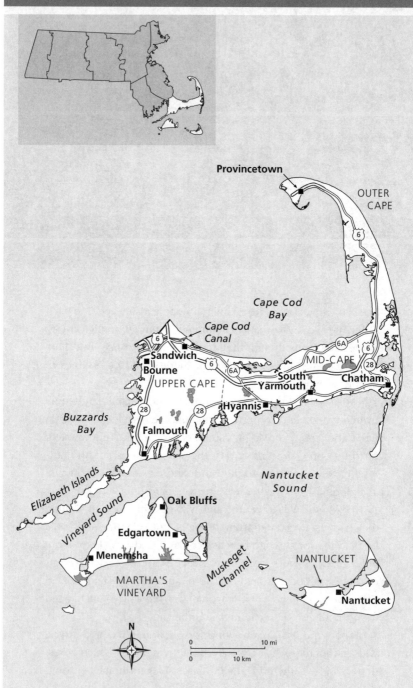

ago sea captains have been restored, some as B&Bs and inns where you can spend the night.

Shaped like a giant bent arm, Cape Cod juts into the Atlantic Ocean, with Bourne at its "shoulder," Chatham at the "elbow," and Provincetown way out at the "fist," the northeast tip. The landscape gets wilder as you head out toward the very end, the place of fabled 100-foot dunes, wide-open beaches, and acres of waving grasses. For some reason, the "shoulder" is known as the Upper Cape and the tip as the Lower Cape (also the Outer Cape). In between is the commercialized Mid-Cape.

The Cape's two island neighbors, Martha's Vineyard and Nantucket, are distinctly different from each other, despite their common whaling heritage. Martha's Vineyard is much larger and has a more varied terrain. Diminutive Nantucket is less touristy and outside of its busy harbor settlement is a wilder place of rolling moors.

The Cape and the Islands are lovelier in the off-season. The summertime hordes can make travel slow on the Cape and disgorge from ferries and cruise ships onto the Islands. Though fall and spring are no longer quite the secret they were, they're much more tranquil times to visit. The surge of tourism dies down to a low roar, and the natives resume their small-town rhythms.

Upper Cape

Before you even get to the Cape, there are things to see. Most people don't give the Cape Cod Canal a second thought, except for how fast they can get over the bridges in heavy traffic. But those two graceful bridges, the **Sagamore Bridge** and the **Bourne Bridge,** won a national award for "most beautiful steel bridges" when they were completed in 1935. From them, you can see for miles over the Upper Cape and watch the sun flooding across the 500-foot-wide expanse, the widest sea-level canal in the world. A constant parade of boats

AUTHORS' FAVORITES ON CAPE COD AND THE ISLANDS

Cape Cod National Seashore	Dunes tours in Provincetown
Cycling on Nantucket	*Ocean Quest* research cruises
Heritage Museums and Gardens	Nantucket Whaling Museum

and ships uses the waterway; some 20,000 a year pass through it, making it one of the world's busiest canals. Myles Standish first suggested a canal here in 1623, but it took until 1914 to get the 17-mile-long route built. The U.S. Army Corps of Engineers oversees the canal and maintains a popular visitor center in Sandwich. But few people stop into the reception area at the administration building just down the road in **Buzzards Bay.**

The white wooden building sits hard by the banks of the canal, dwarfed by the towering legs of the Bourne Bridge. Two red-and-yellow tugs ride at anchor nearby. In the marine traffic controller's office, you can see a large diorama of the canal and watch the controller at work behind a massive bank of computer monitors, radios, and closed-circuit television screens. You'll hear the crackling broadcasts of approaching ships too. A slide show explains how the traffic control system works. The visitor reception area is open from 9:00 A.M. to 4:00 P.M. weekdays, although it may be closed with heightened security alert status; call to confirm (508) 759–4431. From the Sagamore rotary, follow signs for Buzzards Bay to Main Street. Turn left at the first set of traffic lights onto Academy Drive.

The Army Corps of Engineers' **Cape Cod Canal Visitor Center** in **Sandwich** provides a more complete idea of how the canal operates. A short film and interactive touch screens add to the experience. The new visitor center is on Ed Moffitt Drive, next to the Sandwich Marina and is open July through August daily, and September though mid-October Wednesday through Sunday 10:00 A.M. to 5:00 P.M., (508) 833–9678. The old visitor center under the bridge remains open but does not have the range of material that the new center does.

The Corps also sponsors nature walks, bike trips, campfire programs, and similar events in the canal area. Two 8-mile service roads paralleling the canal are nice, flat terrain for bicycling and offer views unseen by drivers. The roads are accessible from more than half a dozen points on the mainland or on the Cape. You can find mainland parking spots behind the Friendly Ice Cream Shop off the Sagamore Bridge rotary, at Herring Run on US 6 between the rotary and Buzzards Bay, and at **Scusset Beach.** You might bike out to Scusset Beach, a long, sandy strip with bathhouses and a snack stand, for the afternoon. On the Cape side, you can park on Freezer Road at Sandwich Marina or at Monument Beach–Pocasset. (Head east from the Bourne Bridge rotary and turn left at the sign.)

If you'd like an even better view of the canal, take a narrated sightseeing cruise along it, perhaps by moonlight or at sunset or accompanied by some rousing jazz music. Hy-Line Cruises runs two- or three-hour **Cape Cod Canal Cruises** (508–295–3883; www.hy-linecruises.com) daily from Onset Bay, spring through fall. Steaming along on a 200-passenger boat with an observation deck,

ANNUAL EVENTS ON CAPE COD AND THE ISLANDS

LATE APRIL

Daffodil Festival,
Nantucket, when the island is abloom with spring bulbs, and activities from bird-watching to picnics welcome visitors; (508) 228–1700.

MID-MAY

Cape Cod Maritime Days,
at various locations, offers lighthouse tours, cruises, visits to historic ships and homes, walking tours, and a variety of other sea-related activities; (508) 362–3225; www.ecapechamber.com/maritimedays

LATE JUNE

Annual Portuguese Festival,
Provincetown, with food, music, dancing, and the Blessing of the Fleet; (508) 487–0500.

AUGUST

Hyannis Pops by the Sea,
outdoor concerts; (508) 362–0066.

MID-AUGUST

Annual Sandcastle and Sculpture Day,
Jetties Beach, Nantucket, open to islanders and visitors; (508) 228–1700.

EARLY SEPTEMBER

Annual Bourne Scallop Festival,
Buzzards Bay Park, brings crafts, entertainment, and, of course, scallops; (508) 759–6000.

MID-SEPTEMBER

Tivoli Day,
Circuit Avenue, Oak Bluffs, Martha's Vineyard, with art, music, and food; (508) 693–0085.

LATE OCTOBER

Happy Haunting,
at the Colonial Inn, Edgartown, on the Saturday nearest Halloween, includes jack-o'-lantern carving and trick-or-treat routes; (508) 627–4711.

EARLY DECEMBER

Christmas-by-the-Sea Weekend,
Falmouth, offers food, music, bazaars, lighthouse tours, and a parade; (508) 548–8500 or (800) 526–8532.

you'll see such historic places as the site of President Grover Cleveland's summer mansion, Gray Gables. Rates for adults range from $11 to $13; children under age twelve ride for half fare on day cruises and free on the 4:00 P.M. cruise. Sunday afternoon Jazz Cruises are $17.

By taking the Bourne Bridge over the canal and onto Route 28, you can make a loop tour of the Cape's chunky "shoulder." The first stop is **Bourne,** where there is a jewel of a little museum, the ***Aptucxet Trading Post.*** This primitive-looking building is a replica of the first trading post in English-speaking North America. It stood here in 1627 and was built by the Pilgrims for trade with the Dutch and Indians. But the post is authentic in many ways. The inside is fitted out with wooden barrels of tobacco, furs hanging on the wall, and wooden scales. It's easy to picture Pilgrims and Indians trading together here. Traders used wampum, beads made of local purple quahog shells that were America's first form of currency. Some architectural details are seventeenth century, such as the beams, wide-planked flooring, and leaded-glass, diamond-pane windows.

Glass cases hold seventeenth-century potsherds, Indian arrowheads, and stone tools and wampum found on the site. Also on the grounds are President Cleveland's Victorian summer railroad station for arriving guests and a replica of an eighteenth-century saltworks with rolling roofs. There are picnic tables on the wooded grounds. The post is open from May through Columbus Day, 10:00 A.M. to 4:30 P.M. Tuesday through Saturday and 2:00 to 5:00 P.M. on Sunday. The museum also opens Mondays in July and August. Admission is $4.00 for adults, $3.50 for students and seniors, and $2.00 for children ages six through eighteen. Call (508) 759–8167. To get to the museum, turn right after crossing the Bourne Bridge and go 1 mile to a cemetery on the left; then turn right under a white railroad underpass onto Aptucxet Road, which jogs right. A windmill stands at the entrance.

Pairpoint is the oldest operating glassworks in the United States. Begun in 1837 as the Mount Washington Glass Company, it's known for its deep rich colors, especially for the "cranberry glass" that is associated with Cape Cod.

Its factory and retail showroom are close to the Sagamore Bridge. You can see glassblowing there Monday through Friday from 9:00 A.M. to 4:00 P.M. Retail shop hours are Monday through Friday 9:00 A.M. to 6:00 P.M., Saturday 10:00 A.M. to 6:00 P.M., and Sunday 11:00 A.M. to 6:00 P.M. Pairpoint is located at 851 Route 6A, Sagamore; (508) 888–2344; www.pairpoint.com.

Because it lies in its own little corner of the Cape, far from busy US 6, ***Falmouth*** is often bypassed by those intent on "doing the Cape" from end to end. Route 28 goes through the center of the village, which still retains its green surrounded by fine homes, and a pleasant compact business district along with a harbor filled with pleasure craft. Here you can sign on for cruises and fishing trips, choosing among several boats including the sailing schooner *Liberté*, which spends July and August on the Cape and the rest of the year in Annapolis, Maryland; (508) 548–2626.

Facing the green is the ***Julia Wood House,*** a Federal home built in 1790 and decorated with furniture from that period. It is open from 10:00 A.M. to 4:00

P.M. Tuesday through Friday, and Saturday 10:00 A.M. to 1:00 P.M. from mid-June to early October. Admission is $5.00 for adults; children are admitted free. You can stroll along the brick-and-flagstone paths of the lovely boxwood-bordered garden anytime, but it is especially nice in May when the azaleas are in bloom or in June when the roses are at their best; just walk in through the front gate. Adjacent in two other buildings are a collection of sailor art and other maritime antiquities and a barnful of old farming tools. They offer Tuesday afternoon walking tours in July and August, occasional trolley tours, and tea in the garden on Thursday afternoon in summer ($12). It is best to call ahead to confirm: (508) 548–4857.

Continuing south on Route 28, turn left onto Route 151 in Falmouth. Just off 151, you'll find a wildlife sanctuary that's full of Christmas spirit year-round—the **Ashumet Holly Reservation and Wildlife Sanctuary.** Here grows the largest native holly collection in New England—eight species and sixty-five varieties. They're all identified along a nature trail surrounding a grassy pond. A walk here is a wonderful discovery of holly's endless variety beyond the familiar red berry. Some hollies are trees, towering 20 or 30 feet tall; others bear orange or black berries. Berries turn color in late October, lingering through March unless robins and squirrels eat them all. Fragrant wreaths and swags of greenery are sold at Christmastime. A barn swallow colony nests in the barn May through August. The sanctuary, at 286 Ashumet Road in East Falmouth (508–563–6390), is open from dawn to dusk. Trail fees are $3.00 for adults and $2.00 for seniors and children.

Heading southwest from Falmouth, before you get to Woods Hole, off Route 28 and via a right turn onto Quisset Harbor Road is a lovely little sanctuary, the **Cornelia Carey Sanctuary.** (Locals call it "the Knob.") The road winds around picturesque Quisset Harbor and its fishing boats before coming to a dead end. Where a sign announces PRIVATE ROAD, there's a fence with a turnstile in front of a large house. Walk through the turnstile and over a stone-fortified causeway. A small wooded area of red cedar and oak opens up to a bare, grassy promontory high up, offering views of Buzzards Bay and the Elizabeth Islands. The Salt Pond Areas Bird Sanctuaries owns the land; call (508) 548–0703 (in the offices of Ermine Lovell Real Estate) for information.

You can take the WHOOSH trolley from Falmouth to **Woods Hole,** where there is very limited public parking. For a schedule, or to buy a pass or discounted tokens, contact the Falmouth Chamber of Commerce; (508) 548–8500 or (800) 526–8532.

The **Woods Hole Oceanographic Institution,** the largest independent oceanographic laboratory in the world, seems to dominate the village of Woods Hole on its water-surrounded little corner of Falmouth. The Exhibit Center and

Gift Shop are at 15 School Street, open Monday through Saturday 10:00 A.M. to 4:30 P.M. and Sunday noon to 4:30 P.M. from May through October; in November and December they're open Tuesday to Friday 10:00 A.M. to 4:30 P.M. They are closed the rest of the the year. Here you will find displays and hands-on exhibits about the deep-diving research station *Alvin* and other vehicles that explore the ocean depths. You can also see a video about the institution and another about *Alvin* and the discovery of the wreck of the *Titanic*. Guided walking tours of the WHOI, as the institution is called locally, leave at 10:30 A.M. and 1:30 P.M. weekdays from late June to early September from the information center at 93 Water Street. You'll get a tour of the facilities, including the pier, where you may have a close-up look at the institution's research vessel *Atlantis,* and other areas of the campus not usually open to the public. Tours are free, but you must have a reservation; (508) 289–2252; www.whoi.edu.

To take part in some marine research yourself, sign on for an excursion with **OceanQuest,** on Water Street in Woods Hole; (508) 385–7656 or (800) 376–2326. These hands-on ninety-minute cruises are good for families, since there is a job for everyone, and kids may get addressed as "doctor" as they record a new oceanic discovery. Passengers are divided into two groups, one learning to take measurements of ocean temperature, turbidity, and other environmental factors while the other examines the "catch" hauled up from the ocean floor by the dredger. Mid-trip the two groups swap jobs. The staff is excellent, making sure that each passenger shares in the activities and has a good learning experience. Adults pay about $20, children ages three to twelve $15. Trips leave at 10:00 A.M., noon, and 2:00 and 4:00 P.M. Monday through Friday in July and August, and Saturdays at noon and 2:00 P.M.; www.oceanquest.org.

The **National Marine Fisheries Service Aquarium** on Albatross Street is free, open from mid-June through Labor Day, Tuesday through Saturday from 11:00 A.M. to 4:00 P.M. During the school year, it's open weekdays, the same hours. It may be open other hours as well, so it's worth calling or stopping by to check. Be there at 11:00 A.M. or 4:00 P.M. to see the seals fed, but you can watch the seals even when the facility is closed; (508) 495–2001.

The **Woods Hole Historical Museum**, on Woods Hole Road as you enter town, is open Tuesday through Saturday from mid-June to mid-September, 10:00 A.M. to 4:00 P.M. Along with the displays of local history at the Bradley House, it has a Small Boat Museum and offers walking tours of the village at 4:00 P.M. on Tuesdays in July and August. Admission is free; (508) 548–7270.

The owners of the beautiful **Spohr Garden** in Woods Hole generously allow visitors to enjoy its blooms. It is a few blocks off Woods Hole Road at Oyster Pond Road; you can park on Fells Road. The gardens are particularly striking in April when the daffodils are in bloom.

Less than a block from the Eel Pond drawbridge, in the center of Woods Hole, is *Shuckers World Famous Raw Bar and Cafe,* at 91 Water Street; (508) 540–3850. Reasonable prices and really good seafood keep locals coming back, but we go straight for the thick, satisfying chowder. It's a meal all its own.

Following Route 28 north from Falmouth to *Mashpee,* you will pass the visitor center of the *Waquoit Bay National Estuarine Research Reserve,* open Monday through Friday 10:00 A.M. to 4:00 P.M. and Saturday in July and August from 1:00 to 4:00 P.M. This reserve includes a beach, a state park recreation area, an island with ten campsites, an upland forest tract, salt ponds, barrier beaches, dunes, and open water along 15 miles of shoreline. The center often has evening programs and interpretive walks; (508) 457–0495; www.waquoitbayreserve.org.

At the southern shore of Mashpee, about 2 miles from the intersection of Great Neck Road and Great Oak Road, is *South Cape Beach State Park,* part of the Estuarine Reserve, with miles of beach and a $2.00 parking fee. While it is filled with sunbathers on nice summer days, the rest of the time, it is quiet, the preserve of the piping plover and surf fishing enthusiasts. Great Flat Pond Trail begins near the parking lot, a level walking path that leads through this shore environment.

On the way to the state park, you will pass *Mashpee National Wildlife Refuge* and the *Jehu Pond Conservation Area,* with more walking trails. A wide bike lane borders the road here, and you can rent bikes from Corner Cycle, 115 Palmer Avenue, near the Village Green in Falmouth; (508) 540–4195.

The 3.6-mile *Shining Sea Bikeway* connects Falmouth and Woods Hole, skirting Vineyard Sound and passing the attractive *Nobska Lighthouse.* This path connects with the scenic 23-mile road loop through picturesque Sippewissett.

To see Nobska and other lighthouses from the sea, including Martha's Vineyard and Buzzards Bay lights, take the occasional lighthouse cruises offered by *Patriot Party Boats,* at Falmouth Inner Harbor; (508) 548-2626 or (800) 734–0088; www.patriotpartyboats.com. They also offer two-hour sight-seeing and fishing trips without reservations, as well as scheduled water taxi service to Martha's Vineyard.

A bit out of town on the way to Sandwich is *Cape Cod Winery,* at 681 Sandwich Road, East Falmouth; (508) 457–5592; www.capecodwinery.com. The ten-acre gently sloping vineyard is open 11:00 A.M. to 4:00 P.M. late May through mid-December, Thursday through Sunday during July and August, Saturday and Sunday in spring and fall. Tours are given Saturday. Check for times. Six varieties of grapes are grown, made into wine, and bottled here.

We're not sure whether Falmouth has an inordinate number of good places to eat or whether that's how far we get on Cape Cod before hunger overtakes us. By looking past the more obvious places, you can find some very good food here, indeed.

Chapaquoit Grill is among these, at 410 West Falmouth Highway; (508) 540–7794. The food is a happy fusion of Caribbean, southwestern, Asian, and Italian into a lively New American menu. Nightly specials always include pasta, seafood, and meat entrees. Pizzas are baked over cherry and apple wood in the brick oven.

We also really like the ***Peking Palace.*** This is not just another Chinese restaurant in a resort town. While there are plenty of Cantonese and Szechuan dishes on the menu, the chef really shines with the Mandarin specialties: crown chicken with macadamia nuts and black mushrooms, mango chicken, or shrimp served in a sweet tomato sauce with walnuts. Entrees are between $9.00 and $12.00, and the restaurant is open daily from 11:30 A.M. to midnight, at 452 Main Street; (508) 540–8204.

A little hard to find (but isn't that what "Off the Beaten Path" is all about?) is ***The Nimrod,*** 100 Dillingham Avenue, Falmouth; (508) 540–4132. Its setting in a stately home sets the stage for its two upscale dining rooms set with linens, candles, and fresh flowers. More tables are on the large deck and often there is live entertainment—a pianist or jazz combo. The food lives up to the setting, especially the Shrimp Nimrod with duxelles and crabmeat stuffing. Open year-round, Nimrod serves lunch and dinner.

On an entirely different note, for good (read that nongreasy) fried seafood, go straight to the ***Clam Shack,*** at 227 Clinton Avenue; (508) 540–7758. It's just what it says it is, and you can take your fried clams (whole, juicy clams, not stray pieces) outside to eat while you watch the steady parade of small craft in the harbor. The Clam Shack is open daily, May through September, and accepts only cash or traveler's checks.

Also in the informal mode, ***Betsy's Diner,*** at 457 Main Street, will carry you straight back to the 1950s; (508) 540–0060. Turkey dinners, homemade pies, and breakfast served all day are accompanied by vintage tunes from the juke-box to complete the experience.

Immediately after Route 28 passes Route 130 heading east in ***Cotuit,*** you'll see a red colonial building on the left, the ***Cahoon Museum of American Art.*** The setting of this small museum heightens the flavor of its engaging collections. Once a tavern and stagecoach stop, the house was built in 1775. The six galleries have original low plaster ceilings, wide-planked floors, nineteenth-century stenciled walls and floorboards, and period wooden furniture. These serenely antique surroundings give the feeling that the paintings hang in a private home. Primitive artists Ralph and Martha Cahoon bought the house for their studio in the 1940s. The museum opened in 1984, with the Cahoons' paintings as the heart of the permanent collection. Ralph was fond of painting mermaids, posing them whimsically in Cape settings of ocean, lighthouses, and ships. These paintings just have to bring a smile to your face, as you see mermaids cavorting in hot-air balloons shaped like fish and birds, or doing their laundry using a whale for a washboard. Also on exhibit are some of the largest and most intricate sailors' valentines, set in gold-framed, octagonal shadow boxes. These beautiful pieces, traditionally bought in the West Indies by sailors for their wives and sweethearts, were made of hundreds of tiny pink, white, and purple seashells formed into patterns of flowers and other elaborate designs. The collection also includes the work of primitive itinerant portrait painters, marine artists, Hudson River School landscape artists, and American impressionist painters. The museum is open from 10:00 A.M. to 4:00 P.M. Tuesday through Saturday, Sunday 1:00 to 4:00 P.M., and is closed January. Call (508) 428–7581. Admission is $3.00; members and children under age twelve enter free.

From Cotuit, Route 130 leads north to the town of **Sandwich.** This attractive, colonial-looking village is famous for Sandwich glass, which was made here. Admirers and collectors of American glassware should stop to visit the fourteen small galleries of the **Sandwich Glass Museum** for some fine examples of the products of the company founded here in 1825. Pressing glass was a new technique then, and the artists and craftsmen here perfected its many different variations, from threaded glass to engraving and colored overlays. More than 5,000 pieces are on display, along with exhibits that show how glass was worked in the factory. Signs and labels not only explain how the glass was made, but also delve into life in the past. We learned, for example, that cup plates were designed to hold a cup while tea cooled to drinking temperature in the saucer. Tea was drunk from the saucer until the invention of handles on teacups, when cup plates went quickly out of style. Admission is $4.75 for adults, $1.00 for children ages six through twelve. The museum is open April through December, daily 9:30 A.M. to 5:00 P.M., and February and March, Wednesday through Sunday 9:30 A.M. to 4:00 P.M., and is closed in January. It is located at 129 Main Street; (508) 888–0251. The museum shop sells fine reproductions of Sandwich pieces.

In the center of town overlooking Shawme Pond, **Dexter Grist Mill** claims to be the oldest still in operation. Built in the 1640s, the mill grinds corn flour using authentic grindstones powered by a waterwheel. The volunteers who operate the mill explain the entire process, including the selection of the grain, how the stones are set to obtain a specific grind, and the mechanical process and problems of a water-powered system with wooden gears. One of the best parts of this mill is that you can take its product with you—by the pound. Complete with a list of recipes authentic to this coarse grind, the cornmeal can be shipped to your house so it won't spoil over the rest of your vacation. You can buy it without touring the mill, as it's for sale at the gate where the tickets are sold for the gristmill. Here you may also purchase a ticket package for $4.00 that includes this site, the Hoxie House, and the Thornton Burgess House. This gate is also a popular spot for artists to set up easels to paint and draw the lovely scenery by the pond and the picturesque village. The mill is open mid-June through September, Monday through Saturday from 10:00 A.M. to 4:45 P.M. and Sunday from 1:00 to 5:00 P.M.; (508) 888–4910.

On your way to visit the Thornton Burgess House, stop off just up the road at 1 Water Street to refuel at the *Dunbar House.* The indoor dining room, warmly paneled with dark wood and decorated with antique prints and paintings, exudes restfulness as classical music plays. On the outdoor patio, nicely tended gardens with a few playful squirrels line the canopied dining area. Blackboard specials might include a rich cream-of-chicken soup, chicken savory, and a traditional ploughman's lunch of cheeses, fruits, and hearty bread. Always available is the traditional cream tea with scones, as well as the indulgent selection of desserts such as Queen Anne cake or English toffee cake. In addition to the impressive selection of teas, a true Brit would be quite pleased to find a good variety of other authentic beverages here as well, including cool and refreshing lemon barley water.

Dunbar House also has a well-stocked gift shop, full of hard-to-find imported British goods, including teas and cooking ingredients. The tearoom is open from 11:00 A.M. to 4:30 P.M. daily, and the gift shop has extended hours during the summer; (508) 833–2485; www.dunbarteashop.com.

Almost across the street at 4 Water Street (Route 130) in Sandwich, you will find the *Thornton W. Burgess house,* where the famous children's story character Peter Rabbit was created. In the home, you can see Burgess's works completed and in progress, as well as art and personal memorabilia of the creator of Peter Rabbit and his host of woodland friends. Tours of the house/museum are offered Monday through Saturday 10:00 A.M. to 4:00 P.M. from April through October and on weekends in December. In July and August, there is a live-animal storytime for children. Admission is $2.00 for adults, $1.00 for children; (508) 888–4668, (508) 888–6870; www.thorntonburgess.org.

Up the road a bit is the saltbox-style *Hoxie House,* at 18 Water Street. Built in 1675, it is among the oldest on Cape Cod (no title records remain to prove the point). When you enter the home, diligently restored to its original period by the town in 1960, volunteers will explain its history and contents, as well as the life and times of its past residents. We were especially interested in the explanations of the unique multiuse furniture in the house and various period cooking techniques. Open Memorial Day through Columbus Day, Monday through Saturday from 10:00 A.M. to 4:45 P.M. Tickets ($3.00 for adults, $1.50 for children) include the Dexter Grist Mill; (508) 888–1173.

Allow at least two or three hours to explore **Heritage Museums and Gardens** during your historical tour of Sandwich. To get there, follow Grove Street behind Shawme Pond (behind the Grist Mill) until you see the signs. In addition to amazing gardens, walking paths, and museums of early Cape settlement, **Heritage Plantation** is home to a 1912 antique carousel, which adults and children can ride. Classic and antique car enthusiasts will find a two-level display barn housing thirty-seven antique motorcars and several rare modern vehicles, such as the Delorean (made popular by its appearance in the movie *Back to the Future*). You can walk around and peer into the cars, which are in mint condition, a thrill for kids and for their grandparents who remember riding in them. The grounds are expansive, and there are small buses to transport those who are not up to all the walking. Adult admission is $12.00, seniors $10.00, and children ages six through sixteen $6.00. Open April through October 10:00 A.M. to 5:00 P.M. daily, with reduced hours the rest of the year; (508) 888–3300.

Enough attractions—not to mention a splendid beach—fill Sandwich that you'll want to spend the night in this attractive town. To treat yourself after a long day, soak in one of the two-person, ultramassage whirlpool bathtubs at the **Belfry Inne,** 6–8 Jarves Street. We always reserve a room in the Abbey, one of the inn's three buildings. Each of its six rooms is graced with its own original stained-glass window—this is a converted church—and each is unique and exquisitely decorated.

The rooms open onto a balcony overlooking the dining area of the **Belfry Bistro,** which serves contemporary eclectic fare in the nave of the former church. Using as much of the detail of the church as possible, the owners have created an attractive and intimate dining room. We liked the appetizer of mussels served with sautéed chourico, garlic, diced tomato, and a wine butter sauce. The Belfry salad—fresh pears with gorgonzola over arugula and mixed greens—began dinner promisingly. Swordfish, pan-seared with black-and-white sesame seeds, was perfectly cooked and nicely set off by the sticky purple rice and blood orange sauce. Appetizers are $8.00 to $14.00 with entrees from $23.00 to $29.00. You can make reservations for the inn, which also includes eight rooms in the Village House and eight more in the Victorian Drew House right next door, or reserve a table at the bistro by calling (508) 888–8550 or (800) 844–4542, or by visiting www.belfryinn.com.

Don't let the informal atmosphere of **The Marshlands Restaurant** lead you to think they are casual about the food they serve. The shrimp platter is superb and the people cheerful and friendly. And, unlike many, it's open all year, on Route 109; (508) 888–9824.

Over in East Sandwich, you'll find the **Green Briar Jam Kitchen and Nature Center,** where they still make jam the way they have since 1903. If you tour the kitchen, you'll feel as if you've stepped into your grandmother's kitchen. Copper counters line the blue-and-white expanse, and sunny windows brim with pink geraniums. A many-burnered, 1920 cast-iron gas stove runs the length of the kitchen, flanked by a Hoosier cabinet and big wooden barrels of sugar. During a jam-making class, steam rises in your face, releasing the delicious smells of warm fruit. The classes are given year-round. A gift shop sells more than a hundred kinds of homemade jams, jellies, and preserves, from popular strawberry, raspberry, and blueberry to beach-plum jellies and marmalades. In the fall and winter, the kitchen makes cranberry conserve, tomato relish, and mincemeat.

A Sandwich woman, Ida Putnam, started the Green Briar Jam Kitchen, using many recipes from her friend Fannie Merritt Farmer's famous cookbook. Naturalist and author Thornton Burgess roamed the jam kitchen's woods as a boy, later basing his *Old Briar-Patch* and *Smiling Pool* on spots he found there. The Green Briar Jam Kitchen and Nature Center, at 6 Discovery Hill Road in East Sandwich, gives tours April through December, Monday through Saturday from 10:00 A.M. to 4:00 P.M. and Sunday from 1:00 to 4:00 P.M., and January through March, Tuesday through Saturday from 10:00 A.M. to 4:00 P.M.; (508) 888–6870; www.thorntonburgess.org.

The Green Briar Nature Center is owned by the Thornton W. Burgess Society, which also operates the Thornton W. Burgess Museum, on Water Street. The society has a very active year-round schedule of nature and environmentally oriented programs for both kids and adults. Most of these, especially those for young people, are hands-on, outdoor activities in the woods and ponds. Call (508) 888–6870 for specific programs during the period when you expect to be in town.

Recently, the society took on the role of manager of the **East Sandwich Game Farm** on Old County Road, an abandoned site where the commonwealth once raised pheasant and quail for its hunting programs. The land is used to further the educational programs of the society in nature study, ecology, and historic preservation. Trail maps are available at the Green Briar Nature Center, above.

You don't have to travel too deeply into the Cape to sample some old-fashioned Cape Cod charm; you'll find it at **Beehive Tavern,** 406 Route 6A, East Sandwich; (508) 833–1184. Rustic and friendly, the Beehive serves up good food at budget-conscious prices. They are known especially for their lobster pie, fresh blueberry pie, and Bee Sting ice cream. They are open all year but don't take reservations, so in the summer dine early or plan on a wait.

For a warm, romantic atmosphere that is also very welcoming to families, stop at **Amari,** on Route 6A in East Sandwich, close to the Sandwich/Barnstable line. Here you'll find your favorite Italian dishes, all prepared with the freshest produce and more than a touch of creativity. The friendly, well-informed staff adds charm, and the open-concept grill and kitchen, with a wood-fire brick oven, adds the taste of the Old World to the chef's original dishes. Most entrees range between $10 and $15. Call (508) 375–0011 for reservations or the daily specials. Amari opens at 4:30 P.M. daily, and at noon on Saturdays and Sundays for lunch, too.

Mid-Cape

A gorgeous barrier beach called **Sandy Neck** stretches over the town line between Sandwich and Barnstable. Calmer than the pounding surf of the Cape Cod National Seashore, this beach is backed by lots of dunes and beach grasses. Hiking trails wind through the dunes. Alas, the days of walking on dunes are virtually gone; fragile dunes easily erode underfoot, and if you walk on the dunes, you'll be asked to leave. But you can't hurt the view. To reach Sandy Neck, turn left on Sandy Neck Road off Route 6A. It costs $10.00 to park on weekends from Memorial Day until July 4; then the fee is charged daily until Labor Day. The small parking lot fills up rapidly on weekends, holidays, and hot days. For information, call the Department of Recreation at (508) 790–6345. If you'd like a view of the splendid **Great Marshes** on Sandy Neck's south side, drive a little farther east on Route 6A and turn left onto either Bone Hill Road or Millway in Barnstable. In season, a $10 parking fee is charged until 4:00 P.M. Parking is then free until closing at 9:00 P.M.

As Route 6A crosses from Sandwich into **Barnstable,** it also crosses a salt-marsh and **Scorton Creek,** a tidal estuary. A road leads south alongside it to a put-in for small boats. This is a pleasant place to paddle, either inland into the bird-filled marsh or out into Barnstable Harbor. If you choose the latter course, to your right will be the Great Marshes, which you can explore. But if the tide is high, be careful paddling in any of the marshes or you could find yourself stranded when the water level drops. It's best to stray from the channel only on a rising tide. Local papers all carry the tide tables.

The Tao Water Art Gallery, at 1989 Route 6A in **West Barnstable** (508–375–0428; www.taowatergallery.com), shows contemporary fine art from mainland China in a 5,600-square-foot gallery, one of the largest on Cape Cod. Other artists from elsewhere in the world are featured as well in the Tao Water's regular exhibits.

Antiques shops are a common sight along Route 6A, and so are gardens, one of which dwarfs the cottage at Blueberry Hill Farm. The diminutive shop of **The Olde Cottage Garden** (508–362–0404) is set in a shake-roofed cottage that is almost lost in the surrounding profusion of foxgloves, delphinium, heliotrope, poppies, and evening primrose. June roses climb beside the porch. The garden is just west of Salt Meadow Lane.

More gardens await at *Cobb's Cove Inn,* a secluded hideaway off Route 6A. When the weather is warm, guests enjoy their multicourse breakfast on the terrace, surrounded by flowers, with birdsongs for music. Life is just as idyllic inside, where guest rooms have king- or queen-size beds, whirlpool tubs, fluffy terry robes, and—for those in the spacious third-floor room—a canopy bed and sweeping views of Barnstable Harbor and Cape Cod Bay. Public rooms invite winter reading—winter breakfasts are served in the library—or just curling up in a comfortable chair to watch the fire crackle in the fireplace. The inn is on Powder Hill Road (P.O. Box 208), Barnstable Village, MA 02630; (508) 362–9356 (fax is the same); www.cobbscove.com.

Behind the low, shingled *St. Mary's Episcopal Church,* on Route 6A in Barnstable, is an astonishing series of gardens, where you may wander through roses set around a well, past brilliant red azaleas, along a stream bank swathed in ferns, or in walled terrace gardens reminiscent of ancient monasteries. A unique brick garden house shelters benches, stone pools provide focal points, and polychrome saints gaze placidly over the bright beds of flowers. Come at any time during the growing season, since the gardens are designed to bloom in sequence, from dogwood to asters. The garden is free, but a donation box is there if you wish to help with its upkeep.

As you travel east on the Cape, it's much more fun and scenic to take the windier Route 6A—the *Old King's Highway*—than to go barreling along US 6, the Mid-Cape Highway, which reveals almost nothing along the way. Route

Run, Alewives, Run

Each spring thousands of alewives, the silver-sided herring abundant all along the Atlantic Coast, return to freshwater ponds to spawn. Before the Cape was settled, these fish used natural waterways for their migration, jumping falls and working their way up rapids, and in some places, they still do. But in others, where dams, the canal, or even natural changes to the landscape have interfered, engineers have created artificial watery staircases for the alewives to climb. In April or early May, you can watch these fish at Herring Pond, off Herring Pond Road in Bournedale (the part of town on the mainland side of the canal), which you can reach from U.S. Route 6, about a mile south of the rotary, or at Stoney Brook Herring Run in Brewster, by the Stoney Brook Grist Mill. In Harwich, you'll find another constructed run in the Conservation area next to Bell's Neck Road, off Depot Road.

Everything's Coming Up Roses

In June Cape Cod seems to be covered in roses, from the elegant hybrids that grace the front gates of former captains' homes to the wild beach roses, *Rosa rugosa*, that line the shore. Spectacular though they are, these are not the only flowers that decorate the roadsides throughout the growing season. Earlier in the spring are daffodils, which have been planted along the roadsides, followed by banks of azalea and rhododendron and by the showy blossoms of magnolia trees. Bright gardens are visible over picket fences everywhere as you drive or walk in the summer, and in the fall whole landscapes turn bright crimson with cranberries.

6A passes right through the main streets of three attractive northside villages: Barnstable, Yarmouthport, and Brewster, lined with old sea captains' houses, general stores, and inns and restaurants. You might in particular poke about the antiques shops in Barnstable Village, taking time to stop into the **Trayser Memorial Museum** of local history, located in the handsome old brick customhouse that was in service from 1856 until 1913. After that it became a post office until 1959. The museum is open from mid-June through mid-October, Tuesday through Sunday from 1:30 to 4:30 P.M.; call (508) 362–2092 to confirm times, which may change.

Cape Cod becomes quite narrow in this central section, so you can be in **Hyannis** quickly by following one of the several roads to the south. Lots of commercialism and strip malls pack this area densely. Thousands of tourists come hoping to catch a glimpse of the Kennedys, who for years have had their family compound in Hyannis Port. There had never been a place for Kennedy fans to visit until 1992, when the Hyannis Chamber of Commerce opened the **John F. Kennedy Hyannis Museum** at 397 Main Street, in the Old Town Hall. Large black-and-white and color photographs as well as videos show the young Kennedy family swimming and boating off Hyannis Port and JFK walking his solitary miles along the beach, as he did during his presidency. Despite the small size of the museum's collection, it's a memorable visit. It is open summertime Monday through Saturday from 9:00 A.M. to 5:00 P.M., Sunday noon to 5:00 P.M. Hours are limited mid-October through Memorial Day. Tickets cost $5.00 for adults and $2.50 for seniors and children ages ten through sixteen; admission is free for children under age ten. For information call (508) 790–3077, or visit www.jfkhyannismuseum.org.

While in town, potato-chip junkies may want to trace some premium chips to their source. **Cape Cod Potato Chips,** which are sold all over New England, gives free factory tours, along with free samples, Monday through Friday from 9:00 A.M. to 5:00 P.M. Take Independence Drive off Route 132 to find the factory, where chips are still made the old-fashioned way; (508) 775–3358 or (888) 881–CHIP (888–881–2447).

Ferries for Nantucket Island leave from Hyannis; you can tell when one is about to board by the number of cars rushing to get to the landing. We suggest getting there early to avoid the rush by whiling away the time at *The Black Cat,* 165 Ocean Street, Hyannis; (508) 778–1233. It's right across from the Hy-Line ferry dock on Hyannis Harbor, and you really can't find fresher seafood. A clubby atmosphere pervades the lounge, and the soft lighting and decor are warm and welcoming in the main dining room. The service is often only passable, but the menu—an assortment of fish, meats, and pastas—is very well prepared. In summer, opt for one of the outdoor tables to watch the tourists and locals parade by and the ferries come and go. It's within walking distance of downtown and features jazz on Sunday nights and entertainment on weekends. It's open year-round, a good sign that its quality is consistent.

Right in the thick of things, *The Roo Bar,* is at 586 Main Street; (508) 778–6515. It's a city-style bistro, where you can stop for a glass of wine or dig into an entree platter of New American cuisine. You can watch the chef at work in the open kitchen, complete with brick oven. They offer more than one hundred wines and fifty beers. If you seek an intimate evening, this may not be the place, but the recent addition of a new dining room has made it a bit quieter than it used to be. Stop here to get a real feel for the center Cape's we're-on-vacation style.

More sedate and relaxing is *Eclectic Cafe,* 606 Main Street; (508) 771–7187. This open-air seasonal eatery really knows how to put a meal together. Intimate and romantic with an open kitchen, Eclectic is pricey, but you may not mind once you sample the cuisine. Depend on the very well-informed staff to help you choose from the menu to create a memorable experience.

One of the best new resorts on the Cape is the *Cape Codder Resort & Spa* close to US 6 in Hyannis. The hotel has been massively rejuvenated since its days as the Four Points Sheraton, with new restaurants, completely refitted rooms, and the addition of an 8,200-square-foot wave pool with two-foot waves, waterslides, and even a waterfall. Other facilities include tennis, volleyball, bocce, and a well-equipped exercise room. A full-service spa has been added, and the resort offers special-value spa packages.

We especially like the hotel's eleven acres of gardens and terraces. The grounds allow easy access between rooms and the many facilities on this big property. The resort's location, close to downtown Hyannis, the Nantucket Ferry, and the sea, makes it a convenient place to stay. Buses stop outside every twenty minutes in season, and it is only a mile from the beach.

Standard rooms start at $179 weekdays, $199 weekends during high season—low prices on the Cape for all the amenities offered. Off-season rates (who needs the ocean when you have the wave pool and more reliable weather inside?) start at $119 weekdays and $149 weekends. Family vacation packages are offered year-round and include two nights and $30 worth of meal vouchers for a couple and up to two kids under age seventeen for less than the price of two nights' lodging. The resort is at the intersection of Bearce's Way and Route 132, just off US 6; (508) 771–3000; www.CapeCodder Resort.com.

Also at the Cape Codder, informal family dining is available at the *Hearth 'n Kettle,* serving what the Catania family's restaurants are well known for: "hearty, healthy, and wholesome" fare at reasonable prices. It opens daily at 7:00 A.M., serving breakfast, lunch, and dinner. You'll find more upscale dining in *VJ's Grille Room,* which features quality steaks and elegantly prepared local seafood, from 5:30 P.M. daily. The *Grand Cru Wine Bar* is a stylish, friendly place for a glass of wine or bistro-style fare.

Locals on their way to and from Craigville Beach stop at *Craigville Pizza & Mexican,* 618 Craigville Beach Road, Hyannis Port; (508) 775–2267. There they devour pizzas, calzones, buffalo wings, and cheese nachos in great amounts. It's been there for decades, open year-round.

Speaking of service, you can't ask for a more accommodating, do-handsprings-to-keep-you-happy staff than at *Clancy's of West Yarmouth,* 175 Route 28, West Yarmouth; (508) 775–3332. Open year-round, Clancy's has memorable cuisine and the prices are reasonable. Dark woods, warm lighting, and a varied menu invite lingering over dinner, even if there is a line forming at the door. The blue cheese dressing is the last word on salads, and we defy anyone to finish the seafood platter. If you can find room, sample their traditional Grapenut Custard for dessert. Get there early in high season, since Clancy's is well known to Cape regulars.

There were once so many sea captains' houses along Main Street in *South Yarmouth* that it was known as "the Captains' Mile." A number have been turned into inns. One of the nicest is the *Captain Farris House,* an 1845 Greek Revival home in South Yarmouth set peacefully just 2 blocks from the Bass River. Two acres of lawn surround the large, white house trimmed with plum-colored shutters and a huge wraparound veranda set with Adirondack chairs and settees. The house blends an antique sensibility with such modernday luxuries as all-new bathrooms and Jacuzzis. Guest rooms are decorated in exquisitely chosen colors like muted rust, silver, and gold overglazes, soothing to the eye and softened by yards and yards of damask draperies. The eight rooms, plus two in another house, are decorated with a mix of antique and contemporary pieces, and some have private decks or private entrances. Doubles begin at about $165. A central open-air courtyard with a small fountain and flowers makes a lovely setting for breakfast and lunch. A formal parlor with an antique baby grand and a small library are also available for guest use. The innkeeper creates his own menus around the seasons, starting breakfast with fresh juices and fresh fruits, then serving a hot entree. Past creations have included cornmeal pancakes with strawberry-rhubarb sauce and whipped cream, and a turkey hash flavored with garlic and rosemary and topped with poached eggs. The inn is at 308 Old Main Street, Bass River Village; (508) 760–2818, (800) 350–9477; www.captainfarriscapecod.com.

In **West Dennis,** just across the Bass River from South Yarmouth and overlooking its own breakwater-protected beach, **The Lighthouse Inn** is a family-owned country inn with accommodations in shingled cottages and the main house. Although it's far from dowdy, it has that warm, relaxing aura of old-fashioned beach resort hotels, where families stayed for weeks at a time, with its wicker-furnished library and sunporch and large, bright dining room. On the property are a working lighthouse, tennis courts, lawn games, and a heated saltwater pool, although the seawater is warm here. The inn is family-friendly, with an InnKids program of daily activities and a supervised kids' dining room for parents who would rather dine alone and at a later hour. Rooms with breakfast begin at $240, plus $25 per person if the five-course dinner is included. Children's rates begin at $25 for ages three through nine, including dinner. Rooms in the fall begin at $160. This is a no-tipping property. In summer, the dining room is open to the public for lunch and dinner, with dinner entrees averaging $20. The Lighthouse Inn is at 1 Lighthouse Inn Road, West Dennis; (508) 398–2244, fax (508) 398–5658; www.lighthouseinn.com.

By now, you may be ready to return to the quiet of Route 6A, which you can do by following nearly any road to the north. The Cape is not very wide at any point, so it's always an easy matter to switch from the fast lane of the south shore to the slow lane on the north. You can do this without ever leaving the town of Yarmouth, which like several Cape towns, stretches from the north to the south shores. Just to make things more confusing, the villages of South Yarmouth and West Yarmouth are in the south, while Yarmouth and Yarmouth Port are on Route 6A to the north.

Anyone who has seen the PBS *Mystery* series will instantly know the name of Edward Gorey, the somewhat eccentric artist who drew the artwork for the opening of the show. In his lifetime he did more than that, however. He also designed the costumes and sets for the Broadway production of *Dracula* and the artwork in more than one hundred books, including the macabre *The Gashly-*

crumb Tinies, which runs through the alphabet describing the deaths of twenty-six children. Actually a quiet and generous man, he lived alone until his death in 2000. His home, **Edward Gorey House,** has now been opened to the public as a testament to the man and to his passion, animal welfare.

Friends of Gorey have established a foundation and filled the house in **Yarmouth Port** with his work and his eccentric collections of doorknobs, cheese graters, and bowls filled with rocks. A special room for kids illustrates the work of the animal welfare organizations that he supported. Open May through December, Wednesday through Saturday 10:00 A.M. to 4:00 P.M. and Sunday noon to 4:00 P.M., and the rest of the year, Thursday through Saturday 11:00 A.M. to 4:00 P.M. The house is off Route 6A on the Yarmouth Port Common, at 8 Strawberry Lane; (508) 362-3909; www.edwardgoreyhouse.org. Admission is $5.00 for adults, $2.00 for children ages six through twelve.

For a contemporary Mediterranean dinner, look for the yellow clapboard house that contains **Abbicci,** at 43 Route 6A; (508) 362-3501. As you choose from the a la carte menu, keep in mind that the portions are healthy, so you may need to restrain yourself to save room for the outstanding desserts. It's hard to save room with the likes of sautéed veal scaloppine, prosciutto and sage with a white wine demi-glace, or osso bucco alla Milanese on the menu. Pastas run from $18 to $21, *secondi* from $18 to $31. Lunch is served Monday through Friday, 11:30 A.M. to 2:30 P.M., dinner from 5:00 P.M. daily.

A turn to the south at the post office in **Yarmouth** takes you to the **Faith F. Tufts Memorial Gate House,** from which you can access a network of woodland walking trails. Trail guides are in the box if there's no one there, and you can drop in your 50-cent trail fee (25 cents for children). At the gate house is a well-kept little herb garden hedged in boxwood and a picnic table shaded by a huge copper beech tree. A short walk will lead you to the **Kelly Chapel,** built in 1873 in South Yarmouth and moved here.

If you watch the roadside closely as you pass Osprey Lane in **Dennis,** you'll see a small sign for the **Burial Ground of Nobscussett Indians.** It is approached through a tunnel of hedgerow on the opposite (south) side of the road. No stones mark the final resting place of Chief Mashantampaine or his followers, but the area is surrounded by a granite and rod fence.

The town of Dennis wraps around the eastern end of Yarmouth, so it gets more than its share of the beautiful north shore beaches. Follow nearly any road north from Route 6A to find one.

You'll see signs for **Howe's Beach, Corporation Beach,** or just plain "Dennis Beaches." Parking at any of these is $15 in season. Lifeguards are there from 9:00 A.M. to 4:00 P.M. daily, and no pets are allowed on the beaches.

If you turn inland (south) on Old Bass River Road, shortly after crossing into Dennis, turning onto Scargo Hill Road, you'll find signs leading to the stone **Scargo Tower.** From the top of its thirty-eight steps, you can overlook Scargo Lake and Cape Cod Bay. On clear days you can see both Plymouth (to the left) and Provincetown (to the right).

Few visitors know that sharing a driveway with the Cape Playhouse on Route 6A in Dennis is the **Cape Cod Museum of Art.** The museum is dedicated to preserving and exhibiting the works of Cape artists and it now has more than 1,000 pieces in its collections. The media exhibited include everything from oils to photography and sculpture. The works on display are of outstanding quality and reflect the many faces and moods of the Cape and its people. In addition to its own collections, the museum also hosts changing exhibits of works by contemporary artists and special shows.

Along with the art and sculpture (be sure to visit the outdoor sculpture garden), the museum has an extensive program of music performances. The museum is open year-round Tuesday through Saturday 10:00 A.M. to 5:00 P.M. and Sunday noon to 5:00 P.M. It is also open Monday 10:00 A.M. to 5:00 P.M. Memorial Day through Columbus Day. Admission is $8.00 for adults; free for children age eighteen and under. Route 6A, Dennis; (508) 385–4777; www.ccmoa.org.

Heather Baxter's cinnamon buns rank high among our favorite Cape Cod breakfasts, and you can sample them in nearby **Brewster.** And since a long day stretches ahead of us, we always stock up on a few things to tide us over— including snickerdoodles, a traditional Cape cookie. Heather's scones, muffins, round hermit cookies, and biscotti fill the racks at her **Hopkins House Bakery,** and you can eat them at the one small table inside or pull up a bench in the pretty garden out front, redolent with scents of lavender and rosemary. Open Thursday through Sunday from 8:00 A.M. to 4:00 P.M., June through October, Hopkins House Bakery is at 2727 Main Street (Route 6A), Brewster; (508) 896–3450. A small shop of country crafts and antiques adjoins the bakery.

The absolute best place to learn about the outdoor wonders of the Cape is the **Cape Cod Museum of Natural History.** A small shingled building surrounded by beach roses and salt marsh, the museum was founded in 1954 as a children's museum. Exhibits are still interpreted with children in mind. Children can pick up seashells and whale bones, play a birdsong identification game, and put on their own animal puppet shows. Many native Cape birds and animals are displayed in an engaging manner. Nature trails lead through woodland and out to a barrier beach. There are picnic tables outside the museum, which offers all kinds of excellent natural-history programs year-round. Located at 869 Main Street, Brewster, the museum is open from 9:30 A.M. to 4:00 P.M.

daily June through September, Wednesday through Sunday in April and May, and Wednesday through Sunday 11:00 A.M. to 3:00 P.M. October through March. Tickets cost $8.00 for adults and $3.50 for children ages three to twelve. Call (508) 896–3867; www.ccmnh.org.

Throughout the year, the museum sponsors walks, canoe and kayak explorations, birding trips, boat excursions with naturalists, special programs on nature topics, art classes, and field trips to outstanding natural destinations in the state. These are geared to a variety of ages. Some are free with admission; others involve nominal fees.

South Trail begins across Route 6A from the museum, traversing upland woods, a salt marsh, and an unusual forest of beech. From April through June, Stoney Brook, which follows part of the trail, is a run for alewives returning to freshwater to spawn. Expect to see ospreys along parts of this trail during nesting season. **Wing Island Trail** also begins at the museum, crossing an upland forest of pitch pines and a boardwalk across a salt marsh before arriving at a barrier beach. Near the beach is a unique sassafras grove, and, in a field, you will find a recently built solar calendar of standing stones, demonstrating how modern concepts of time measurement grew from ancient astronomic calendars.

A short distance east on Route 6A lies the **New England Fire and History Museum** (508–896–5711). This museum is a collection of small-town buildings set around a little green, with a children's play area in the middle. You'll find a big barn, a blacksmith shop, the Union Fire Company (once under the direction of Benjamin Franklin), and an 1890 apothecary shop. The barn houses early hand-pulled and horse-drawn fire engines, with huge spoked wheels, leather buckets, and handsome brass bells and lanterns. A lighted diorama recreates the famous 1871 Chicago fire, complete with clanging bells and smoke. Downstairs is the world's only 1929 Mercedes-Benz fire engine, as well as a collection of fire hats donated by the late Boston Pops conductor Arthur Fiedler, who loved fire trucks. The museum was closed for extensive renovation for the 2006 season, but will reopen in 2007. It was regularly open daily all summer, but it's best to call ahead for current hours and admission rates.

Biking enthusiasts should definitely try their wheels on the **Cape Cod Rail-Trail** bike path, a 26-mile stretch from East Harwich and Dennis to Wellfleet that follows the old right-of-way of the Old Colony Railroad. The easy, flat terrain passes some lovely scenery: stands of cedar and scrub pine, horse farms, cranberry bogs, salt marshes, beaches, and kettle ponds. Despite the rail-trail's popularity, this is still one of the great things to do on the Cape. One of the nicest things about the rail-trail is that you can use it to bike to the beaches along the way, thereby escaping the parking aggravation.

You can join the trail almost anywhere you like and can bike for as long as you want. Access is from more than a dozen points, clearly marked by signs on US 6 and Route 6A. The southerly trailhead is at a parking lot on Route 134, just south of US 6 in South Dennis; the northern end comes out in Wellfleet. There are plenty of take-out stands, ice-cream shops, restrooms, and bike-rental shops along the way. For information about the rail-trail, call Nickerson State Park at (508) 896–3491.

Where the trail crosses Route 6A in Brewster is **Cobie's,** which has been serving up fried clams, lobster rolls, and ice cream since 1948. The crabmeat salad roll is filled with chunks of snow crab meat, for $8.95 the last time we tucked into one. On Sunday Cobie's serves a fisherman's platter of clams, scallops, shrimp, and cod. Take your plate to a picnic table on the deck or in the pavilion. This is the kind of old-fashioned quality roadside stand you thought had given way everywhere to fast-food chains. Open from 11:00 A.M. to 9:00 P.M. daily May through Labor Day, at 3260 Main Street (Route 6A), Brewster; (508) 896–7021.

Cobie's is within easy cycling distance of **Nickerson State Park,** a vast tract—nearly 2,000 acres—of rolling upland forest surrounding eight ponds that are unique because no brooks or streams feed them. These are "kettle ponds," created when melting glaciers left large chunks of ice behind more than ten thousand years ago, when Cape Cod was formed as a ridge of terminal glacial moraine. The ponds provide canoeing, swimming, fishing, and birding opportunities, and the rest of the park has paved cycling paths, hiking trails, and more than 400 campsites, divided among eight campgrounds. Most sites can be reserved in advance (518–884–4959 or 877–422–6762), but 165 are not reservable. These are distributed each morning at a 10:00 A.M. site call, which may involve a wait of several days. Park attendants can usually predict when you take your number how many days you will have to wait for a space, so you don't have to be there every morning. The park is open year-round, with winter camping allowed. Campsites are $15 for Massachusetts residents, $17 for nonresidents; (508) 896–3491.

The vast tract of land that now comprises Nickerson State Park was once a game preserve, part of the estate of Samuel Nickerson, a Chicago banker whose ancestors had purchased their Cape Cod land directly from the Native Americans in the 1600s. Samuel and his wife built a spacious mansion, Fieldstone Hall, in Brewster on a rise of land overlooking Cape Cod Bay. Along with the mansion and the game preserve, the property included a windmill, a stone tower, and a carriage house. Fieldstone Hall became the home of Samuel's son Roland, and the original building burned down in 1906, just two weeks before his death.

Roland's widow, Addie Nickerson, rebuilt the house on the old stone foundation, but in the slightly more modern tastes of the early twentieth century.

Her new home had a richly carved staircase and leaded-glass windows, popular at that time. The family donated the game preserve to the Commonwealth of Massachusetts to create Nickerson State Park.

Today the mansion, stone tower, and outbuildings comprise **Ocean Edge Resort,** and although the 400-acre property is now peppered with modern guest-room and villa clusters that mar the sweeping view to the sea that the Nickersons enjoyed, the mansion has been nicely converted. Across Route 6A is an eighteen-hole PGA championship golf course, and two tennis centers offer workshops and clinics for players of all ages. Guest rooms are spacious and well decorated, and the resort offers a number of special sports and other programs for children. The 700-foot stretch of adjoining beach is reserved for guests. Guest rooms begin at $375 in the summer; special packages offer savings. Ocean Edge Resort is at 2907 Main Street (Route 6A), Brewster; (508) 896–9000, (800) 811–3457; www.oceanedge.com.

Outer Cape

Chatham juts out at the Cape's elbow and so is almost surrounded by water, giving it some of the most spectacular views and nicest beaches on the entire Cape. To admire the view, drive out Shore Road along the ocean's edge, winding up at the Chatham Lighthouse.

One of a pair of twin lighthouses, built together so mariners could distinguish this point from the single lighthouse at Truro, Chatham Light was built in 1877. The other, which stood 100 feet to the north, was later moved to Nauset. During **Maritime Days** in mid-May, this and other lighthouses are open for tours. For more information on lighthouse tours and the week's other activities, contact the Cape Cod Chamber of Commerce at (508) 362–3225, or consult the Days' Web page at www.ecapechamber.com/maritimedays.

Although Chatham may sometimes seem like a preserve for the Cape's old-money gentry, it's a real town, with an active fishing fleet. To see the boats and watch them unload their catch, arrive in the afternoon at the **Chatham Fish Pier** on Shore Road. From late May throughout summer and fall, you can buy very fresh seafood right here on the wharf, at **Nickerson's Fish and Lobster Market.** Be sure to notice the attractive sculpture of fish, crustacea, and mollusks at the top of the landing, titled *The Provider,* created by Sig Purwin and dedicated to the fishing industry.

There's so much in Chatham that you could spend a week here and not do everything. Of the half-dozen historic landmarks, a good place to start is with the oldest.

A treasure trove for learning about Chatham's history is tucked away in a solitary wood-frame house, the **Old Atwood House.** Five generations of a sea captain's family lived here, from about 1752. Nineteenth-century pieces and memorabilia fill the parlor, borning room, keeping room, music room, and kitchen with a fireplace. A whole gallery is full of portraits of Chatham sea captains. Among those seafarers were Captain Isaac White, who made a record, 120-day New York-to-Shanghai run on his clipper ship *Independent,* and Captain Oliver Eldredge, hired as a cook for eight men at the age of nine.

Black-and-white photographs show historic local scenes: the railroad depot, the coastline, and Twin Lights. There are lots of maritime artifacts too, such as a bottle of real whale oil. One room showcases hundreds of seashells on glass shelves, shining pink and white in the sunlight. Another room is devoted to noted Cape Cod author Joseph C. Lincoln. A barn in back displays the realistic murals of Alice Stallknecht Wight, each portraying Chatham townspeople and religious themes, such as Christ preaching from a dory. All this costs only $5.00 admission, $3.00 for students; admission is free for kids under twelve. The Old Atwood House is located at 347 Stage Harbor Road, about three-fourths of a mile from the rotary at the Congregational Church on Route 28 (508–945–2493). The museum is open June through mid-October, Tuesday through Saturday 1:00 to 4:00 P.M. In July and August, it opens at 10:00 A.M.

Only a little "newer" is the **Old Grist Mill,** off Shattuck Place, which was built in 1797. The wind-powered mill ground corn for early residents when wind speeds were 20 to 25 miles an hour—or higher with a little reefing of the sails on the huge sweeping arms. It's open weekdays in July and August, from 10:00 A.M. to 3:00 P.M.

Every summer Friday night, **brass band concerts** unfold in Kate Gould Park on Main Street, a decades-long tradition whose pleasure is undimmed by the thousands who come. People spread out on blankets and lawn chairs and bring their babies, dogs, popcorn, and coolers. Lights dramatize the gleaming white bandstand and snappy red uniforms. The band plays old favorites, inviting the audience to sing along, do the bunny hop, and waltz. These evenings take on a magical quality as dusk falls, with floating clouds of brightly colored balloons and children waving glow-in-the-dark light sticks.

Chatham is one of the rare "walking" towns left on the Cape, a place where you can stroll among the shops and browse the restaurant menus in a pleasant village setting. Restaurants are almost all privately owned—there's only one franchise eatery in town—and you will find a wide variety here. To learn the season's dining news, we always stop to chat with the chef/owner at **Amara's Italian Deli and Pastry Shop,** at 637B Main Street, almost hidden on the ground floor behind the CVS drugstore. This bright cafe is redolent with good things baking, and with the aromas of espresso and cappuccino. Pastries are irresistible, and the bread is real Italian, with a crunchy bite. Custom-made subs may include the usual or the unusual, such as roasted vegetables and chicken cutlet. An antipasto bar, Sicilian pizza, and gelato round out the menu, available every day from May through Columbus Day from 10:00 A.M. to 8:00 P.M.; (508) 945–5777. Amara's faces a large parking lot (with public restrooms), accessible from Main Street or from Stage Harbor Road, a good place to park while you wander around town.

The screen door slams often with the many arrivals at **Marion's Pie Shop,** a family bakery for more than forty years on the west side of town, at 2022 Main Street (508–432–9439). Everything is made from scratch. Irresistible smells emanate from freshly baked cinnamon rolls and hand-cut doughnuts, cranberry-nut and zucchini-pineapple breads, and old-fashioned two-crust pies such as apple, peach, and blueberry. Chicken and clam pies make great take-home dinners.

Set amid gardens with Italian fountains is **The Captain's House Inn,** 369 Old Harbor Road, Chatham; (508) 945–0127 or (800) 315–0728; www.captains houseinn.com. Its nineteen elegant rooms are furnished in antiques and fine reproductions. Rooms are at the luxury level, some with whirlpool tubs. Breakfast is served at individual tables, a relief for those who don't relish the company of strangers at breakfast. Traditional afternoon tea offers scones and jam tarts.

At the very tip of Chatham, past the lighthouse, you'll find **Monomoy National Wildlife Refuge,** on Morris Island (508–945–0594). Its two barrier islands, North Monomoy Island and South Monomoy Island, were once a single 7-mile-long island that was split in two by the blizzard of 1978. These starkly beautiful islands are splendid spots for birding and hiking. Their wild, windswept terrain includes tidal flats and salt marshes, thickets and dunes, and inspiring ocean vistas from every angle. The sea winds will clear your brain cells thoroughly of any city anxieties. Thousands of birds use the islands as a staging area, and close to 300 species have been spotted here. The many shorebirds include marbled godwits, piping plovers, oystercatchers, whimbrels, and terns.

The only access to North and South Monomoy Islands is by private boat or guided tour. The Massachusetts Audubon Society, based at the Wellfleet Bay Wildlife Sanctuary (508–349–2615) offers occasional tours of the islands or of the seals that frolic in their waters. Tours are offered year-round on Saturday or Sunday, with much greater frequency in summer. Call for a current schedule and to reserve a place, because they fill up in advance. Cruises run $35 to $55 for nonmembers.

The most-frequently operating access is provided by the Monomoy Island Ferry, which leaves right from the Monomoy National Wildlife Refuge headquarters on the boat *Rip Ryder.* They specialize in seal-watching and fishing trips, and will also ferry passengers to North Monomoy Island for hiking or fishing access (from $10 per person, round-trip). Reservations are strongly recommended, (508) 945–5450; www.monomoyislandferry.com. They operate specialty cruises in conjunction with the Cape Cod Museum of Natural History (508–896–3867) with a more pedagogical approach. One two-hour cruise takes visitors around Morris Island to watch fishermen hauling traps and working shellfish beds before stopping on North Monomoy to learn about its bird population. For a truly memorable excursion, the Monomoy Island Overnights include sleeping in the light keeper's house, with ample opportunities for bird-watching and seal spotting. Contact the museum for a schedule and reservations (508–896–3867).

Golfers will enjoy the newly opened 6,860-yard championship **Cape Cod National Golf Club** in Brewster; (508) 240–6800. Its wooded hills and kettle holes create dramatic varieties in elevation and several ocean views. Four sets of tees offer challenges to all levels of players.

Orleans, north of Chatham, is certainly not off the beaten path for avian tourists: Close to 300 species visit every year, and more live here as year-round residents. To see many of them, head for Nauset Beach. In June and July, you can visit one of the state's largest colonies of least terns, north of the beach, and west of them is Nauset Marsh and New Island, nesting ground for common terns, American oystercatchers, and black skimmers. Come here in August and September and you will see thousands upon thousands of shorebirds migrating southward. If you visit in October or November, walk south along the beach to Pochet Island, where you may be rewarded for your long walk with sightings of hawks and owls. Return for a windy walk in the middle of winter to see eiders, scoters, and harlequin ducks.

During beach season, **Nauset Beach,** one of the Cape's finest and longest, charges $15 per car ($5.00 on weekends between Memorial Day and mid-June) for all-day parking, but if you are renting a cottage in Orleans, you can get a weekly pass for $50 or a seasonal one for $110. Many local lodgings have discount coupons for their guests. At the entrance to the beach are restrooms and changing rooms with showers, as well as a snack bar. You can rent umbrellas here, too, half-price after 2:00 P.M. The beach and all facilities are wheelchair accessible; (508) 240–3775.

On the way to the beach you will pass the often-overlooked **Meeting House and Museum** of the Orleans Historical Society, at 3 River Road, where it intersects with Main Street. Among the usual collections of local historical items are a number of Native American stone tools and weapons, and artifacts from a German U-boat attack off Nauset during World War I. Here also are artifacts from the shipwrecked *Sparrowhawk,* which you will have seen if you visited the Pilgrim Hall Museum in Plymouth. The museum is open in July and August on Thursday, Friday, and Saturday 10:00 A.M. to 1:00 P.M. or by appointment. They also sponsor several scheduled tours and festivals from May through September. Call (508) 240–1329.

The Historical Society also maintains the *Jonathan Young Windmill,* dating from the 1700s, in Cove Park, overlooking Town Cove, not far from the rotary intersection of Routes 6 and 6A.

Orleans is a town that's chockablock with restaurants and shops. Two of the nicest stores, although they're no secrets, are right on Route 6A. The *Birdwatcher's General Store* (508–255–6974, 800–562–1512; www.birdwatchers generalstore.com) is a bird-watcher's dream come true. Never in one store will you see so many birding items, from field guides, binoculars, feeders, and fountains to prints, note cards, paintings, and posters. *Tree's Place* (508–255–1330; www.TreesPlace.com) is an art gallery and crafts showroom in one. Fine regional paintings are on exhibit, while the shop has some lovely, high-quality goods, including pottery, jewelry, decorator ceramic tiles, art glass, and Russian lacquerware boxes.

For morning coffee and pastries, you can't find anyplace better than the *Cottage Street Bakery,* at Routes 6A and 28. This tiny shop is filled with the warm smells of freshly baked European pastries and gourmet coffee blends. Among its innumerable enticing wares are French pastries, Danish, walnut rye bread, lemon poppyseed muffins, and cranberry scones. An antique Hoosier cabinet displays the bakery's very own cookbook, which you can purchase. Call (508) 255–2821.

Before you leave Orleans, step into the *French Cable Station Museum,* at the corner of Cove Road and Route 28, built in 1890 to house the extension of the transatlantic cable from France to Eastham. A jumble of original equipment lies piled on tables in several rooms, and there are also historic photos of the cable being laid. The curators demonstrate how a cable message was translated from wavy lines to letters. News of the wreck of the paddle steamer *Portland* on the Cape was telegraphed from Orleans to France and then to Boston via New York because all phone lines were down in a winter storm. News of Lindbergh's landing in Paris arrived here first. During World War I, the cable station was guarded by marines because General Pershing's orders were routed from Orleans to France. The museum is open in July and August from 1:00 to 4:00 P.M. daily except Sunday, and Friday through Sunday, same hours, in June. Admission is free, but donations are accepted. Call (508) 240–1735.

Main Street in Orleans becomes Rock Harbor Road when it crosses US 6 and leads to historic *Rock Harbor,* now a habitat for shellfish, birds, and fish, and a place to walk on the sandflats at low tide. But it was once a very busy port for packet ships sailing out of Boston. A ten-ton sloop sailed this route as early as 1808, soon joined by others carrying passengers and freight between the city and the Cape. Here on December 19, 1814, the local militia repulsed a British landing party from the HMS *Newcastle*, whose purpose was to burn the village and its vessels. Rock Harbor is on the Cape Cod bike trail, which uses Rock Harbor Road through this section. You can rent bicycles in Orleans from **Orleans Cycle**, 26 Main Street; (508) 255–9115.

Although there are plenty of upscale restaurants in Orleans, fishermen can feel right at home at **Captain Cass Rock Harbor Seafood**, on Rock Harbor Road (no phone), which is open June through October. Strung with buoys and nets, the restaurant looks like an old fishing shack, and don't worry if you spill anything on its tables covered with black-and-white-checkered oilcloth or on its battered wooden floor. Lobster rolls ("no filler") are its specialty, along with fish, clam, and scallop plates. The restaurant is open for lunch and dinner.

The **Salt Pond Visitors Center at the Cape Cod National Seashore** (508–255–3421; on US 6 eastbound) has recently been thoroughly refurbished to educate visitors about many aspects of the Cape's greatness. Here you'll find exhibits on fine art inspired by its beauty and natural history displays and activities. Films on the geological formation of the Cape maritime history, Thoreau's time here, and on the first transatlantic cable give visitors an understanding of the significance of sites, as do many materials for sale in the shop. You can also pick up trail maps here to guide your explorations of the several nature trails that depart from the visitor center, or ask about guided nature tours and interpretive programs that are offered frequently through the summer. You might follow in the footsteps of Henry David Thoreau, visit some retired lighthouses, or see a shellfishing demonstration. Another tour takes you to the **Captain Edward Penniman House**, an unusually ornate home built in 1867 for a New Bedford whaling captain. Designed in French second empire style, it features a mansard roof, an octagonal cupola, and an arch made of whalebone jaws framing its entrance. The visitor center is open 9:00 A.M. to 4:30 P.M. daily with extended summer hours.

The Inn at the Oaks, a home and carraige house, awaits you at 3085 County Road (US 6), Eastham; (508) 255–1886; www.innattheoaks.com. Here Pam and Don Anderson make sure that their guests get a taste of Britain in New England. The house was built in 1869 and originally owned by Sarah Chipman, who was married to a sea captain. The inn has been renovated recently and is expecially child and pet friendly. Classic breakfast options are joined by Don's family recipe for abelskivers, a puffy pancake from Denmark. The inn is convenient to the extensive nearby bike trails as well as a bike-rental shop. Several of the rooms are set up especially for larger families, but do be warned that there are no televisions, so bring children with imaginations.

When you see the sign on US 6 for Wellfleet Center, take a left at the light onto Commercial Street. A short distance down on the left will be a small wooden footbridge crossing a salt marsh. The bridge is known as **Uncle Tim's Bridge.** It offers a wonderful vista of Wellfleet's coastal scenery: a tidal creek, a wooded rise, and Wellfleet Harbor to the south.

Wellfleet is called "the Art Gallery Town" because there are so many galleries here, almost two dozen. They're clustered on Main Street or within a few blocks, and so you can make a nice walking tour of them. Artists in every medium are represented, and you'll see the work of nationally known Cape artists as well as foreign artists. A popular tradition on many Saturday nights is attending cocktail party openings at which you can meet the artists. Strolling from one of these openings to another on a warm summer night is a wonderful way to spend the evening. For a guide to the galleries, write the Wellfleet Art Galleries Association, P.O. Box 916, South Wellfleet, MA 02667, or pick one up at the town information booth off US 6 in Wellfleet.

For breakfast, lunch, and dinner, a local favorite is **The Lighthouse,** right on Main Street (508–349–3681). The Lighthouse is always busy with customers who know where to find a hearty, freshly cooked breakfast with good coffee to match, served at comfortable wooden tables. Open 7:00 A.M. to 10:00 P.M.

While you're driving along Main Street, you'll see the pretty blue cupola of the First Congregational Church. In the church steeple is the only **town clock** in the world that strikes on ship's time (four bells, six bells, and eight bells, just as in *Moby-Dick*).

The **Wellfleet Bay Wildlife Sanctuary** (508–349–2615) is one of Massachusetts Audubon's largest and most active. Its thousand acres of pristine salt marsh, woods, fields, and brooks are fine places to wander on their 5 miles of nature trails. The program offerings are rich and of wide appeal. Besides birding and botany walks, there are canoe trips, sunset and whale-watching cruises, and family hikes. A three-hour cruise to Nauset Marsh takes you to the setting of *The Outermost House,* Henry Beston's book about a year spent living alone among the dunes. Nauset Marsh is also home to thousands of shorebirds and Massachusetts's largest tern colony. Hardy souls will love the wintertime cruises from January to April to see harbor and gray seals. Thousands of these playful-looking mammals winter off the Massachusetts coast. Reservations are required. Wellfleet Bay is on West Road, just off US 6.

Truro is the quintessential Outer Cape. You could drive through it without knowing you were here. Rural and remote, Truro is not much more than a stretch of dunes. In the dunes are shacks where solitary writers and artists once sought inspiration, among them Harry Remp and Eugene O'Neill. Cape Cod

An Unintended Gift

A plaque on Cornhill Road in Truro commemorates the first theft recorded in Massachusetts, and explains the name of the road. It recounts that Myles Standish and his scouting party, on November 16, 1620, found seed corn that had been buried there by Indians, and they promptly carried off a basketful. Later, they looked for and found similar mounds under which the corn was buried, for a total of about ten bushels. The Pilgrims were glad to have this vital food, but history doesn't mention whether the Indians who had stored it and depended on it were equally pleased.

narrows so much at this point that you can see water on both sides. Some of the Cape's earliest cabin colonies, built in the 1920s and 1930s, still stand in Truro along Route 6A. Truro has the smallest population of any Cape town, only about 1,600. A tiny town center holds little more than a post office and store, the Cobb Library, and the Blacksmith Shop restaurant, once the workplace of Truro's only blacksmith. Not many people come to Truro. And that's how the natives like it.

For a scenic drive, take Depot Road off Route 6A north to Mill Pond Road, which becomes Old County Road. Old County Road's windswept hills and ridges are called "the Hogsbacks" because they looked like animals in a pen to the early settlers. Edward Hopper once had a studio off Old County Road.

Follow Route 6A north again and turn right onto South Highland Road, which will bring you to Lighthouse Road, the entrance to the **Highland Light** (508–487–1121). This handsome black-and-white lighthouse is the Cape's oldest, built in 1797 and rebuilt in 1857. An overlook of the beach below will show you the same views that Thoreau described on his visits here in the mid-1800s. Storm erosion threatened Highland Light with toppling right into the sea, and a citizen fund-raising campaign made it possible to move it a few hundred feet to safety. Now visitors can climb the light and learn about its history from mid-May to mid-October, daily 10:00 A.M. to 5:30 P.M. Tickets are $4.00; children must be at least 51 inches tall to climb. A combo ticket of $6.00 allows visitors to see the **Highland House Museum** (508–487–3397), devoted to local history.

"Off the beaten path in **Provincetown**" is an oxymoron. Summer crowds jam this resort town so densely that people walk twelve abreast on Commercial Street. Still, P-town is a carnival of variety and audacity, its alternative lifestyles, thriving gay community, and dozens of galleries, boutiques, sophisticated restaurants, nightclubs, and arts offerings serving as a magnet for the masses. There's no other place like it in all of Massachusetts.

Provincetown is further from the beaten path before Memorial Day and in the glorious fall days of September and October. While some of the lodgings and businesses are open only in the height of summer, many do remain open and are crowd-free in the off-season.

The lively arts scene and live-and-let-live attitude are Provincetown's two key draws, and both are found in abundance along Commercial Street, a long and crowded promenade that hugs the inner shore. On the east end especially are a multitude of galleries, displaying everything from the exquisite to the truly strange. At night, look toward the west end of the street for small clubs and cafes with live music. Performance times and dates vary, and places open and close, so you'll have to rely on local advice and your own explorations. Once we found a small club where we heard some of the best live jazz singing since Ella Fitzgerald. Keep your ears and mind open and you'll probably find something you like.

If the energy required on Commercial Street wears you down, drive out to **Race Point,** which never disappoints. The narrow road out to the lighthouse winds through dunes and hillsides covered with waving grasses and wind-beaten scrub. You can smell the salt heavy in the air and feel the cleansing wind in your face. In any season, no matter what the weather, Race Point is starkly wild and beautiful. Thoreau, who made a walking tour of the Cape in 1849, wrote that "a man may stand there and put all America behind him." So may you.

A look at an aerial photograph of Provincetown and the end of the Cape shows the violence with which the Atlantic Ocean beats this exposed pile of sand. Huge wind-driven mounds of sand lie like gigantic waves about to wash over the eastern beaches. Fortunately for visitors, this violence is less visible from footpath level, where the terrain is a lot more inviting than threatening. These fragile, windblown dunes were once favored places for crude cabins where locals retired in summer.

To really appreciate the unique and beautiful dunes, book an exploration with **Art's Dune Tours,** corner of Commercial and Standish Streets; (508) 487–1950 or (800) 894–1951; www.artsdunetours.com. Traveling through the National Seashore Park and sand dunes, you are, literally, transported to an otherworldly part of P-town: dune shacks, indigenous species of plants and animals, and the incredible light that only appears in the dunes. Special sunrise, sunset, and moonlight tours show them in different lights, each creating a new land- and seascape. Rob Costa, whose father started the business more than fifty years ago, is an enlightened guide who really loves this place—and it shows. Tour prices are $20 for adults, $15 for children ages six through eleven. Sunset tours are $30 ($19 for children).

Another thing that never disappoints is **whale watching.** Seeing these gentle giants up close is a moving experience—one you'll never forget. Cruises go to Stellwagen Bank, the whales' feeding ground. A number of cruise lines dot the wharves, but the Dolphin Fleet boats are staffed by scientists from the Center for Coastal Studies, experts in whale research. The Dolphin Fleet pioneered whale watching on the East Coast. The scientists have identified and named several hundred humpback whales. Scientist-led cruises are sensitive to the whales' behavior and are less likely to disturb the creatures' feeding or breeding activities. The Dolphin Fleet offers cruises from April through October, with eight or nine cruises a day May through September, leaving from MacMillan Wharf. Advance reservations are advised in summer, especially on weekends. Summer fares are $30 for adults and $22 for children ages five to twelve. Call (800) 826–9300 or (508) 240–3636.

The hook at the Cape's end forms Provincetown Bay, sheltered from the rougher waters. *Flyer's Boat Rental, Inc.,* at 131-A Commercial Street, on the western end near the Coast Guard wharf, has a wide range of craft to get you out onto its waters. Our favorite is the plastic sea kayak, of basic design. It's a wonderful way to scout along the harbor, skim the beaches, and explore the outer reaches of the sandy arm as far as the lighthouse. Bear in mind that you should wear a bathing suit, since these little kayaks have self-draining holes in the hull and you will get wet. The cost is $25 a half-day, $40 a day. Flyer's also has Sunfish, 16-foot powered skiffs, and traditional and racing sailboats. Sailing lessons are also available; (508) 487–0898 or (800) 750–0898.

The terrain at the end of the Cape is essentially flat, with an occasional hillock rising no more than 20 feet or so. A landscape like that begs to be explored by bicycle, even for those who don't cycle regularly. *Provincetown Bikes* is at 42 Bradford Street; (508) 487–8735. The shop can fix you up with good broad-tired bikes that work well in the sand (starting at $9.00 for a two-hour rental), or go all out for a bicycle-built-for-two for $16 for two hours. The shop also has helmets and other gear—and can service your own bike if you brought one. *Arnold's,* 329 Commercial Street (508–487–0844), also has bikes for rent.

Cycle out to *Herring Cove Beach* to pick up the bike trail on the north end of the parking lot. It will take you along Race Point, and you can follow it along the shore through the dunes to Race Point Road. Go to the end of the road and the beach, then return to town either by the same route or via Race Point Road, Conwell Street, Arch Street, and Commercial Street.

That tall tower you've been seeing across the bay during your travels on the Cape is the *Pilgrim Monument and Provincetown Museum,* a tribute to the Pilgrims, who actually landed first in Provincetown in November 1620, not in Plymouth. Dedicated in 1910, the monument is the tallest all-granite structure in the United States, at 252 feet tall. You can climb to the top for an unparalleled view of Cape Cod and the distant Boston skyline. Outside the monument are seven acres of grounds, where you may enjoy a picnic. Adjacent to its base is a museum with exhibits about the Pilgrims, the *Mayflower,* and Provincetown's early fishing and whaling history, including a captain's cabin from a whaling ship. The museum also holds specimens of birds and polar bears brought back by Admiral Donald MacMillan, for whom MacMillan Wharf is named. To get to the monument, take the Shankpainter Road exit from US 6, make an immediate left, and then take the next right onto High Pole Hill. The monument is open daily from 9:00 A.M. to 4:15 P.M. April through November and remains open until 6:15 P.M. in July and August. Admission is $7.00 for adults, $5.00 for seniors and students with ID, and $3.50 for children ages four through fourteen; (508) 487–1310; www.pilgrim-monument.org.

Beachcombers should head for **Long Point,** a low spit of sandy beaches and dunes. This desolate wind- and sea-whipped place was part of the town settlement at one time until its residents had a better idea and floated their houses across the harbor to safer moorings in the present town. You can catch a water shuttle to Long Point from Flyer's Boat Rental or you can walk, following Commercial Street along the waterfront to the end, then crossing the stone breakwater that protects the sensitive marshlands at the inside corner of the harbor. The beach here offers the best chance to find handsome, small, multicolored seashells and to watch the many varieties of seabirds that live on and migrate through these shores.

Off the bustle of Commercial Street, we like staying at **The Fairbanks Inn,** 90 Bradford Street; (508) 487–0386 or (800) 324–7265; www.fairbanksinn.com. Classic 1776 buildings have been tastefully restored to their former elegance, discreetly adding the modern amenities of television and showers. All but two rooms have private baths. Oriental carpets, period antiques, and patina-rich woods give the inn a beautiful welcoming glow; the floorboards and paneling are from Captain Fairbanks's ship. Innkeepers Alicia Mickenberg and Kathleen Fitzgerald have created an atmosphere of tremendous style and panache. Continental breakfast is accompanied by newspapers, and plenty of reading material is everywhere. A patio, porch, and rooftop sundeck make this a great place to just hang out, and the beautifully kept grounds are all atwinkle at night. Rates range from $139 to $269 in peak season.

Victorian decor accented by period antiques and wainscoting characterize the forty guest rooms at **Crowne Pointe Historic Inn,** 82 Bradford Street; (508) 487–6767 or (877) 276–9631; www.crownepointe.com. The inn abounds with so many inviting and cozy nooks that you almost wish for a rainy day so you can curl up with a good book. Little details—such as extra-fine bed linens and custom-made mattresses—set the inn apart. It's open all year, and our favorite season is after mid-September or in May, when rates are lowest (from $120) and P-town is its quietest.

Dining out is one of the greatest pleasures of Provincetown, and many visitors, especially in the spring and fall, come expressly for the food. You might begin an eating tour of the town at *The Red Inn,* 15 Commercial Street; (508) 487–0050. This Federal-style building is located in the sedate west end of town, past the bend in the road near the Coast Guard station. Gracious hospitality and a menu of fine continental cuisine (the rack of lamb is enough for two and delectable) combine to ensure a lovely dining experience. Stop by in daylight when you can enjoy the flower- and herb-filled courtyard, and select your water-view table. Lunch and dinner are served year-round.

Although they are best known for their giant Porterhouse steaks, we head for the fresh cod, especially when it's roasted on a bed of rosemary-scented potatoes. Expensive, but memorable. Rooms in the two-century-old inn begin at $125 on weekends, rising to $315 in July and August. It's a favorite venue for weddings and commitment ceremonies.

More down-to-earth—at least in its prices—but still rich in imagination is *Bubala's by the Bay,* 183 Commerical Street; (508) 487–0773; www.bubalas .com. Great views and an equally impressive all-day kitchen make it a favorite with local residents. Breakfast waffles and omelets are creative; lunch and dinner menus feature seafood, salads, burgers, and other usuals, but each executed in upscale style. Bangkok pasta with prawns, herb-crusted rack of lamb, or pepper-coated ostrich are just a few examples, all at sensible prices. Picasso-style murals and brilliant yellow make the decor as bright as the menu. Bubala's is open 8:00 A.M. to 11:00 P.M., May through October.

Right in the thick of everything in P-town is *The Lobster Pot,* 321 Commercial Street; (508) 487–0842. First-timers think they're entering through the back door when they walk in through the kitchen. But the dramatic entrance gives you a chance to witness a few feats of seafood legerdemain en route to your seat. The venue may be earthy, but the food is great (lines may be long in high season) and the view of MacMillan Wharf is excellent from the upstairs lounge. Prices are moderate; closed in January.

Chester Restaurant, at 404 Commercial Street (508–487–8200; www .chesterrestaurant.com), serves Wellfleet oysters, Vermont quail, and lobster right off the boat. Local sea scallops may be served with a fennel-potato ragout, or free-range chicken with a compote of lemon and dates. Most entrees are between $20 and $30. Reservations are recommended.

A terrific breakfast spot is the *Cafe Edwige,* at 333 Commercial Street; (508) 487–2008. It's an airy, upstairs loft space with light woods, art deco accents, and paintings by local artists. Creative pancakes and omelets are specialties, as are pastries and fruit and yogurt dishes.

Edwige omelets are so beautifully presented that our friend, Bill, when served one, said he couldn't decide whether to frame it or eat it. Healthful breakfasts are de rigueur, with everything from tofu frittatas to broiled flounder accompanied by stir-fry veggies. Edwige doesn't stop with breakfast, however. New American menu selections might include the planked codfish in ginger-carrot broth, lobster and Wellfleet oysters over pasta, or Asian-style sesame noodles. Along with the creative cuisine goes solicitous service, but you'll need to call ahead or expect a wait. Breakfast is served from 8:00 A.M. to 1:00 P.M., dinner from 6:00 P.M. The cafe is open April through late October.

For those who long for the bright lights and high buzz of the city when darkness falls, Provincetown has it all, and in one spot. *Crown & Anchor* is a complex of accommodations, entertainment, and more. From the poolside bar to the stylish cabaret, this is where the action is. Guest rooms are stylish, and the restaurant—*Central House Bar & Grill*—is a standout in a town where dining ranks high. It's in the middle of things, at 247 Commercial Street; (508) 487–1430; www.onlyatthecrown.com.

Martha's Vineyard

Closer to the mainland than Nantucket, Martha's Vineyard is only forty-five minutes by ferry from *Woods Hole.* For information call the Woods Hole, Martha's Vineyard, and Nantucket Steamship Authority (508–477–8600; www.steamship authority.com), which services both islands. (Summer car reservations must be made months in advance.) The one-way peak-season ferry fare to Martha's Vineyard from Woods Hole is $6.50 for adults, $3.50 for children ages five through twelve, $3.00 for bikes, and $62.00 for a car. Leaving from Falmouth, the cruise ship *Island Queen* makes seven round-trips daily from late June through early September, with a more limited schedule spring and fall. Fares are $12.00 for adults, $6.00 for children under age thirteen, $6.00 for a bicycle, and $15.00 per day to leave a car in their Falmouth lot; (508) 548–4800; www.islandqueen.com.

Or you can reach the island at *Oak Bluffs* from New Bedford via the passenger ferry operated by New England Fast Ferry Company. The fares are higher than on the Steamship Authority ferry from Woods Hole, but if you are traveling from the Providence or southern Massachusetts areas, it saves a lot of driving; (866 683–3779). Nine ferries daily in peak season alternate between Oak Bluffs and Vineayard Haven ports. Once on the island, you can rent a bike at any of a number of places close to either ferry landing, or take a Yellow Line bus on its circuit from Vineyard Haven to Oak Bluffs and Edgartown, via the beach road.

The mass of tourists descends on Vineyard Haven, where the Woods Hole ferry docks. They also converge on Oak Bluffs, to see the Flying Horses Carousel—the nation's oldest—the nineteenth-century gingerbread cottages, and the open-air Methodist Tabernacle. The rest of the island is generally less crowded. Shuttle buses service Martha's Vineyard in summer. If you have a sturdy pair of legs, you can bike around—the island is 20 miles long and 10 miles wide.

A short distance from the ferry terminal is an island institution, the **Black Dog Tavern,** at Beach Street Extension (508–693–9223), with a seaside porch dining room. Local seafood dishes, meats, and freshly baked breads and desserts from its own bakery are offered.

Off the southeast corner of Martha's Vineyard, the island of **Chappaquiddick** embraces some of the remotest and wildest territory on the island, reachable only by four-wheel drive. From Edgartown, take the **Chappy On-Time Ferry,** which holds only three or four cars and takes less than two minutes to cross the inlet. A few miles down the Chappaquiddick Road, the second dirt road you come to forks left. Follow it, and you'll find **Mytoi,** a Japanese-style garden of several acres with a small pond, wooden footbridge, and several acres of blooming plants and trees nestled in a pine grove. Mytoi is a Trustees of Reservations property; admission is free.

Continuing down the Chappaquiddick Road to School Road and then to Wasque Road brings you to **Wasque Reservation,** a 200-acre reserve owned by the Trustees of Reservations. Wasque edges the Atlantic in a landscape of heath and dunes. There's a gatehouse and a lot where you can park and walk to the beach and nature trails. Hooking 4 miles northward from Wasque, **Cape Poge** is a wind-ripped barrier beach reachable only by four-wheel-drive vehicles. At its tip stands the Cape Poge Light. Admission to Wasque is $3.00 per person. For information call (508) 693–7662 or (508) 627–7689.

For more places to walk and enjoy the quiet natural areas of the island, pick up a copy of *Vineyard Visitor,* a free publication of the *Martha's Vineyard Times.* A handy pullout centerfold shows individual trail maps for fourteen walking paths located on Land Bank properties throughout the island. Trail maps are also available at the Cape Poge gatehouse, from which the Trustees of Reservations operates many tours and programs; (508) 627–7689.

Tiny downtown **Edgartown** is crammed with resort amenities: boutiques, restaurants, and ice-cream stands. Yet just 2 blocks up, the resort roar quiets to streets of white sea captains' houses with neat green or black shutters and white picket fences.

The unofficial town center has long been ***The Colonial Inn,*** North Water Street; (508) 627–4711 or (800) 627–4701, or through DestINNations New England at (800) 333–4667. Many of the rooms overlook the sea; all have private baths, phones, and TV. The wide veranda is the quintessential seaside vantage, with white wicker chairs. The staff simply couldn't be nicer; it seems as if their only interest in the world is in making sure you are comfortable and happy there. Rates begin at about $225 in summer, including continental breakfast. The inn is open mid-April to November.

Newes From America Pub, at The Kelley House, Kelley Street (508–627–4397), was built in the mid-1700s and is known for its fine collection of microbrews. The creative menu features lighter foods and pub grub. An island favorite is a rack of five brews and an Island Poor Boy sandwich.

As you tour Martha's Vineyard, it may surprise you to see a white-tailed deer or a wild turkey cross the road. But the island is a great haven for wildlife, and one of its most stunning achievements is the osprey-nesting program. You can see the 40-foot poles erected as nesting platforms for these huge birds at the ***Felix Neck Wildlife Sanctuary*** (508–627–4850) on the Edgartown–Vineyard Haven Road. From two breeding pairs in 1971, their numbers had grown by 1990 to almost eighty pairs; in 1989 the osprey was removed from the list of endangered species, the first one in Massachusetts removed because of recovery. There's also a small museum here as well as nature trails.

Another place to enjoy the out-of-doors—and a more remote preserve—is ***Cedar Tree Neck.*** A car-disabling dirt road leads to a tiny parking lot where a short wooded trail takes you to the beach. An almost-constant wind has twisted the trees into intriguingly blasted-looking shapes. Finally you come upon a peaceful vista of sandy beach, dunes, and bayberry circling a lagoon— especially nice at sunset. Take Indian Hill Road off State Road several miles west of Vineyard Haven.

Quintessential Martha's Vineyard is expressed by the ***Field Gallery,*** an art gallery in a field in the center of ***West Tisbury.*** Some twenty larger-than-life dancing white figures inhabit the lawn, expressionist-like with thick, rounded limbs and curving forms. There are a massive chicken with a tiny head, a figure blowing a trumpet, a hatted figure with a little dog, and a colonial figure on horseback. The sculptures are the work of island artist Tom Maley, who exhibits the work of others in the adjacent gallery. The Field Gallery is such an island institution that people like to get married here.

Also in West Tisbury, on Stoney Hill Road, is ***Chicama Vineyards,*** which takes advantage of the island's unique warm autumn and mild winter to grow European wine grapes. You can take a tour at noon, 2:00, and 4:00 P.M. from

Memorial Day to Columbus Day, or visit the shop for a tasting year-round. Days and hours vary widely with the season, so it's best to call ahead or pick up the vineyard's brochure on the boat; (508) 693–0309.

The **Allen Farm** on South Road in **Chilmark** has been a family farm since the seventeenth century, and Allens still run it, these days keeping a herd of some 150 New Zealand sheep. The wool goes into gorgeous hand-knit sweaters of a comforting weight, as well as scarves, hats, blankets, and shawls—all sold in a sunny gift shop behind a neat stone wall. The shop is open noon to 5:00 P.M. daily from May through Labor Day and during the holiday season; (508) 645–9064.

The **Native Earth Teaching Farm** (94 North Road, Chilmark) is a small organic working farm that opens its doors three days a week to visitors who would like to meet their food in the lovingly cultivated farm habitat. The diverse offerings include vegetables, fruit, and animal products that are for sale at the farm stand, but the real attraction is a family-friendly farm where you can ask experts what they do to keep squash beetles away, or just what a kohlrabi is, anyway. The answer may well come in the form of a demonstration. There is no fee, though they do ask for a donation to help with expenses. Open Wednesday, Saturday, and Sunday 10:00 A.M. to 6:00 P.M.; If you want to drop in off-season, call to make sure they're open (508–645–3304).

The road to **Menemsha,** on the western edge of the island, winds through field and forest and ends abruptly at a stone wall that could pitch you right into the sea. In this miniature fishing village with a tiny harbor are more boats than houses. The village has a post office, a fish market, a restaurant, and a gas station, and that's about it. A small beach facing due west is a popular spot for celebrating the sunset, one of the few places on the East Coast where the sun sinks into the sea. (Key West, stand aside.)

Home Port, North Road, Menemsha (508–645–2679), is an island institution—it opened in 1931—with great harbor views and sunsets and fresh-off-the-boat seafood. Nothing fancy, with paper placemats and stuffed fish on the wall and no liquor license, so BYOB. Platters run $40 to $60 but include appetizer, salad, fresh-baked breads, nonalcoholic beverage, entree, and dessert. You will need a reservation. Open mid-May to mid-October from 5:00 P.M. daily.

While busloads of tourists tramp along the path to the **Gay Head Cliffs,** these spectacular white-chalk cliffs should not be missed. They run for 1 mile along the coast, with a dramatic backdrop of russet-colored beach vegetation and the stout, handsome brick spire of the Gay Head Light. The cliffs were the country's first registered National Natural Landmark.

Living is easy on Martha's Vineyard, so if that makes you long for the Big Easy, head for **Lola's Southern Seafood,** adjacent to the Island Inn on Beach Road, Oak Bluffs; (508) 693–5007. The sprawling house creates a languid ambience, and entertainment may be jazz, blues, or dancing. If you still have room after working your way through the bread basket, order mammoth portions of nicely seasoned blackened catfish, jambalaya, or crab cakes. Caesar salad, a basket of rolls, corn bread, and real southern biscuits plus collard greens and potatoes accompany the fixed-price entrees. You'll need a reservation; open daily from 10:00 A.M., spring through fall, and Wednesday through Saturday from 5:00 P.M. in winter, when Sunday brunch is also served 10:00 A.M. to 2:00 P.M. In the summer there is live music from 9:30 P.M.

Passengers arriving from New Bedford may disembark in Vineyard Haven, a tad more down-to-earth than the somewhat-precious Oak Bluffs. If you arrive by ferry and would like to see the island, we suggest the thorough and reasonably priced tours offered by **AdamCab,** in Edgartown at (508) 627–4462 or (800) 281–4462.

Nantucket

Nantucket is somehow even more an island than Martha's Vineyard. Isolated 20 or so miles at sea, it's two and a half hours by ferry from the mainland. If you get stranded by a winter gale (and people do), you're really stranded. Because of its flat terrain and smaller size—16 miles long by 6 miles wide—the island is manageable on a bike, which will get you outside the crowded town of Nantucket. There are also buses and taxis.

You can bring your own bike on the ferry or rent one when you arrive from **Young's Bicycle Shop** at 6 Broad Street; (508) 228–1151. You can also get a free map here with streets and cycling paths. Be sure to observe the one-way street signs, since you are considered a vehicle when on two wheels, and will be ticketed. If you must go the wrong way, do it as a pedestrian. Cobblestones make some streets in town uncomfortable for road bikes.

Both car ferries and the faster catamaran service run year-round from Hyannis to Nantucket and in the summer between Nantucket and Martha's Vineyard. Summer passenger ferries and high-speed catamarans are operated by Hy-Line Cruises; for reservations (which are recommended) call (508) 778–2602 or (888) 778–1132; www.hy-linecruises.com. There are five high-speed departures daily, year-round that cost $64 for adults, $45 for children, plus $10.00 for a bike, all round-trip. The three slower ferry trips cost about half that. The Steamship Authority operates the year-round automobile ferry (although visitors will find a car more of a nuisance on the island than a help) with economical passenger rates on the regular ferry of $28 (round-trip; $14.50 for children) and $12 for a bike. The Authority also runs the FastFerry, which runs $59 round-trip for adults. We take our bikes and leave the car in

Hyannis. For reservations (necessary only for cars) or schedules, call (508) 477–8600.

It's a lot faster to fly to Nantucket than to take the ferry: a twelve-minute flight from Hyannis. Cape Air flies more than ten times a day to Nantucket, as well as to Martha's Vineyard and Boston, and from Boston to Provincetown. Call (800) 352–0714 or visit www.flycapeair.com for reservations and departure times. The planes are small enough for a baby to offer his or her bottle to the pilot, but the oversea route gives you an aerial view of Nantucket that shows what is meant by "the little gray lady of the sea." From the air, all the houses look gray against the subdued landscape of heathered moors.

To see Nantucket from its historical perspective, the best way to begin is to visit the museums of the **Nantucket Historical Association,** or better yet, to take one of their walking tours. Offered twice daily from June into early September, the hour-and-a-half amble helps you appreciate history in its living context (call for current schedules: 508–228–1894). The association has six properties in its care—two houses, a mill, an old jail, a Quaker meetinghouse, plus its brand new **Whaling Museum.** The latter's centerpiece is the suspended skeleton of a sperm whale that washed ashore in 1998, and the vital economic and artistic significance of this massive mammal is made abundantly clear in the museum's exhibits. Short films and frequent minilectures fill the museum's schedule, as do changing exhibits; call or see their Web site to be sure to catch one (www.nha.org). Tickets to the whole complex are $18.00 for adults, $9.00 for children six to seventeen. Walking tours are an additional $10.00 per adult and $4.00 per child. The museums are open mid-May to mid-October, Monday through Saturday 10:00 A.M. to 5:00 P.M., and Sundays noon to 5:00 P.M. The Whaling Museum is open into December, with more limited hours.

Maria Mitchell was the nation's first woman astronomer. The king of Denmark awarded her a gold medal in 1847 when she discovered a comet. The house she was born in was a typical Quaker house built in 1790, a two-story dwelling with weathered shingles on Vestal Street. Now it's the **Maria Mitchell House** (1 Vestal Street; 508–228–2896). The small rooms of the family home have plain plaster walls and some Mitchell family memorabilia. To read Maria Mitchell's fascinating story, pick up a copy of *More than Petticoats: Remarkable Massachusetts Women,* by Lura Seavey (The Globe Pequot Press).

Near the birthplace house, at 7 Milk Street, is the **Hinchman House Natural Science Museum,** which contains exhibits on local flora and fauna and offers numerous guided nature walks and educational programs for adults and children; (508) 228–0898. The Maria Mitchell Association also runs astronomy programs and exhibits at the Vestal Street Observatory year-round and welcomes visitors to observe the skies at the Loines Observatory on perfectly clear Friday nights at 9:00 P.M., with additional opportunities in summer on Monday and Wednesday. This costs $10.00 for adults, $6.00 for children. Loines is on the Milk Street Extension across from the cemetery; call (508) 228–9273 to verify night and time, which change periodically. The *Aquarium,* at 28 Washington Street (508–228–5387), features exhibits on local waters and sea life, and its programs include *Marine Ecology Field Trips* several times a week during the summer.

The observatories and science library are open year-round, with limited hours in the off-season, and the science museum, Mitchell House, and Aquarium are open mid-June through Labor Day, Monday through Saturday 10:00 A.M. to 4:00 P.M. (the house, library, and observatories are closed Monday). A pass is available to visit all the museums, $10.00 for adults, $7.00 for children; or separate tickets for each museum can be bought for $4.00 to $5.00 for adults, depending on the site.

Nantucket is rich in marine environments, from the protected waters of the harbor and the salt marshes to the wave-battered southern shore. Beds of eel grass provide a safe environment where young fish develop, while the rocky jetties are home to hard-shelled creatures such as mussels and barnacles, as well as lobster. At Madaket Harbor you can sometimes find tropical fish in the summer that have traveled to Nantucket with the Gulf Stream.

Nantucket's *Old North Church* stands on a hill, which raises its needle-like spire even higher above the treetops of the streets below. As you might imagine, the view is wonderful, reaching from Great Point to Siasconset to Madaket. Exhibits at each level of the climb give you a chance to catch your breath. The church and tower are not open all the time, but certainly are during the Daffodil Weekend in April, and often on Saturday. Check at the Chamber of Commerce at 48 Main Street. The church is at 62 Centre Street.

An often-overlooked spot a short distance from town is the *Nantucket Lifesaving Museum,* a replica of the 1874 lifesaving station. Years ago, shoal-bound Nantucket harvested so many wrecks that it was called "the Graveyard of the Atlantic." A newspaper clipping recounts the dramatic 1829 rescue of the crew of the *H.P. Kirkham,* 15 miles offshore in a winter storm. Sepia-toned old photos show other wrecks and a horse-drawn lifeboat on the beach. Quarter-boards hang on the walls—ships' wooden nameplates with gold letters and elaborately carved floral designs. The museum is 2.5 miles out on Polpis Road, on the left by a marsh. It's easy to miss by car, but on a bike you'll quickly spot the white stone marker with the museum's name at the entrance. Hours are 9:30 A.M. to 4:00 P.M. daily, June 15 to Columbus Day. Admission is $5.00 for adults, $2.00 for children over age five; (508) 228–1885.

Nantucket Harbor is enclosed by a giant fishhook of sand that encompasses some 18 miles of shoreline, the *Coskata-Coatue Wildlife Refuge.*

These miles and miles of barrier beach are open country of salt marsh and tidal creeks, pine and holly, and clam flats. Coskata-Coatue is home to a vast array of wildlife and birds, among them snowy owls, eiders, herons, and egrets. Rare and endangered least terns and piping plovers nest on the beach. The refuge is much favored for surf casting, picnicking, and bird-watching. You can drive to its entrance out the Wauwinet Road, but from there you'll either have to walk or use four-wheel drive. From the gatehouse, it's a 1-mile hike to the beach. For information call (508) 228–5646.

Natural history tours are generally given twice daily, June through October. The tour by over-sand vehicle has limited space so reservations are a must. You may see rare bird species or learn about the unique ecosystems of the dunes, beaches, and marshes. Also available is a tour to the top of Great Point Lighthouse for a view from the very tip of the island. The $40 cost ($15 for children under fifteen) goes to help preserve the sanctuary. To make reservations call (508) 228–6799.

Despite this island's tiny size, fully one-third of it has been set aside as open space by the Nantucket Conservation Foundation and the Nantucket Land Bank. Their actions ensure that the island's fragile beauty will be protected from the heavy pressures of tourism and development. One such property is **Sanford Farm,** a great place for hiking, out on Madaket Road. On Polpis Road, just past the Wauwinet Road turnoff, is the **Windswept Cranberry Bog,** a small working bog where you can watch the harvest in October. For a map of land bank properties, write the Nantucket Land Bank Commission, 22 Broad Street, Nantucket 02554, or call (508) 228–7240. The Nantucket Conservation Foundation, at 118 Cliff Road, P.O. Box 13 Nantucket 02554 (508–228–2884), sells a guide to its properties for $3.00, or you can download it at no charge from their Web site (www.nantucketconservation.com).

A scattering of quaint, interesting villages dots the island. Siasconset, called **'Sconset** for short, began as a fishing village of one-room shacks in the seventeenth century. 'Sconset's tiny, weathered cottages cluster together like a dollhouse village, festooned with rambling roses—a pretty sight in summer. There's a nice public beach but few conveniences besides a gas station, market, post office, and a restaurant, **Chanticleer** (508–257–6231), serving upscale, fresh cuisine in a rose-covered cottage. It's open Mother's Day through Columbus Day, and entrees begin at $35.

Nantucket has dozens of restaurants and, in general, better restaurants than Martha's Vineyard. In Nantucket town, there's a restaurant on every block, and the only hard part is choosing one (and affording the inflated prices of some).

For an upscale menu with lots of creative options and beautifully prepared dishes, leave the main streets to seek out **American Seasons,** at 80 Centre Street;

(508) 228–7111. Celebrating American ingredients and cooking styles, the chef may offer a pan-roasted sirloin of veal, sliced and served in an architectural arrangement, or molasses-marinated pork with a smokey undertone paired with polenta. Large cubes of fresh tuna may be encrusted in coarse pepper and served over a lobster curry. They don't serve espresso after dinner "because it's not American," but this rule fortunately didn't seem to exclude the crème brûlée or the cappuccino mousse they offer for dessert. Entrees average $25 to $30.

For a breakfast big enough to take you through lunch as well, and for dinners that are just as satisfying, try *Arno's at 41 Main Street;* (508) 228–7001. The menu offers a nice blend of local tradition with New American. Casual, with no pretensions, this is a place you'd be comfortable taking children and still expect a very nice dinner at very reasonable prices.

Freshness and simplicity are the watchwords at *Centre Street Bistro,* 29 Centre Street; (508) 228–8470. They don't accept credit cards. Entrees might include roast duck breast with mushroom ravioli or seared salmon over crisp vegetables and wontons, with spiced citrus soy glaze, and run $18 to $25.

In the summer and on festival weekends spring and fall, it can be hard to find a room on the island; expect a two-night minimum on weekends. Island B&Bs range from simple and homey to quite elegant; all are pricier than similar establishments would be on the mainland. *Periwinkle Guest House* is convenient to the ferry landing, at 9 North Water Street (P.O. Box 1436, Nantucket, MA 02554); (508) 228–9267 or (800) 872–6830, fax (508) 325–4046; www.the periwinkle.com. Its rooms are light, with the classic white woodwork and pastel decor of the island, comfortably furnished in cottage style. Some have shared baths, and breakfast is a do-it-yourself continental. It's one of the few with single rooms, which are priced from $65 in winter to $85 in summer. Doubles range from $215 to $450 in the summer, $95 to $325 in the winter. Don't expect an innkeeper—we never met one in the two nights we stayed there.

Up the street is the more upscale *Carlisle House Inn,* furnished in antiques, canopy beds, Oriental carpets, and inlaid paneling. Rooms vary in size, but most are quite large and none is claustrophobic; all are very tastefully decorated and beautifully maintained. Breakfast is continental, but elegant, in keeping with the house itself. The innkeeper has a fine-tuned sense of humor, and the atmosphere has a warmth you'll notice from the moment you step inside. Rates range $60 to $165 for a double room off-season (which includes April and May) to $85 to $285 in the summer. It's at 26 North Water Street; (508) 228–0720; www.carlislehouse.com.

To experience the setting in which successful island captains and shipbuilders lived a century-and-a-half ago, book a room at the *Jared Coffin House,* at 29 Broad Street, a short walk straight ahead from the ferry landing.

The main house has been supplemented by several others of equal (or greater) architectural and historic distinction, where you will find fine paneling, antiques, large rooms, and the hospitable touch of luxury. Those traveling alone will appreciate the single rooms here, priced from $155. Doubles begin at $215 and all rooms have private baths; (508) 228–2405 or (800) 248–2405.

More Places to Stay on Cape Cod and the Islands

The Dan'l Webster Inn,
149 Main Street,
Sandwich;
(508) 888–3622 or
(800) 444–3566;
www.danlwebsterinn.com
A modern inn with traditional furnishings—canopy beds, wing chairs, fireplaces.

**Shoreway Acres
Resort Inn,**
Shore Street,
Falmouth;
(508) 540–3000 or
(800) 352–7100,
fax (508) 540–9337;
www.shorewayacresinn.com
Refreshingly priced for the Cape, with rooms under $160 even in high season, $80 off-season, often including breakfast buffet.

Admiralty Inn,
51 Teaticket Highway
(Route 28),
Falmouth;
(508) 548–4240 or
(800) 341–5700,
fax (508) 457–0535.
You'll have to drive (or bike) to town or beach, but it's a good base with high-season motel rooms at $120 to $200.

Liberty Hill Inn
77 Main Street (Route 6A,
Old Kings Highway),
Yarmouth Port;
(508) 362–3976 or
(800) 821–3977,
fax (508) 362–6485;
www.libertyhillinn.com
A B&B in an elegant 1825 home with amiable owners and rates as low as $100 a night in the off-season.

Blueberry Manor,
438 Main Street
(Route 6A),
Yarmouth Port;
(508) 362–7620.
A classic 1700s captain's house "modernized" in the following century, furnished in antiques, with rooms from under $135 to $195, in season.

The Whalewalk Inn,
220 Bridge Road,
Eastham;
(508) 255–0617.
Upscale property with country antiques, fine linens, and soft colors, and a garden where you can breakfast in the summer.

Corsair and Cross Rip,
33 Chase Avenue,
Dennisport;
(800) 889–8037 or
(508) 398–2279;
www.corsaircrossrip.com
A pair of upscale motels with impeccable attention to detail, a hospitable staff, and

fine dining on site. Two pools plus a private beach right on the ocean, coin-operated laundry, fully equipped kitchenettes, babysitting available, and many other extras.

Provincetown Inn,
1 Commercial Street,
Provincetown;
(508) 487–9500 or
(800) 924–5388;
www.provincetowninn.com
It may look tired from the outside, but its hospitable owners are not. At the end of town, it's away from the crowds and within walking distance of the lighthouse.

The Look Inn,
13 Look Street,
Vineyard Haven;
(508) 693–6893.
In a restored farmhouse dating to 1806, this B&B is casual, with shared baths and continental breakfasts at $125 per room in summer.

For bed-and-breakfast lodgings, contact Bed and Breakfast Cape Cod;
(508) 255–3824,
(800) 541–6226;
www.bedandbreakfastcape
cod.com
Representing more than sixty locations.

More Places to Eat on Cape Cod and the Islands

Vining's Bistro,
upstairs in the Wheeler
Building, 595 Main Street,
Chatham;
(508) 945–5033.
Imaginative dinners with
excellent salads, wood-grilled
chicken, and sautéed
vegetable and pasta
combinations. Dinner only,
from 5:30 P.M.

Christian's,
443 Main Street,
Chatham;
(508) 945–3362.

Upstairs is a year-round
intimate piano bar/restaurant
with a terrace for alfresco
summer dining. Downstairs,
the more formal New American restaurant is open daily
from 4:00 P.M., winter Thursday through Saturday. Specialty is "Sea of Love"—a
heady mélange of shrimp,
lobster, and scallops with
sundried tomatoes and artichokes, served over pasta.

Impudent Oyster,
15 Chatham Bars Avenue,
Chatham;
(508) 945–3545.
A casual eatery known for its
fresh fish, with many grilled
choices. Pesca Fra Diavola is
a blend of local littlenecks,
scallops, and shrimp in a
spicy Italian tomato sauce,
served over fettuccine.

Pate's Restaurant,
1260 Route 28,
Chatham (toward
Barnstable);
(508) 945–9777.
The lamb chops, cooked
over an open-hearth grill, are
outstanding, as is the Caesar
salad; open daily from
5:30 P.M.

The Cheese Corner,
56 Main Street,
Orleans;
(508) 255–1699.
Sandwiches on good bread,
along with soups, chowder,
and salads to eat there or
carry out.

TO LEARN MORE ABOUT CAPE COD AND THE ISLANDS

Cape Cod Chamber of Commerce,
P.O. Box 1001,
Hyannis 02664–1001;
(508) 362–5230;
www.hyannischamber.com

Falmouth Chamber of Commerce,
20 Academy Lane;
(508) 548–8500 or (800) 526–8532;
www.falmouthchamber.com

Martha's Vineyard Chamber of Commerce,
Beach Road,
P.O. Box 1698,
Vineyard Haven 02568;
(508) 693–0085;
www.mvy.com

Nantucket Island Chamber of Commerce,
48 Main Street,
Nantucket 02554;
(508) 228–1700;
www.nantucketchamber.org

Orleans Chamber of Commerce;
(800) 240–2484 or (508) 865–1386;
www.capecod-orleans.com

Provincetown Chamber of Commerce,
307 Commercial Street;
(508) 487–3424,
fax (508) 487–8966;
www.ptownchamber.com
e-mail: info@ptownchamber.com

CRUISES, WHALE WATCHING, AND FISHING

Hyannis Whale Watcher Cruises,
Barnstable Harbor;
(508) 362–6088 or (888) WHALE-
WATCH (942–5392);
www.whales.net

Cape Cod Canal Cruises,
Town Pier,
Onset Center;
(508) 295–3883;
www.hy-linecruises.com/canal

Hyannisport Harbor Cruises,
Ocean Street Dock,
Hyannis;
(508) 778–2600;
www.hy-linecruises.com/hhc

Zapotec,
Kennebec Avenue,
Oak Bluffs,
Martha's Vineyard;
(508) 693–6800.
Southwestern and Mexican
dishes blend with innovative
combos in the Southwest
style. Most entrees are
$15.00 to $18.00; children's
menu at $8.00.

Four Seas Ice Cream,
360 South Main Street,
Centerville;
(508) 775–1394.
Extraordinary homemade
ice cream so smooth that
a friend describes it as
cold silk.

Old Jailhouse Tavern,
28 West Road,
Orleans;
(508) 255–5245.
A casual family dining room
in a contemporary setting,
with good food and
excellent service.

The Pancake Man,
952 Main Street,
South Yarmouth;
(508) 398–9532.
A good place for an
inexpensive breakfast. In
addition to the eggs, ham,
sausage, and bacon, you
have a wide variety of
pancakes, waffles, and
French toast to choose
among. Kids' menu.
Sandwiches served after
11:30 A.M.

Pizzas by Evan,
1220 Iyanough Road
(Route 132),
Hyannis;
(508) 790–3554.
Really good sausage pizza
and Cummaquid roll-up
made of turkey, cranberry
sauce, stuffing, mayonnaise,
lettuce, and tomato.

**Arnold's Lobster
& Clam Bar,**
3580 US 6,
Eastham;
(508) 255–2575.
Excellent seafood place with
raw bar and inexpensive
lunch specials.

Jimmy Seas Pan Pasta,
32 Kennebec Avenue,
Oak Bluffs;
(508) 696–8550.
It may not be much to look
at, but it's the place for pasta
with a wide variety of
toppings and extras.

Southeastern Massachusetts

Southeastern Massachusetts, or Bristol County, holds some of the prettiest and most unspoiled territory in the state. Tucked into a corner between Rhode Island and Plymouth, it encompasses miles and miles of farmland, where quiet cornfields line both sides of the road. Small rural towns like Dighton, Rehoboth, and Berkley appear as little surprises here and there.

The coastal villages east of New Bedford are picturesque gems. Founded mostly by shipbuilders, they're proud of their history and have preserved it well. These villages became favored summer resorts for residents of New York and Boston, among them Oliver Wendell Holmes, who summered in Mattapoisett. In Marion, you can still see the great Victorian summer homes erected along a long waterfront avenue, with broad acres of lawns.

The most high-profile cities are Fall River and New Bedford. Both have prestigious pasts. Fall River led the world in textile production in the nineteenth century, and many of its old mill buildings now serve as offices and shops. New Bedford was one of the greatest whaling ports in the world and today has a lingering flavor of whaling's heyday in its historic district's cobblestoned streets and gas-style lamps.

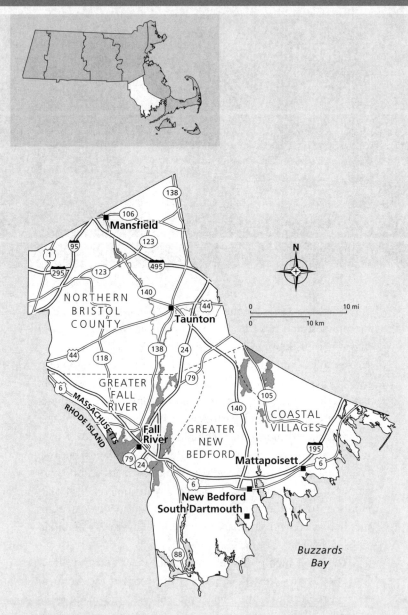

N

0   10 mi

0   10 km

138

106

Mansfield

123

1

95

295

123

495

NORTHERN
BRISTOL
COUNTY

140

44

Taunton

44   118

138   24

GREATER
FALL
RIVER

79

105

6

140   COASTAL
VILLAGES

MASSACHUSETTS

RHODE ISLAND

GREATER
NEW
BEDFORD

195

**Fall
River**

Mattapoisett   6

79   24

6

New Bedford
South Dartmouth

88

*Buzzards
Bay*

Northern Bristol County

As you walk or drive about ***North Easton,*** northeast of Mansfield, it's a little startling to see Gothic behemoths of stone, complete with gargoyles, looming from every corner. Altogether, there are five ***buildings designed by Henry Hobson Richardson,*** as well as nine landscapings by Frederick Law Olmsted, three Augustus Saint-Gaudens sculptures, two John La Farge stained-glass windows, and three National Historic districts—such wealth that architects come from Chicago and Australia just to see it.

How did it happen? It all goes back to Oliver Ames, who founded the world's largest shovel company here in the early 1800s. By 1850, more than 60 percent of all the world's shovels were Ames shovels. During the Civil War, President Lincoln personally asked Oliver Ames to supply the Union army with his shovels. Ames's descendants subsequently shoveled the profits into elaborate mansions and civic gifts, commissioning Richardson to design them. One such building is the ***Old Colony Railroad Station,*** on Mechanic Street, which serves as a town history museum. Here you can get a walking/driving–tour map. The towering ***Oakes Ames Memorial Hall*** and the ***Oliver Ames Free Library*** on Center Street also are HHR creations. Besides these larger structures, Richardson designed the stone ***Gate Lodge*** and shingled ***Gardener's Cottage.*** The museum is open from 1:00 to 5:00 P.M. the second Sunday of every month. For information write the Easton Historical Society, P.O. Box 3, North Easton 02356, or call the curator at (508) 238-3143.

Across the banks of the Taunton River to the east is a large rock with ancient inscriptions on it—a curiosity whose origins have mystified scientists for three centuries. It's displayed under glass in a small, white pavilion in ***Dighton Rock State Park*** in ***Berkley.*** The faded characters are definitely there, kind of pointy and hieroglyphic-looking. But who wrote them? More than twenty theories have been advanced. The front-runners, explained in large panels, are the marks originated from American Indians, Phoenicians, Vikings, or Portuguese explorers. The park overlooks the Taunton River, with picnic

AUTHORS' FAVORITES IN SOUTHEASTERN MASSACHUSETTS

Battleship Cove, Fall River	New Bedford Whaling Museum
Rotch-Jones-Duff House	

tables in the shade. It is open from 8:00 A.M. to 6:00 P.M. daily in summer, but closes earlier in spring and fall; call (508) 822–7537. To get there, take exit 10 from Route 24 and follow the signs.

Hidden away in Attleboro is a wonderful family destination called **Capron Park Zoo.** The zoo here is small, but it has some exotic animals from Asia, Africa, Australia, and New Zealand. A small rain-forest exhibit is complete with waterfall, artificial fog, and recorded jungle sounds. There's a playground for the kids, green lawns with picnic tables, and a lovely rose garden. The park is on Route 123 off Interstate 95 at exit 3. It's open from 10:00 A.M. to 5:00 P.M. daily from April to October, and 10:00 A.M. to 4:00 P.M. daily the rest of the year. Admission is $3.50 for adults and $2.00 for seniors and children ages three through twelve; (508) 222–3047; www.capronparkzoo.com.

The historic little town of **Rehoboth** sits all alone on the map in an area of Massachusetts that is surprisingly undeveloped, considering its location so close to Providence. A thriving little town at the time of the Revolution, Rehoboth centered around its mills, whose big water-powered wheels were used to grind grain and saw wood.

Only the stone foundations remain of the mills, but next to Rehoboth's white clapboard church today is the **Carpenter Museum,** at 4 Locust Avenue, off County Street, which is off U.S. Route 44. Locust Avenue looks as though it were the church's driveway. Although the museum is open only March through November on Sunday afternoon between 2:00 and 4:00 P.M., it is worth a stop. Its collections focus on local history and include a kitchen with old cooking equipment, a dining room, a general-store exhibit, and a collection of wood-working tools. An herb garden is maintained by the Garden Club, and the collections are owned by the Rehoboth Historical Commission, which publishes an interesting little pamphlet on local historical sites. The booklet is available at the museum or at the **Goff Memorial Library,** down the road a piece, which also

ANNUAL EVENTS IN SOUTHEASTERN MASSACHUSETTS

EARLY MAY

Annual Maritime Heritage Festival,
New Bedford, includes classes on boat-building, knotwork, and even the carving of figureheads;
(508) 997–0046.

EARLY AUGUST

Fall River Celebrates America
with a food fair, fireworks, and a parade of ships;
(508) 676–8226;
www.fallrivercelebrates.com

has a genealogy and local history room upstairs. If you cannot visit on Sunday, you can arrange to see the museum by appointment by calling (508) 252–3031.

If you'd like to stay in this quiet village, consider the **Perryville Inn,** a B&B at 157 Perryville Road, Rehoboth; (508) 252–9239. It is in a classic clapboard house with a gabled window and covered front porch for sitting and pondering how time has treaded so gently past this little corner of the state.

Greater Fall River

Although it's one of the outstanding maritime attractions of New England's coast, we've never had to stand in line to see any of the ships in **Battleship Cove.** The showpiece is the battleship USS *Massachusetts*, sister ship to the USS *Arizona* and once home to 2,300 servicemen. You can tour the ship and get lost quite easily—it's longer than two football fields and as tall as a nine-story building—and stop for a cheeseburger, sandwich, or fish and chips in the Officer's Wardroom restaurant. The ship, scheduled for scrapping in 1962, was saved by its former crew members as the state's memorial to those who lost their lives in World War II. Also in the cove are a destroyer, a submarine (contrast the cramped quarters here with those on the huge battleship), a Japanese "special attack" boat, a "Huey" helicopter from the Vietnam War, and two PT boats. The complex is open daily from 9:00 A.M. to 5:30 P.M. in the summer, closing at 5:00 P.M. in spring and fall and 4:30 P.M. in winter. Admission is $14.00 for adults, $12.00 for seniors and veterans, $8.00 for children ages six through fourteen, and free for those under six and active military in uniform; (508) 678–1100 or (800) 533–3194; www.battleshipcove.org.

Fall River lost its leading position as a textile producer to lower-costing southern labor. The story of the city's great rise and fall in prosperity is told at the **Fall River Heritage State Park,** in an eight-acre waterfront setting designed to look like an old mill. From a farm village, the city grew rapidly to encompass more than a hundred mills, and production easily outstripped that of competitors Lawrence and Lowell. Poignant black-and-white photographs show the immigrant mill workers, many of whom were children. Here you will glimpse the moving history of the many ethnic groups who powered the mills. The park is at 200 Davol Street West, next to Battleship Cove. It is open from 10:00 A.M. to 4:00 P.M. daily. If you are traveling a distance to visit, it's wise to call ahead, because they are short staffed and the attendant may be elsewhere on the grounds (look around if the door is locked); call (508) 675–5759.

Among the many immigrant groups of mill workers were large waves of Portuguese and Polish, who left a lasting imprint on the city. The Portuguese have a home-front stronghold on **Columbia Street,** complete with eight-sided cobblestones and black iron lampposts. Old women in black with lace mantillas walk along with bowed heads; laundry hangs between the triple-decker houses, and the street is redolent with Portuguese bakeries, fish markets, coffee shops, and restaurants. Try the authentic *Sagres Restaurant* (181 Columbia Street; 508–675–7018), an impossibly good deal, and with live fado music Friday and Saturday, to boot! The heart of the street is *Chaves Market* (508–672–7821), where almost every customer speaks in the lilting tones of Portuguese. You can buy almost anything Portuguese here: octopus, conch shells, chourico, sugar-coated almonds, *vinho verde,* Portuguese cookies and sweet bread, paella pans, and porcelain samovars and centerpieces.

One block away from the Heritage Park is the *Marine Museum at Fall River.* In its heyday, Fall River was a major port of call for steamship liners on the Fall River Line, which operated from 1847 to 1937. Floating palaces with every luxury on board carried vacationers from New York and Boston. On view in this museum are many mementos of this age, including steamship china and chairs and a chandelier. A 28-foot model of the *Titanic* here was used in the 1952 movie about the disaster. There are also *Titanic* artifacts and memorabilia. The museum is at 70 Water Street. Summer hours are 9:00 A.M. to 5:00 P.M. Monday through Friday, noon to 5:00 P.M. Saturday, and noon to 4:00 P.M. on Sunday and holidays. In winter, hours are 9:00 A.M. to 4:00 P.M. Wednesday through Friday and noon to 4:00 P.M. weekends. Tickets cost $4.00 for adults, $3.50 for seniors, and $3.00 for children ages five to twelve. Call (508) 674–3533 or visit www.marinemuseum.org.

Back in the day when all those gray stone factory buildings actually housed booming, rattling industry, an English mill worker by the name of Hartley thought there might be a better life and profit to be made in selling cheap, portable, ready-to-eat meals to his laboring companions. And the individual meat pie of his homeland fit the bill perfectly. This being America, the stock at *Hartley's Original Pork Pies* expanded to suit the tastes of others come to Fall River. Today Hartley's still sells regular meat pie, plus French-Canadian pork, Portuguese chorizo, a Friday-friendly salmon, and down-home chicken pie fillings. At $1.50, they suit modern fast-food eating quite well, and make an especially elegant picnic food for the beach when supplemented with produce from a roadside farmstand (several are found off the roads heading south to the beaches). Open daily mid-morning until 4:15 P.M., Hartley's is at 1729 South Main Street; (508) 676–8605.

To enjoy a scenic drive, take U.S. Route 6 off Route 88, follow it south to Kirby Road, and begin a driving tour that makes a natural loop around the east branch of the Westport River, taking you to *Dartmouth.* Along the way, you'll see farms with silver silos, stone walls, and pastureland sloping to the sea. Turn right on Kirby Road, then turn left onto Main Road, which brings you through the center of **Westport,** past its town hall and Quaker Meeting House. Main Road becomes Westport Point Road as it approaches Westport Point Village, an enclave as quaint as its seafaring origins. On a little warren of tiny streets rise eighteenth- and nineteenth-century homes of sea captains and tradesmen, all dated and identified with signs (e.g. WILLIAM AND SAMUEL BRIGHTMAN, MARINERS, CA. 1788/1830; ABNER SISSON, HOUSEWRIGHT, CA. 1841).

Go back up to Drift Road on the right and take it over to Route 88 south. Route 88 ends just before **Horseneck Beach,** a spectacular stretch fronting the ocean on a narrow peninsula at the mouth of the Westport River. (For more information on this dune-backed beach, call Horseneck Beach State Reservation at 508–636–8816.) Leave the peninsula via East Beach Road, which brings you east of the river to Horseneck Road. Up on the left, with a panoramic view of sweeping pastureland that stretches unbroken down to the sea, is **The Bayside,** at 1253 Horseneck Road (508–636–5882), a good country restaurant. This one bills itself as "the best dinky little restaurant in the Commonwealth." And dinky it is—you can traverse its narrow dining room in two steps. Wide windows let you admire the view. Everything is "made from scratch," from sandwiches and burgers with hand-cut french fries to pan-fried smelts and fresh-baked pies.

Bordering the east branch of the Westport River, **Westport Rivers Vineyard and Winery** is New England's largest vinifera (wine grape) vineyard. On 110 acres of farmland, this small, family-run business grows grapes similar to those in France's Burgundy region. Among the wines produced are chardonnay, pinot blanc, Riesling, and sparkling wines. If you eat in upscale Boston restaurants, you'll probably have noticed Westport on their wine lists, and its fame is spreading fast. The winery and tasting rooms are housed in a renovated dairy barn and a Victorian farmhouse. The tasting room and art gallery are open from 11:00 A.M. to 5:00 P.M. daily. Tours are given at 1:00 and 3:00 P.M. on weekends. For information call (508) 636–3423 or visit www.westportrivers.com. To get there, follow Horseneck Road north and turn left onto Hix Bridge Road; the winery is at number 417.

Greater New Bedford

From Horseneck Road, turn right onto Slade Corner Road, which brings you into the historic little village of **Russells Mills,** a neighborhood of **South Dartmouth.** In the center of the village, on Russells Mills Road, you'll find **Davoll's General Store** (508–636–4530), a local provisioner that dates to 1793.

If you backtrack from Russells Mills Road and go left onto Rock O' Dundee Road, it will bring you to Potomska Road and the **Lloyd Center for**

Environmental Studies. This is really a hidden jewel. Set on the picturesque Slocums River estuary, its coastal-zone habitat makes it an amateur naturalist's and birder's paradise. You can wander the salt marshes, swamps, and forests on a handful of nature trails. On the research building's third floor, an observation deck gives lordly views of the estuarine lowlands, Buzzards Bay, and the Elizabeth Islands. Inside are casual, low-key exhibits on native wildlife and water pollution, along with the skeleton of a pilot whale. Beautiful photographs show the river and species of birds and butterflies. Downstairs is a roomful of aquariums and a tide-pool tank. A wide variety of educational and natural-history-oriented programs are offered. The center is at 430 Potomska Road; call (508) 990–0505 or visit www.thelloydcenter.org. Hours are May through October, Monday through Friday 8:00 A.M. to 4:00 P.M., Saturday and Sunday 11:00 A.M. to 4:00 P.M.; the rest of the year it's closed on Sunday and Monday holidays (the grounds are open daily).

Continuing out on the neck of land that is Dartmouth, follow Little River Road to Smith Neck Road and turn left for three more interesting stops. On your right, at the sign for Round Hill Condominiums, look down toward the ocean. You'll see a rambling stone mansion that was built by the son of Hetty Green, the fabled "Witch of Wall Street." Heiress to a New Bedford whaling-and-shipping family fortune, she shrewdly invested her way to one of the largest personal fortunes in the country by the turn of the twentieth century. Hetty was a miserly sort who dressed in tattered black rags. She was so miserly, in fact, that when her son broke his leg, she refused to consult a doctor, and he became crippled for life. Perhaps partly for revenge, the son and his sister spent their mother's money as fast as they could. Building the mansion, which rivals those of Newport, certainly helped. Now, it's condominiums. You can also see it from Round Hill Beach in the off-season (October to May), when you can drive down the condominium access road to the beach.

To learn more about this unusual woman, visit ***Hetty Green, A Miserly Woman's Museum,*** at 52 Union Street, New Bedford; (508) 996–0326; www .hettygreen.com.

Just up the road a piece on the left, you'll come to a giant white wooden milk bottle with green-and-white awnings. It's ***Salvador's Ice Cream,*** a vintage lunch stand built in 1936. After sixty-nine years in the Salvadore family, "the can" has been bought and lovingly restored by the Gauvin family, who won an award for their work; they even restored the original cow on top, last seen before the 1938 hurricane. Now it dispenses cones, dishes, sundaes, burgers, and stuffed quohogs ("stuffies") at the edge of a pasture with grazing sheep. The stand is at 460 Smith Neck Road; call (508) 994–4193. It's open 11:30 A.M. to 9:00 P.M. daily for the summer season.

Also near South Dartmouth, the village of **Padanaram** is so sprightly and chic that you'll ask what it's doing in an old Yankee boatbuilding town. Padanaram is home to the world-famous wooden yacht company Concordia, and yachtspeople from all over the globe put in to port here. Along two tiny blocks of Elm Street cluster some fine shops and restaurants that make for a nice stroll. Among the wares might be everything from imported foods to Icelandic sweaters, dollhouses, antiques, handcrafted furniture, china, and gifts.

Despite the claims of other New England ports to whaling fame, **New Bedford** stands as the city of whaling heritage par excellence. Now that New Bedford has a more industrialized downtown, it's hard to picture just how vital whaling once was. But by the 1840s, New Bedford was one of America's largest whaling ports and employed 10,000 seamen. Many Portuguese came to whale and fish, and today their descendants make up half the city—the largest Portuguese population in Massachusetts. Herman Melville, who has made sure we will never forget the days of whaling, described New Bedford in *Moby-Dick* as a place of "brave houses and flowery gardens." New Bedford today has the largest fishing fleet on the East Coast. The fleet ties up on the waterfront, just below the original cobblestoned section of the city, now a historic district. While the northern part of the city is heavily Portuguese, the southern section is home to a large Latin American population.

New Bedford's busy working waterfront is the scene of much activity and more kinds of ships than you're likely to see in any one place anywhere else. You can take a walking tour of the waterfront called **Dock Walk,** starting from the **New Bedford Waterfront Visitor Center,** at Pier 3 just off MacArthur Drive (508–979–1745 or 800–508–5353; www.rixsan.com/nbvisit), where you can pick up a brochure or join a guided tour. The National Park Service operates another center downtown in an old bank (33 William Street; 508–996–4095), with an abundance of information and walking trail maps. Besides Coast Guard cutters, scallopers, and draggers, ships on the tour include the *Lightship New Bedford,* a 65-year-old, red-and-white Coast Guard lightship with two masts and double lights, one of only seventeen remaining lightships. Lightships helped ships find land where lighthouses could not be built. Two more historic ships are the schooner *Ernestina,* a 101-year-old Gloucester fishing vessel, and the 1925 coastal steamer *Nobska,* the last of its kind. Plans are under way to refurbish the *Nobska* for coastal cruises.

There are two small vest-pocket parks on the piers, one honoring a Norwegian immigrant, Rasmus Tonnessen, who came to New Bedford in 1929 and founded New Bedford Ship Supply, a major supplier to fishermen that still operates today. In **Tonnessen Park** stands an unusual bronze statue of a sea god holding a cod and a sturgeon. Winding all the way around the 10-foot base are creatures of the seven seas: a giant clam, a swordfish, a dolphin, an eel, a starfish, a sea turtle, a rock crab, and others. The statue honors fishermen lost at sea. The tour also points out an ice company, fish-processing plants where fishing boats are unloaded by "lumpers," and the **Bourne Counting House,** a granite building that dates to 1848 and was owned by wealthy whaling investor Jonathan Bourne. Dock Walk guided tours leave the waterfront visitor center daily at 10:00 A.M. and 2:30 P.M. in July and August.

At the New Bedford State Pier, you'll see the elegant lines of the schooner *Ernestina,* built in 1894 and used in history-making Arctic explorations. You can tour the boat. For more information call (508) 992–4900 or visit www .ernestina.org.

Just across the street from the waterfront in New Bedford, surrounding Union Street, begins the cobblestoned historic district. Opposite each other stand the two most important whaling attractions. Established in 1907, the **New Bedford Whaling Museum,** at 18 Johnnycake Hill, is the largest museum in the United States devoted to whaling. On display in its many galleries are items depicting every aspect of the industry—from tools and harpoons, logbooks and journals, figureheads and quarter-boards to the giant skeleton of a hump-back whale and a half-scale model of the whaleship *Lagoda* that you can climb aboard. The scrimshaw pieces include a sled made with ivory runners, a birdcage, and many kitchen tools with ivory handles. An exhibit of Herman Melville memorabilia illustrates the whaling experiences that formed the basis of his famous novels; it includes a 1930 edition of *Moby-Dick* illustrated by Rockwell Kent and an original 1851 edition of the novel. Marine paintings show nineteenth-century harbor scenes, famous whaling ships, dramatic chases, and whales biting dories in half. The museum is open year-round from 9:00 A.M. to 5:00 P.M. daily and until 9:00 P.M. on summer Thursdays. Admission is $10.00 for adults, $9.00 for seniors and students, $6.00 for children ages six to fourteen. You can buy a combined ticket for the Whaling Museum and the New Bedford Art Museum. Call (508) 997–0046 or visit www.whalingmuseum.org.

Melville visited the **Seamen's Bethel,** at 15 Johnnycake Hill, and described it in *Moby-Dick*. His pew is labeled. A somber place, the bethel is most famous for its prow-shaped pulpit. Marble cenotaphs memorializing men lost at sea line the walls and galleries. The bethel is still used today, and you may even chance on a Portuguese wedding. It is open May through October from 10:00 A.M. to 5:00 P.M. daily, with reduced hours the rest of the year.

From its original waterfront blocks, New Bedford spread south and west in the nineteenth century, with shipowners and whaling investors building their houses south of Union Street, which runs straight up from the waterfront. Sadly, few of these houses remain in an unaltered state. But there could not be a more shining reminder of the past than the **Rotch-Jones-Duff House & Garden Museum,** at 396 County Street, a few blocks west of the historic district. The architect Richard Upjohn designed this house in 1834 for William Rotch Jr., a prominent whaling merchant. Later, another whaling merchant owned it. The house stands out as one of the nation's finest examples of the Greek Revival style. The interior reflects the owners' histories via period antiques from the mid-nineteenth century into the twentieth. You wander from Victorian parlors with Italian-marble fireplaces and gold-leaf mirrors to Rotch's opulent Greek Revival sitting room. Other house appointments include silk linens,

Seamen's Bethel, New Bedford

eighteenth-century furniture, and a collection of Faberge-style eggs made by Mrs. Duff. The grounds showcase a wildflower walk, a dogwood allée, and a boxwood parterre garden with pink, white, and red roses. In summer, concerts of acoustic music are held on the grounds. From Memorial Day through September, the house is open for tours from 10:00 A.M. to 4:00 P.M. Monday through Saturday and from noon to 4:00 P.M. Sunday, with fewer open days the rest of the year. Admission is $4.00 for adults, $3.00 for students and seniors, and free for children under twelve; call (508) 997–1401 or visit www.rjdmuseum.org.

Acushnet Avenue runs through the heart of the Portuguese North End. Lining the street are dozens of Portuguese shops, restaurants, and bakeries. To sample some Portuguese pastries, stop in at **Lydia's Bakery,** at 1656 Acushnet Avenue (508–992–1711), where you may choose from more than fifty varieties. Just off Acushnet Avenue, **Antonio's,** at 267 Coggeshall Street (508–990–3636), serves up such traditional Portuguese dishes as shrimp Mozambique, with huge, handmade Portuguese rolls to sop up the garlic sauce. Other dishes include *cacoila,* meat stews, seafood casseroles, and grilled meats, all served with ample portions of rice and roast potatoes, priced from $5.00 to $22.00.

If you love to shop for good food and want nothing but the best, stop in at **Sid Wainer & Sons Specialty Produce & Specialty Foods** at 2301 Purchase Street (508–999–6408), which sells the freshest and best food from around the world. Sid Wainer & Sons buys winter truffles from France, cold-pressed olive oils from Italy and Spain, some dozen kinds of olives, and all kinds of cheeses, pâtés, chocolates, coffees, Asian foods—too many to list. Shelves of fresh raspberries, blueberries, edible nasturtiums and pansies, portobello mushrooms, baby arugula, corn, lettuces, potatoes, and peppers tempt the senses. Buying specialty foods from all over the globe and wholesaling worldwide to the finest restaurants and chefs, the store makes up custom orders for its regulars, such as a pound of rose petals or an order of apricot-honey jam. The wholesale outlet has a retail showroom where you can shop for these goodies from 9:00 A.M. to 5:00 P.M. Monday through Saturday.

In the south end of the city, tucked away in a residential area, the **Lisbon Sausage Company** makes its own smoked *linguica, chourico,* and other meats, which it wholesales around the country. You can buy the meat, too, at prices that compare quite favorably to the supermarket. As soon as you walk through the black wrought-iron gates, the pungent, spicy smells of sausage assault you. Behind the metal counter, through a glass wall, you can see white-coated workers hanging up yards and yards of freshly made sausage loops. The store, at 433 South Second Street, is open from 7:00 A.M. to 3:30 P.M. Monday through Friday and from 8:00 to 11:00 A.M. Saturday. Call (508) 993–7645. Mail orders are also taken by phone or online at www.amarals.com (don't miss their Web site's theme song!).

Across the harbor from New Bedford is **Fairhaven,** an often-overlooked place. Fairhaven flourished in the eighteenth century as a shipbuilding town, supplying whaling ships to the burgeoning trade from New Bedford. The original settlement area, called Poverty Point, consists of several blocks centered on West, Cherry, and Oxford Streets, situated off Main Street north of US 6. Many weathered old houses of the ship chandlers, merchants, and shipwrights of that time still stand. One is now the **Edgewater Bed & Breakfast,** originally built in the 1760s by a merchant who supplied the whaling and shipbuilding industries, and added onto in the 1880s. The Edgewater sits on a point of land overlooking the New Bedford Harbor scene. The water views from inside the house are splendidly set off by large, arched windows with inviting window seats. At night, the harbor lights make a pretty picture too. Rooms in the newer part of the house are larger and have nice antique touches, such as patterned wallpaper, a pencil four-poster, and a claw-foot bathtub. Two suites have working fireplaces. Rooms in the older section are smaller and more cramped, but still nice, each with private bath. Double rooms with breakfast are $80 to $110. Write the inn at 2 Oxford Street, Fairhaven 02719, or call (508) 997–5512.

A walking tour of **Poverty Point** takes you to some of the old whaling houses and turns up several interesting historical sites, such as the place where Joshua Slocum, the first man to circumnavigate the globe solo, set sail in 1895. (Edgewater innkeeper Kathy Reed has brochures describing the walking tour.)

Elsewhere in Fairhaven are architectural treasures given to the town by millionaire Henry Huttleston Rogers. One is the *Unitarian Memorial Church,* one of the finest examples of English Gothic architecture in America.

Coastal Villages

Mattapoisett was famous the world over for its whaling ships and built ships of all kinds for more than a century, with six shipyards lining the waterfront. Mattapoisett men made the ship *Acushnet,* on which Melville crewed in 1840. Mattapoisett's waterfront is quiet now. But it's an attractive one, and a few wood-and-shingled eighteenth-and nineteenth-century houses still stand along narrow little Water Street. All have neatly lettered black-and-white signs identifying the owner and date, including the 1798 carpenter's shop and the 1832 block shop. A small green park, Shipyard Park, looks out on the harbor.

Town history is on view at the *Mattapoisett Historical Society Museum and Carriage House,* 1 block up at 5 Church Street (508–758–2844). The museum is housed in an 1821 church with pews and pulpits, an interesting backdrop. The collection, mostly donated by town residents, varies strikingly. Sea captains brought back such exotic things as Pacific seashells, silk and feather fans from many countries, a Chinese lacquered writing desk, and two painted and gilded glasses used by Napoleon on Saint Helena. Military memorabilia span the Revolutionary War, the Civil War, and the War of 1812. Up on the balconies you'll find a collection of dolls and toys, period furniture, and a stand full of antique canes, many with ivory tops. An attached building holds antique vehicles and farm tools, among them carriages and buggies, the town's first water wagon, a corn sheller, a bean winnower, a cranberry separator, and a corn chopper. The museum is open from 1:00 to 4:00 P.M. Wednesday through Saturday, July 5 to August 31, and by prior arrangement Tuesday, Wednesday and Friday the rest of the year. Admission is $3.00 for adults and $1.00 for children ages six to sixteen.

On Route 105 in Marion, north of Mattapoisett, you'll find *The Wave,* a family restaurant in more ways than one: It's a family business with a family-oriented menu and atmosphere. "We don't say we're a gourmet restaurant," the owners are quick to point out, in a refreshing bit of honesty, but they do serve good, reliable seafood and Italian dinners at prices that won't break the bank. Go for the chowder first; it's not thickened to cream-sauce consistency, and it's full of clams. Open 7:00 A.M. to 11:00 P.M. daily; (508) 748–2986. They don't accept credit cards.

Continuing east along the coast brings you to *Wareham.* The first stop here, at 8 Elm Street, is the *Tremont Nail Company* (508–291–7871), the nation's oldest nail factory, listed on the National Register of Historic Places. Using hundred-year-old nail machines, the company still makes old-fashioned nails from cut sheets of high-carbon steel, rolled and tempered. Cut nails can penetrate any wood without splitting it and have better holding power than conventional nails. The company was founded in 1819, and the current mill dates back to 1848. Although there are no tours, you can stand on a wooden platform and look in the windows any weekday from 7:30 A.M. to 5:00 P.M. while you listen to the rumbling and chugging of the nail-cutting machines. The mill is still warmed by a few potbellied stoves. The full line of nails is sold across the street in the *Old Company Store,* formerly the cooper shop. Nails, running from a ¾-inch clout nail to an 8-inch boat spike, include rosehead, clinch, fine finish, and wrought-head. The store also sells colonial-style hardware, paints, gifts, jellies, crackers, and penny candy. A film explains the company history and a little bit about nailmaking. Outside the factory is a herring run. Call (508) 295–0038 for information.

The village of Onset within the town of Wareham runs along the waterfront, passing sandy beaches and quiet vistas. If you'd like to stay awhile here, you can book a room in a turn-of-the-century Victorian estate set right on the beach, the *Point Independence Inn.* The mansion has seven antiques-filled guest rooms, all with private bath, and unparalleled ocean views. Wicker pieces and Adirondack chairs invite you to lounge on the sunporch or private beach, or in a gazebo on the lawn. Breakfast offers juices, fruit salad, all kinds of muffins, and bagels. Room rates begin at $200 for peak-season. For reservations contact the inn at 9 Eagle Way; (508) 273–0466 or (866) 827–4466.

Before leaving Wareham, take a tour of its lovely Victorian waterfront at Onset Bay, along West and South Boulevards, which lead onto Onset Avenue and take you to the town pier. Enormous Victorian summer cottages festooned with turrets and gables appear along this stretch, the sidewalk accented by black iron lampposts and cobblestoned sidewalks; a small park with a gazebo reaches up the hill.

More Places to Stay in Southeastern Massachusetts

Hampton Inn,
53 Old Bedford Road,
Westport;
(508) 675–8500;
www.hamptoninn.com
Well-kept rooms with refrigerators, irons, twenty-four-hour coffee; doubles from $70.

Independent lodgings are few in this area, but several budget chains, including Days Inn and Comfort Inn, have good properties nearby.

More Places to Eat in Southeastern Massachusetts

Cup of the Bay Cafe,
3 West Central Avenue,
Onset;
(508) 295–3527.
Despite a name that conjures up ambiguous images of salty coffee, this cafe serves up a well-brewed cup, plus pastries, soups, and vegetarian sandwiches 6:00 A.M. to 3:00 P.M. daily.

Davy's Locker,
1480 East Rodney
French Boulevard,
New Bedford;
(508) 992–7359.
Popular with locals for its ample plates of fresh seafood, Davy's is open every day from 11:30 A.M. to 9:00 P.M. (10:00 P.M. on Friday and Saturday).

Old Grist Mill Tavern,
390 Fall River Avenue,
Seekonk;
(508) 336–8460.
The setting is lovely, over a water-powered mill surrounded by green lawns and gardens; the food is traditional New England fare.

Turk's Seafood,
82 Marion Road (US 6),
Mattapoisett;
(508) 758–3117.
Giant portions of fried clams, fish-and-chips, or clam cakes with chowder at low-low prices. Fine food, not frills, at $5.00 to $9.00.

TO LEARN MORE ABOUT SOUTHEASTERN MASSACHUSETTS

Bristol County Development Council,
70 North Second Street,
P.O. Box BR–976,
New Bedford 02741;
(508) 997–1250;
www.bristol-county.org

Fairhaven Office of Tourism and Visitors Center,
43 Center Street,
Fairhaven 02719;
(508) 979–4085.
They run walking tours in the summer.

New Bedford Waterfront Visitor Center,
Pier 3,
New Bedford 02740;
(508) 979–1745 or (800) 508–5353;
www.ci.new-bedford.ma.us/Destination
NewBedford.htm

Worcester County

Once you travel west of Interstate 495, you've crossed a psychological barrier that is acutely felt by those who live here. Residents feel scorned, spurned, and ignored by Bostonians. Bostonians, in turn, think they've entered a primitive, provincial place of no interest or importance.

Worcester, New England's second-largest city, has historically been seen at best as a poor cousin to Boston. But Worcester is a pleasant surprise, with a handful of excellent museums and a rich past. Worcester is where the dining car was invented, as well as the valentine. The Worcester Centrum is now the rock music palace of New England.

Worcester County stretches all the way from New Hampshire to Connecticut and Rhode Island. Within its borders are not only the big-city environs of Worcester but also territory ranging from old industrial towns to apple orchards and wineries, together with a clutch of rural small towns featuring some of the loveliest town commons in New England.

Although the towns of Royalston and Athol lie in the northwest corner of Worcester County, travelers in this area are liklier to group it with a visit to the Pioneer Valley. So we have described its attractions at the beginning of the next chapter. We apologize to Worcester County for disregarding its boundaries

and abducting some of its prettiest landscapes. Perhaps we're subconsciously hoping to lay claim to the two stunning waterfalls found there, one of which is only a few minutes from our own farm, just over the boundary line.

Old Sturbridge Village Area

The world has beaten a path to **Sturbridge,** specifically the entrance gates of **Old Sturbridge Village,** and rightly so. It is New England's premier period restoration, creating a mid-nineteenth-century village from historic homes, shops, mills, and public buildings—even a covered bridge—collected from throughout New England. This village is inhabited by costumed interpreters who go about the everyday lives of the people who would have lived here, stitching quilts and bonnets, hammering iron into hooks and hinges, making bread and cheese, cooking over an open hearth, planting and harvesting crops, and making buckets. Despite the number of visitors each year, the village—especially the back areas—never seems crowded. Even the green has a leisurely feel to it, and if you follow the paths beyond it to the **Freeman Farm** and the newly added **Bixby House,** home of the village blacksmith, you will find even fewer people in this quiet corner.

The "modern" enclave of mills here comes as a surprise to many people, who expect to see the farm and home industries of quilting, sewing, bread-making, and cooperage, and even early skilled trades such as blacksmithing and tinsmithing, but don't realize how important the miller was in a community from the time of New England's earliest settlement. This industry had already begun to make life easier for the farmer and his wife by the early 1800s, harnessing water power to grind grain, card wool, and mechanize the laborious job of shaping timbers and sawing boards. Go down behind the carding mill and into its lower floor to see how the water powers the wheels. Cross the little bridge over the millrace to see how the gristmill operates on the weight of water, not its velocity.

AUTHORS' FAVORITES IN WORCESTER COUNTY

Old Sturbridge Village

Higgins Armory Museum

Worcester Historical Museum

The **Tavern at Old Sturbridge Village** offers four dining options, from the rustic Taproom to three dining rooms decorated in styles of the early 1800s. The Federal Parlor has a working hearth used for cooking demonstrations on Wednesday evening. A bake shop, open daily from 8:00 A.M. to 5:30 P.M., is also in this newly built center at the village entrance. Access to all these eateries does not require entrance to the museum area. Reservations are advised for any of the special tavern evening programs, which include music and "visits" with historical characters (508–347–0395). The **Bullard Tavern,** on the green inside the museum, offers an unromantic buffet of traditional New England dishes, such as potpies, baked beans, Indian pudding, and corn bread, as well as a year-round cafeteria.

Old Sturbridge Village has a vast museum shop where, amid the predictable scented candles and other souvenir items, you can find kits for period crafts and a fine selection of books on early skills, New England, and New Englanders. Admission to the village is $20.00 for adults, $18.00 for seniors, and $6.00 for children ages three through seventeen. Plan to spend the day in order to see everything. More than half the historic buildings are wheelchair-accessible. Or better yet, spend two days and take advantage of free admission for the second day, which must be within ten days. The village is open Tuesday through Sunday from 9:30 A.M. to 5:00 P.M. April through October, 10:00 A.M. to 4:00 P.M. in spring and fall, and shorter hours in the winter. In midwinter the village is open only on weekends; (508) 347–3362.

Hyland Orchard and Brewery is a happy story of a family that reclaimed its farm—in more ways than one. The land their grandfather farmed more than thirty years ago had been sold, and its orchards fallen into disrepair, when two brothers joined with their brother-in-law and best friend to buy it back. "You couldn't even walk through the orchard, it was so overgrown," they recall, but you wouldn't know it today. They saved 400 of the old trees and plant more each year. Along with the orchards, where they grow apples, peaches, pears, and berries, Hyland Farm has a microbrewery, which you can tour—and where you can taste the product. In fact, you can help bottle it if you're over twenty-one. Exotic animals, including emus, miniature horses, and highland cattle, live here, too, and there's a nature trail to a bird sanctuary. The farm is open noon to 7:00 P.M. Tuesday through Sunday, with more limited winter hours, and four times a year there are family-oriented festivals with hayrides, a barbecue, and local bands. It's on Arnold Road, 2 miles off U.S Route 20, Sturbridge; (508) 347–7500, (877) HYLANDS (877–495–2637); www.hylandbrew.com.

On Saturday evenings in the summer, the town of Sturbridge presents free **Concerts on the Common,** on Route 131. The performers are professional musicians in all traditions—we recently heard the Latin trio Bambule, from

ANNUAL EVENTS IN WORCESTER COUNTY

**LATE JUNE AND
MID-SEPTEMBER**

Drover's Roast,
Salem Cross Inn, West Brookfield,
re-creates the 1700s feast cooked over
an outdoor fire, by reservation only;
(508) 867–8337.

LATE JUNE

**Western Massachusetts Highland
Games and Celtic Festival,**
Greenfield, with traditional contests,
music, dance, and Scottish goods
for sale;
(413) 584–9182.
www.wmhg.org

JULY 4

Independence Day Celebration,
Old Sturbridge Village, Sturbridge, with a
family picnic, parade, and reading of the
Declaration of Independence;
(508) 347–3362.

LATE SEPTEMBER

Agricultural Fair,
Old Sturbridge Village,
Sturbridge, where old-fashioned farm
skills are demonstrated;
(508) 347–3362.

Boston, but other shows might be a sixteen-piece "big band" or a German or
New Orleans ragtime band. Concerts begin at 6:30 P.M., lasting for two hours,
and you can bring a folding chair or sit on the grass. Pick up a schedule at the
visitor center or call (508) 347–2506.

On Thursday, Friday, and Saturday evenings and Sunday afternoons in the
summer, you can attend productions at the **Stageloft Repertory Company,**
450A Main Street (US 20). The schedule may include musicals, comedies, or a
thriller; call for a schedule, ticket prices, and reservations, (508) 347–9005, or
visit www.stageloft.com.

To stay in character with the ambience of Old Sturbridge Village, you can
stay or dine at **The Publick House,** facing the green on Route 131. This is a gracious old New England inn at its best, with well-decorated rooms in various sizes
and an outstanding restaurant divided among several rooms. One has a walk-in
fireplace where guests can watch their dinner being cooked in the winter. Traditional recipes are updated to contemporary styles and include newly available
ingredients. Complete dinners are $25 to $35, and the inn serves continuously
from 7:30 A.M. to 9:00 P.M.; (508) 347–3313 or (800) PUBLICK (800–782–5425).

After all the early American-ness of Sturbridge, you may long for something
modern, and the New American menu of **Cedar Street Restaurant** provides

it. Candlelight and fresh flowers set the mood, but casual clothes are welcome. The menu gives more than an obligatory nod to vegetarian sensibilities, with several choices each day. These may include a plate of grilled and roasted vegetables with corn risotto or a stir-fry of vegetables with peanut sauce over soba noodles, served with tofu spring rolls. Those who long for seafood may find seared yellowfin tuna coated in sesame and coriander seeds with sautéed rice cakes. Rack of lamb is roasted in North African spices with apricot-lentil couscous. The restaurant is just off Main Street at 12 Cedar Street, Sturbridge; (508) 347–5800. Serves dinner Monday through Saturday evenings.

Some believe in miracles. Their cast-off crutches and canes flank the white statue of Saint Anne at the **Saint Anne Shrine** in Sturbridge, where red and green votive candles glow in the dimness. The faithful believe a miracle took place here in 1887 when, with the help of Saint Anne, a woman parishioner was healed of dropsy. Ever since, pilgrims have flocked to the shrine in such numbers that an outdoor chapel was built for Sunday Mass.

Even if you don't believe in miracles, a visit here is well worth your while to see the museum of some sixty rare eighteenth- and nineteenth-century Russian icons. The icons feature elaborate artistry in lacquerware, gold and silver filigree, or mother-of-pearl. The most impressive of these exquisite and valuable pieces is a 5-foot-tall triptych in gold and silver of Christ, the Virgin, and Saint Nicholas.

Saint Anne Shrine is at 16 Church Street in the Fiskdale section of Sturbridge; call (508) 347–7461. The museum is open from 10:00 A.M. to 4:00 P.M. Monday through Friday, from 10:00 A.M. to 6:00 P.M. Saturday, and from 9:00 A.M. to 6:00 P.M. Sunday.

The **Oakwood Farm Christmas Barn** (508–885–3558), on Route 31 north in **Spencer,** is a shop in a 150-year-old barn that sells ornaments, wreaths, garlands, music boxes, and nutcrackers. It's open daily from May 1 to January 1.

Just west of Spencer in **West Brookfield** is a uniquely historical restaurant and inn, the **Salem Cross Inn.** The house was built in 1705 by a grandson of Peregrine White, the baby born on the *Mayflower* as it lay in Plymouth Harbor. The inn is richly paneled and extensively furnished with impressive collections of antiques: tin lanterns, portraits, redware, tall case clocks, and old prints, books, and maps. Come dinnertime, you can feast heartily on traditional dishes of beef, pork, chicken, seafood, fish, chowder, and Indian pudding, with meats cooked over the open hearth on a 1700s roasting jack in the fieldstone fireplace. Apple pie bakes in the 1699 brick beehive oven. In summer, an old-time "Drover's Roast" is held, offering a side of beef cooked over an open pit, as it used to be by drovers driving their cattle to market in Boston. On the 600-acre farm, hayrides and sleigh rides are part of the festivities. The Salem Cross Inn is on Route 9 in West Brookfield. Dinner reservations are strongly advised and are required for hearthside dinners on Friday nights. Call (508) 867–2345 or (508) 867–8337.

Also on Route 9 in West Brookfield is a Native American site, **Rock House Reservation.** Trails lead a short distance to a huge overhanging rock face, which was exposed by the last glacier that passed over Massachusetts more than 10,000 years ago. The cliff extends for some distance over a cavelike area at its base, and faces south, which protects the area under it from the coldest winds and also gives it sun in the winter. Its shelter was used as a winter hunting camp, and early digs here turned up implements and animal bones. You can climb to the top of the rock for a better view of how the glaciers moved the earth from around it like a giant bulldozer.

Other rock outcrops lie beside or above the trails, which you can follow on a forty-five-minute loop to the top of an overlook or on shorter loop segments. With luck, you might spot a scarlet tanager or eastern painted turtle in the reservation. Admission is free, and there is often a ranger at the entrance to explain the natural and human history of the site.

Blackstone River Valley

If you did not hear about *Lake Chargoggagoggmanchauggagoggchau-bunagungamaugg* in the fourth grade, now's the time. This is said to be the longest geographic name in the United States. It's an Indian word, translated as "You fish on your side, I fish on my side, nobody fishes in the middle." For short you can call it **Webster Lake,** since that's the town it's near, on Route 197 just west of Interstate 395.

Clara Barton, founder of the American Red Cross, was born in a simple white farmhouse in **North Oxford** in 1821, now the **Clara Barton Birthplace Museum.** Amazingly, Barton never trained as a nurse. One story notes that she tended her bedridden little brother after he fell off a barn roof. She did not found the Red Cross until she was sixty. Before that, she was a teacher, and she was at the front lines in the Civil War. Besides nursing the soldiers and getting blankets and honey for them, she wrote their letters home, using a small wooden field desk that folded up so that it could be carried on a wagon.

The field desk is on view, as is a handmade quilt given to Barton with each of its twenty-seven blocks signed by Civil War officers. Many other pieces of family memorabilia and furnishings fill the house. The 1790 kitchen has an unusual indoor well with an oak bucket hanging from a rope. The museum is located at 68 Clara Barton Road, North Oxford, near I–395 and U.S. Route 20; call (508) 987–5375. It's open from 11:00 A.M. to 5:00 P.M. Wednesday through

Sunday, in summer, and by appointment the rest of the year. Admission is $2.50 for children and $4.00 for others.

Purgatory Chasm State Reservation offers a challenging hike through a huge ravine strewn with giant boulders, and a dramatic chasm that reaches down almost 80 feet. The steep, half-mile loop trail down from the parking lot takes you right through the middle of the gorge and gives your legs and lungs a real workout. Here and there, the boulders form a warren of little chambers and caves that children love to crawl into. The park also has picnic tables and a playground. Purgatory Chasm is on Purgatory Road off Route 146, about 10 miles south of Worcester; call (508) 234-3733. The chasm is closed in winter because of the danger posed by slippery rocks.

Somewhere in New England, you may have seen one of the famous clocks made by Simon Willard. Simon's three brothers, Benjamin, Ephraim, and Aaron, were famous clockmakers too. The brothers Willard lived and worked in a cranberry-red colonial house in ***Grafton,*** now the ***Willard House and Clock Museum.*** To get there, you drive through acres of stone walls and sheep pastures. The house began as one room in 1718 and still has a lived-in quality. You feel like a guest upon entering the stooped and narrow doorway. Clocks tick amiably from every room, periodically chiming in many voices. There are some seventy clocks made by an associated group of clockmakers, the largest such collection from this period in existence.

The Willard brothers invented and made clocks until 1839. Simon invented the "banjo" clock, named for its shape, although he never called it a banjo clock. The brothers became known for their tall case clocks—what most people call grandfather clocks—many with elegant brass finials and brass-filled stop fluting. The most splendid creation, made for the First Church of Roxbury, is a large round wall clock that is topped with a massive gold eagle. There's also a musical case clock, made by Simon, that plays one of seven tunes on the hour. Another Willard hallmark was decorative scenes on reverse-painted glass, such as Mount Vernon or Mary and her little lamb.

The brothers' workshop is much as it was, benches strewn with tools and works, and is the only eighteenth-century American clock shop still in its original location. The museum is at 11 Willard Street, a short distance from Grafton Center; call (508) 839-3500. It's open from 10:00 A.M. to 4:00 P.M. Tuesday through Saturday and from 1:00 to 4:00 P.M. Sunday. Admission is $7.00 for adults, $6.00 for seniors and students, and $3.00 for children twelve and under.

Uxbridge, south of Grafton at the intersection of Routes 16 and 12, sits on the Blackstone River, which was the corridor along which the American Industrial Revolution began. The entire Blackstone Valley is a National Heritage Corridor, with a combination of historical and natural attractions highlighted, preserved, and interpreted. At the ***River Bend Farm Visitor Center,*** at 287 Oak Street, you can learn about the progress of this project, see how the canal locks worked, walk the towpath, or launch your canoe. Look for the excellent booklet "Canoe Guide for the Blackstone River," which maps the entire river with detailed text for paddlers and information on rapids, portages, and the environment. The visitors center is open 10:00 A.M. to 4:00 P.M. daily, and the park is open daylight hours, (508) 278–7604.

At various times during the year, the riverboat **Blackstone Valley Explorer** takes passengers on a cruise through some of the earliest sites of the Industrial Revolution along the Blackstone River and Canal. It runs June through October, Sunday at 1:00, 2:00, 3:00, and 4:00 P.M.; the schedule is variable, so call ahead to confirm and make reservations, which are suggested. All seats are priced around $7.00; (401) 724–2200.

Worcester and Environs

Worcester's heritage is on view at the ***Worcester Historical Museum,*** at 30 Elm Street (508–753–8278). Though it's small, this museum packs a lot into its beautifully designed galleries. Holdings include many artifacts that belonged to Worcester residents in times past, such as furniture, memorabilia, clothing, artworks, and simple household items. Among the artifacts are an eighteenth-century delftware charger, a tricorn hatbox, the Lord's Prayer inscribed on a seashell, and a petrified buffalo horn brought back from the West.

Oil paintings show that Worcester was astonishingly rural until the mid-nineteenth-century manufacturing boom. Patent models represent some of the many clever machines invented in Worcester: a rolling mill, twine reels, a harness motion for a loom. Around 1900, Worcester also became the country's leading producer of lunch wagons. Four custom-made lunch wagon windows are lighted to show off their rich designs painted in red and white. The museum is open 10:00 A.M. to 4:00 P.M. Tuesday through Saturday and is open until 8:30 P.M. on Thursday. Admission is $5.00 for adults age eighteen and older.

Stephen Salisbury was a leading citizen of Worcester, and in 1772 he built an exquisite mansion in downtown Lincoln Square, which was later moved to 40 Highland Street. Besides being one of the few surviving eighteenth-century houses from Worcester's Main Street, the house is so beautiful that people love to get married here.

The ***Salisbury Mansion*** has serenely symmetrical Georgian lines, with beautiful matching fanlight doorways front and rear, a pillared portico, and four tall chimneys. Patterned wallpapers and carpets, as well as paint colors, have been faithfully re-created using extensive family records. These records make the mansion one of the best-documented historic houses in New England.

Downstairs, Stephen ran a "hardware" store that sold imported teas and molasses, flax, sheep's wool, chocolate, ginger, beeswax, pewter, brass, and copper. In the original kitchen hangs the large wooden store sign bearing the Salisbury logo of a samovar. House tours are given Thursday from 1:00 to 8:30 P.M., Friday and Saturday from 1:00 to 4:00 P.M.; admission is $5.00 for adults over age eighteen. For information call the Worcester Historical Museum at (508) 753–8278. Year-round programs include vintage Christmas decorations, classical-music concerts, and afternoon teas.

The romance of knighthood and chivalry lives on at the **Higgins Armory Museum,** one of the best collections of medieval armor in the country. The centerpiece is the Great Hall, which feels like a castle, with its stone Gothic arches, rose-patterned stained-glass window, and cathedral ceiling. An impressive array of shining suits of armor lines the Great Hall from end to end, as do halberds and lances, hauberks, and crossbows.

A sound-and-light show re-creates all the pageantry and heraldry of a tournament, featuring two life-size knights on horseback, their lances atilt. Trumpets blare, hooves gallop, and weapons clash resoundingly. It makes you think of Ivanhoe and Richard the Lion-Hearted.

An armored knight on horseback might wear as much as ninety-five pounds of armor. It's a wonder that anyone could even walk, let alone fight, in a getup like this. Some of the armor is surprisingly beautiful, such as a sixteenth-century Italian suit made of engraved and gilded blued steel, decorated with gold floral motifs.

The collection of several thousand pieces also includes some rare items, such as a Roman gladiator's helmet and Greek Corinthian helmets from around 550 B.C. Look too for the little white dog in armor, sporting a grand red head plume. One whole floor is devoted to hands-on fun for children, including trying on armor, making brass rubbings, and dressing up as Maid Marian or King Arthur. The Higgins Armory Museum is at 100 Barber Avenue; call (508) 853–6015 or visit www.higgins.org. It's open from 10:00 A.M. to 4:00 P.M. Tuesday through Saturday, from noon to 4:00 P.M. Sunday. Admission is $8.00 for adults, $7.00 for children ages six through sixteen and for those over sixty, and free for those five and under.

The **EcoTarium** blends the qualities of a zoo and a science museum, all spread out on spacious grounds ideal for a family outing. Around the grounds runs a bright red narrow-gauge train called the Explorer Express. Animal habitats house polar bears, primates, river otters, snowy owls, and bald eagles. A new tree canopy tour takes you into the treetops on rope bridges (you wear safety cables) to see what it's like to be a treetop scientist. There's a small picnic area and playground. Inside the museum, visitors see animal habitat exhibits such as intertidal zones, ponds and bogs, and African communities. There is a pre-schooler discovery room, a bird-identification game, and several interactive computer and video exhibits on the environment. The museum is open from 10:00 A.M. to 5:00 P.M. Tuesday through Saturday and from noon to 5:00 P.M. on Sunday. Admission is $10.00 for adults and $8.00 for seniors, students, and children ages three to sixteen. Explorer Express tickets cost $2.50 extra, and the seasonal tree canopy walkway tours are $17.00. Call (508) 791–9211. The museum is at 222 Harrington Way in Worcester; (508) 929–2700; www.ecotarium.org.

What do you do with an old toilet? If you're Russell Manoog, a plumbing distributor who followed his father into the business, you save it, along with dozens of other vintage fixtures. Russell exhibits them all at his **American Sanitary Plumbing Museum,** the country's only such museum, opened in 1988.

Russell's father collected antique fixtures for sixty years. The oldest item is a section of a centuries-old wooden water main installed in Boston around 1652. An early, primitive indoor toilet looks more like an outhouse seat. By contrast, an 1891 earthenware toilet is elegantly painted with green and white floral motifs embossed with gold tracings. And an enamel hopper boasts beautiful scenes, painted in blue, of people, trees, buildings, and forests—a duplicate of a hopper at Mount Vernon. Among the museum's chamber pots is one made of white Limoges china that came from the French ocean liner *Ile de France.*

Besides toilets, there are early copper-lined and claw-foot bathtubs, lavatories, kitchen sinks, and sitz baths, along with a large collection of plumbers' tools and blowtorches. An "electric sink" invented in 1928 was the first try at a dishwasher. As part of its "Win the War" line in 1943, Kohler offered an iron kitchen sink, iron being a noncritical material. The museum is at 39 Piedmont Street. Hours are 10:00 A.M. to 2:00 P.M. Tuesday and Thursday, and by appointment, except July and August. Admission is free. Call (508) 754–9453.

Although Worcester and Providence, Rhode Island, both have serious claims to being the birthplace of the diner, there is no dispute that Worcester was the major center of their manufacture between 1906 and the early 1960s. More than 600 of them were manufactured by the Worcester Lunch Car Company, which used to be across the street from the surviving Miss Worcester Diner it built. So it's only right that you should pay your respects to this legacy by stopping in one of the city's well-preserved examples, such as the **Miss Worcester Diner,** just mentioned, at 300 Southbridge Street (508–757–7775) or the 1936 **Boulevard Diner** at 155 Shrewsbury Street (508–791–4535).

In the countryside about 7 miles west of Worcester, Route 9 joins up with Route 56. Follow it north to Paxton and south on Route 31 to a very special spot,

Moore State Park. This 400-acre park was a private estate in the 1930s, land-scaped with thousands of rhododendrons and azaleas. A dramatic, tree-lined drive leads down past open meadows to a swift-running brook, the site of an eighteenth-century mill village. Around a sawmill and gristmill, early settlers built a tavern, a one-room schoolhouse, a blacksmith shop, and a mill owner's house. A self-guided tour winds among the remaining buildings and the crumbling stone foundations and cellar holes of those that are gone. The weathered blacksmith shop still sits along the brook, close to a waterfall, as does the sawmill, one of the oldest standing sawmills in New England still on its original site. Call (508) 792–3969 or (508) 368–0126 for information.

The Rural Heartland

A rural heartland of small towns, farmland, and apple country spreads out across all of Worcester County from the I-495 beltway, near the town of *Harvard,* all the way west to the Quabbin Reservoir. Here you'll find town greens that look the same as they did a hundred years ago, remnants of Shaker settlements, and real working farms. Route 62 west travels right through the middle of this territory, and to see this area you can follow it with only a couple of detours.

Making your way through apple orchards on Route 110, you'll come to signs for *Fruitlands Museums,* a collection of four small museums that are little-known gems. Set high on rolling green hills with a stunning view of Mount Wachusett, the museums are surrounded by woods with nature trails. Down the hill stands the red colonial farmhouse where Bronson Alcott and like-minded others tried out their transcendentalist dream, thinking hard while the women tended the house and crops. Plain and primitively furnished, the *Alcott House* is pervaded by the spiritual feelings of its past occupants. The 1790s *Shaker House* was used as an office by the Shaker community in Harvard. It is filled with exhibits of Shaker handicrafts and industries, such as growing seeds and herbs. There's also a chair that belonged to Mother Ann, the sect's founder, who lived briefly in Harvard. The *American Indian Museum* holds countless decorated shields, clothing, baskets, and pottery. Finally, an ivied brick building houses the *Picture Gallery,* where you can see primitive portraits of children done by itinerant artists, as well as landscape paintings by artists of the Hudson River School.

Even if you don't tour the museums, the grounds are a wonderful place for picnicking. In summer, there are old-fashioned bandstand concerts on the lawn. The museum shop has some unusual, quality handicrafts. There's also a lovely tearoom enhanced by a white lattice doorway and an outdoor patio. The tearoom serves light lunches, snacks, and afternoon tea (3:00 to 4:00 P.M.) with pastries and desserts. The museums, at 102 Prospect Hill Road off Route 110, are open from 11:00 A.M. to 4:00 P.M. weekdays and until 5:00 P.M. on weekends and holidays from mid-May through October. Admission is $10.00 for adults, $8.00 for seniors and college students with ID, and $2.00 for children ages four to seventeen. Call (978) 456–3924 or visit www.fruitlands.org.

You can see some of the houses built by Harvard's Shaker community on Shaker Road, in the ***Shaker Historic District.*** These plain but attractive clapboard dwellings are painted in pastel colors and complemented by stone stairs, barns, and tall pines. Some other Shaker land has been set aside as the ***Holy Hill Conservation Area,*** on South Shaker Road, just off Shaker Road. The sanctuary gets its name from a Shaker holy hill, where religious services were held outdoors. The worship area, sometimes called "the dancing ground," is half a mile up a trail. The grounds also include a stone bridge, a Shaker barn foundation, and a Shaker cemetery. For information call the Harvard town clerk at (508) 456–4100. A trail guide is available for $5.00 at Town Hall on the town common.

Northeast of Worcester between Routes 140 and 110, you'll come to the ***Wachusett Reservoir and Dam.*** The dam here is so large it will remind you of the Grand Coulee Dam—Massachusetts-style, of course. And the reservoir itself is scenic and wild, ringed with tall pines and a rocky shoreline like that in Maine. The dam was built starting in 1900 and at its base is 185 feet thick. The structure stands 415 feet tall. A green park with a fountain lies at the base of the dam, down steep stone steps. There's a wide path along the spillway that makes for a pretty stroll as you look out on white houses hugging the shore.

By following Route 70 toward the south end of the reservoir, you'll come to ***Boylston.*** Here, high on a windswept hill with a breathtaking view of Mount Wachusett and the Wachusett Reservoir, the most ambitious botanical garden in New England is taking shape. The ***Tower Hill Botanic Garden*** is a fifty-year project of the Worcester County Horticultural Society.

Begun in the late 1980s, the botanical garden showcases the best plants of all kinds the gardener can find that will grow in Massachusetts. There are the Cottage Garden, planted with vegetables; the Wildlife Garden, with a pond and bird feeders; and the Lawn Garden, filled with flowering plants and shrubs. Walking and nature trails wind through the 132 acres.

An orchard contains more than a hundred flavorful antique varieties of apples that once grew all over New England. Above the Lawn Garden, a blue stone terrace set with urns steps up to the eighteenth-century white farmhouse that serves as the society's headquarters.

A large and luxurious visitor center holds a library, rooms for programs and classes, and a cafe that serves light fare. The cafe's flagstone terrace, a splendid place to dine, overlooks the Wachusett Reservoir.

The Tower Hill Botanic Garden is at 11 French Drive; (508) 869–6111; www .towerhillbg.org. It's open year-round Tuesday through Sunday, plus Monday holidays from 10:00 A.M. to 5:00 P.M. May through August, they are also open Wednesday evening until 8:00 P.M. Tours are on Sunday at 2:00 P.M. in the summer. Admission is $8.00 for adults, $5.00 for seniors and children ages six to eighteen.

Route 140 is a pleasant, winding country road through mixed forests and farmland, often lined by stone walls. It provides a shortcut, as well as a quiet respite, to those traveling from Route 2 to Interstate 190, bypassing Fitchburg and Leominster. On its way it passes the entrance to **Wachusett Mountain State Reservation** (978–464–2987), with 20 miles of hiking trails and alpine and cross-country skiing. The visitor center is a cozy refuge for hikers, with a huge, four-sided fieldstone fireplace. Views from the top are spectacular: Boston to the east and the Berkshire hills to the west. Wachusett is also a great place for seeing hawks, ospreys, falcons, and eagles, because it's along the migration route of these raptors.

Not far east of the reservation, stop for apples at the **Sagatabscot Orchards** farmstand in West Sterling or for lunch at the **Country Side Cafe** next to the stand at 4 Johnson Road. Tasty liverwurst or ham salad sandwiches along with the usual selection ($3.00 to $5.00) are served up quickly and cheerfully, as are breakfast specials. These might include a zucchini and provolone omelet, an asparagus omelet, or steak and eggs. The cafe is open from 7:00 A.M. until 2:00 P.M. daily; (978) 422–6686.

Outdoor pleasures await at **Wachusett Meadow Wildlife Sanctuary,** a Massachusetts Audubon property. A surprising amount of farmland survives in this part of the state, and here you can see a traditional farm landscape. The farmland is home to bobolinks, whose numbers have declined along with farm acreage. A nature trail passes through a red-maple swamp over a boardwalk with observation platforms for viewing the special plants and animals that live here. Another highlight is the **Crocker Maple,** one of the country's largest maples and more than 300 years old. Though its ancient, gnarled limbs look as if they should spread next to a haunted house, the maple is an impressive sight, especially when its leaves are aflame with color in autumn. Wachusett Meadow is also a good place for snowshoeing. To get to the sanctuary, follow Route 62 west from the center of Princeton and turn right at the Massachusetts Audubon sign, which will lead you to 113 Goodnow Road. The trails are open Tuesday through Sunday, dawn to dusk, and the Nature Center is open Tuesday through Saturday from 10:00 A.M. to 2:00 P.M. Admission for adults is $4.00; for seniors and children three through twelve, $3.00. For information call (978) 464–2712.

Princeton has some excellent restaurants. A quiet gourmet dinner in the countryside is a hallmark of **The Harrington Farm.** This mountainside farm was built on the western slope of Wachusett Mountain in 1763 and still has hand-painted stenciling on its walls. It's surrounded by thousands of acres of protected land ideal for hiking, berry picking, and cross-country skiing. In keeping with its setting, the restaurant's menu gives a country flair to dishes such as grilled pheasant with rosemary, roasted tenderloin with candied shallots, roast pork loin with sautéed apples, and occasional quail and venison entrees. To take advantage of the freshest seasonal ingredients, the menu changes weekly. The restaurant is open Thursday through Sunday from 5:00 P.M.; reservations are recommended. The inn is at 178 Westminster Road; (978) 464–5600; www.harringtonfarm.com.

Tiny **Rutland,** in the heart of farm country about 5 miles south of Route 62, has a most historic property in the **General Rufus Putnam House,** a bed-and-breakfast inn built in 1750. The house belonged to one of George Washington's generals, Rufus Putnam, who served in the French and Indian War, and designed defenses for the American Revolution. The Georgian colonial home is largely untouched and still has its original wide pine floors, raised paneling in every room, and eight working fireplaces. The parlor, library, and dining room are beautifully painted and decorated with period antiques, as are the three guest rooms. The seven and a half acres of grounds include a nature trail through woods and a pond. The four-course breakfast is a feast of fruits and juices, homemade breads, coffee, and eggs or pancakes. Double rooms are $100 to $150. The B&B is at 344 Main Street (Route 122A); (508) 886–0200 or (508) 886–4864; www.rufusputnamhouse.com.

Outside of a movie, you may never have seen a herd of buffalo. But way out on a winding country road in Rutland is a buffalo farm, called **Alta Vista Farm,** where owners Howard and Nancy Mann have been raising buffalo since 1968. They have a herd of sixty-two bison and a small store where they sell bison steaks, roasts, kabobs, corned bison, and ground bison. Bison meat is often recommended for heart patients because it is low in fat and cholesterol, the Manns explain. The store also sells gifts with bison or Indian themes, such as belt buckles, stickers, books, earrings made of buffalo head nickels, and American Indian good-luck shields and dream catchers. Buffalo hides go for $175. You can see the buffalo out in the pasture and visit the store Friday, Saturday, and Sunday from 10:00 A.M. to 5:00 P.M.; call (978) 886–4365. To get to the farm, take Route 56 south 0.8 mile from Route 122A in Rutland Center. Just past a Citgo station, turn left onto Prescott Street, which turns into Hillside Road, and follow it 1.3 miles to the farm.

Although the town of **Barre,** reached via Route 62, has a pretty town common and lots of shops, a more interesting stop is the family-owned **Hartman's Herb Farm,** which sells one of the most extensive selections of herbs you'll ever see. Its catalog lists twenty kinds of thyme, seventeen kinds of mint, and thirteen kinds of basil. The farm sprang back after a massive fire in 1989 that claimed the shop and house, but everything grows greener now, say the Hartmans. The cluster of farm buildings commands a rustic setting down a narrow blacktop road. From the new shop's beamed ceiling hang tied bundles of yellow, pink, and purple flowers and dried herbs. The shop also sells plants and garden accessories, books on herbs, soup and salad herbs, herb dips, herb teas, and such handmade crafts as dried-flower arrangements and wreaths, flower-decorated straw hats, and, at Christmastime, herb wreaths and potpourri. On your visit, don't overlook the farm's resident pig, goats, sheep, rabbits, chickens, ducks, cats, and dog. The farm is particularly resplendent and fragrant at Christmastime, when mulled cider is served. To get there, go west on Routes 122 and 32, turn left onto Old Dana Road, and follow it until you come to the heart-shaped green sign. The shop is open from 10:00 A.M. to 5:00 P.M. daily. If the setting and the farm make you long to linger, you can stay on in one of their four B&B guest rooms. The $85 rate includes a bounteous full breakfast. Lunch is also available Friday from 11:30 A.M. to 2:30 P.M. by reservation; (978) 355–2015; www.hartmansherbfarm.com.

At the junction of Routes 32 and 122, the town of **Petersham,** too, has a picturesque common, complete with bandstand and Greek Revival mansions. The common is surrounded by interesting shops. A short hop from the common on North Main Street, the **Petersham Craft Center** (508–724–3415) offers a wide variety of crafts and art. The galleries in this more-than-seventy-year-old center, housed in an antique white farmhouse, have a homey, community feeling. Their offerings range from watercolors, blue-and-white flowered pottery, and heart-shaped, hand-forged iron hooks to linens, wooden toys, clothing, cotton rugs, and jewelry. The center has a full schedule of classes and programs that have included rug hooking workshops, landscape photography, precious metal and enameled jewelry making, scrapbooking, and journaling. Call for a list of their current programs and workshops, which are offered year-round. The center is open from 11:30 A.M. to 4:00 P.M. daily except Monday.

Directly opposite the common, the **Country Store** is behind the tall white pillars of its Greek Revival facade. Among its merchandise are maple syrup and cheddar cheese, but the best part is the small dining room in back with long tables. You can get delicious fresh-made sandwiches to eat here or to take on a picnic, or you can buy house-made soups or chili. The kitchen closes at 3:00 P.M.; (978) 724–3245.

Few people know that Harvard University has owned land in Petersham since 1907 for the purpose of forestry research. In 1941, a museum opened in the Harvard Forest, the *Fisher Museum of Forestry,* designed to interpret the history of New England forests. The museum is dark inside, to better show the lighted windows housing twenty-three unique dioramas. A preliminary color slide show gives background about the dioramas and showcases some beautifully artistic shots of tree canopies and forest plants.

As you go around the room, each diorama shows a particular phase of history in New England's forests, starting with a dense primeval forest of 1700 and moving on through farming, reforestation, and clear-cutting. Other dioramas portray forestry management techniques, erosion, wildlife habitat, and forest-fire devastation.

In addition to the dioramas' teaching intent, they are rare jewels whose like will never again be created. Hours of hand labor went into each display, and they are filled with purely artistic touches, such as people and vehicles, animals, and birds. The trees and branches look so natural that you'd swear they were real. But even the tiniest pine needles are made of copper. One diorama looks just like a painting of a scenic spot among the trees on Harvard Pond, aflame with the reds and oranges of sunset.

Second-floor exhibits focus on tree injuries, the effects of storms and fungus, ants and blights, and how to read a landscape, among many other fascinating aspects of New England forests. Museum hours are 9:00 A.M. to 5:00 P.M. weekdays all year and noon to 4:00 P.M. Saturday and Sunday from May through October. There is no admission charge. The museum is at 324 North Main Street (Route 32), Petersham; (978) 724–3302; www.harvardforest.fas.harvard.edu.

The *Harvard Forest* covers 3,000 acres, serving as a research and education center for forest biology and environmental sciences. The Natural History Trail, which starts at the museum, is a quarter-mile walk with twenty-one numbered stations and a corresponding map and guide to explain the development of the land. Another trail map, to the 1.5-mile-long Black Gum Trail, interprets seedling beds, the effects of lightning, disease such as chestnut blight, and the life cycles of swamp plants. You can pick up the trail maps at the Fisher Museum or download them from the Web site.

For a lovely oasis in the northern part of the county, stay at *The Inn at Clamber Hill,* a bed-and-breakfast in an estatelike stone-and-shingle "cottage" set in woodlands carpeted in beds of fern. Rooms or suites have queen-size beds, and breakfast breads are freshly baked. Rates start at $155 for doubles with a shared bath, $285 for suites with sitting rooms and private baths. Tea and dinner are served by prior arrangement. The inn is at 111 North Main Street, Petersham; (978) 724–8800 or (888) 374–0007, fax (978) 724–8829; www.clamberhill.com.

The Industrial North

By 1914, the town of **Winchendon** was making so many toys that mail would arrive addressed simply to **"Toy Town,"** its widely known nickname. Winchendon's Morton E. Converse Company, named after its founder, was the largest toy manufacturer in the country and sent wooden rocking horses all over the world. Memorabilia surrounding the town's heyday are exhibited at the **Winchendon Historical Society,** now housed in the Victorian Gothic revival **Murdock-Whitney House.** The house was built by the founder of a major woodenware manufacturer of the 1800s, and has been restored and decorated with antiques of local interest. The wide-ranging collection includes objects from the Revolutionary War, the Civil War, and World War II; eighteenth-century pewter, antique tools, clothing, portraits, and household items. A fair bit of space is still dedicated to Converse toys, from porcelain dolls to little tin drums, easels to tea sets. Converse's success bred other toymakers in the town, which built some renown. In fact, visitors to Toy Town became so numerous that Converse built a resort called the Toy Town Tavern to house them in comfort, as documented in a scrapbook in the collection. The museum, at 151 Front Street, is open from June through October, Wednesday 10:00 A.M. to 4:00 P.M. and Sunday 1:00 to 4:00 P.M.; the admission price of $5 includes a guided tour; (978) 297–2142.

A proud symbol of Toy Town, a 12-foot-long rocking horse, stands under a canopy on Route 12, 2 blocks north of the library. A copy of the 1914 original, this giant replica was made as a parade float to celebrate the company's 150th anniversary.

As you drive down Elm Street in **Gardner** (between Routes 2 and 140), you'll come upon a giant wooden ladder-back chair, so tall that it may remind you of Lily Tomlin's comedy prop for her routine about a little girl in a giant rocker. Townspeople remark that when the wood deteriorated, the chair was rebuilt bigger to maintain its Guinness world record as the world's largest chair. The two-story-high chair symbolizes Gardner's heritage as a large manufacturing center known as "Chair City."

The story of this chairmaking tradition is outlined at **Gardner Heritage State Park.** One man, James Comee, began crafting chairs by hand at his Pearl Street home in 1805. The apprentices he trained went on to open their own companies. A century later, there were almost forty chair companies in Gardner, making more than four million chairs a year. Gardner still makes chairs today.

A video details the craft of chairmaking, and on display are locally made chairs of bentwood, rush, rattan, wicker, and pressed-back oak, as well as Windsor, side, bedroom, ladder-back, and hand-painted and stenciled chairs. There's also an exhibit detailing Gardner's silversmithing history. The museum and park are at 26 Lake Street; call (978) 630–1497 or (978) 632–7897 (the state park office). The park is open Tuesday through Saturday from 9:00 A.M. to 4:00 P.M., as well as Sunday and Monday from noon to 4:00 P.M.

Another legacy of the chair-making heritage is the many *furniture factory outlets* in Gardner, Winchendon, and Templeton, great places to find bargain furniture. For a map and brochure listing them,

Toy Town Horse, Winchendon

contact the Central Massachusetts Convention and Visitors Bureau at (800) 231–7557 or www.worcester.org

At 102 Main Street in Gardner is a vintage diner in mint condition, the **Blue Moon Diner** (978–632–4333). Built by the Worcester Lunch Car Company in 1948, the diner has a handsome blue-and-cream exterior, oak-trimmed booths with blue leather seats, and the original art deco, steel diner's clock. The Italian owner, a former police officer who loves people, makes the rounds of the counter stools, booths, and tables to chat and joke with customers. Besides breakfasts of home fries, eggs, and fresh-fruit pancakes, the diner has blackboard lunch specials such as meat loaf and pork pie, and homemade soups and pies.

Nineteenth-century novels are full of references to women keeping their long, upswept hair in place with ornamental hair combs. Such combs have largely disappeared nowadays, but the **Leominster Historical Society** has the largest hair-comb collection in the country. Once home to a hair-comb factory, **Leominster** was known as "Comb City of the World."

Hundreds of hair combs fill two whole walls. It's hard to believe they came in so many styles. Some are 6 inches high or more, carved of tortoiseshell with scrolled floral designs. Others are made of silver and filigreed in minute detail. And still others are made in the shapes of butterflies or dragonflies and studded with rhinestones or pearls. There's an ivory comb, too, cut with the design of a fire-breathing dragon.

Other exhibits detail the plastics industry in Leominster, comb-making machinery, and the story of Johnny Appleseed, who was born here. While many know Johnny Appleseed only as a folk hero, he was a skilled nurseryman who distributed thousands of apple trees to settlers and started many nurseries throughout the Midwest. The historical society's museum is at 17 School

Street, just behind City Hall (978–537–5424) and is open from 9:00 A.M. to noon, Tuesday, Wednesday, and Saturday, or by appointment. There is no admission charge.

Ever since the first plastic—celluloid—was manufactured 130 years ago, plastic has found uses from toys to medical products to spaceflights. The country's only museum to chronicle the history of plastic is the *National Plastics Center and Museum* in Leominster, where the first celluloid plant was built. A "Plastics Hall of Fame" honors pioneers in the industry. Children can play with thousands of Legos and DuPlos and learn how plastics become popular toys they can recognize. A new exhibit showcases plastics and the environment, especially concerning recycling. A micromolder grinds up plastic milk bottles into souvenirs visitors can take home. The museum is at 210 Lancaster Street (Route 117). Hours are 11:00 A.M. to 4:00 P.M. Wednesday through Saturday; closed Saturday in July and August. Tickets cost $5.00 for adults and $3.00 for seniors over sixty-five and children ages four through eleven. Call (978) 537–9529 or go to www.plasticsmuseum.org for information.

TO LEARN MORE ABOUT WORCESTER COUNTY

Blackstone River Valley National Heritage Corridor Commission,
(401) 762–0250;
www.nps.gov/blac

Central Massachusetts Convention and Visitors Bureau,
30 Worcester Center Boulevard,
Worcester 01608;
(508) 755–7400 or (800) 231–7557;
(800) 231–7557;
www.worcester.org

WORTH SEEING IN WORCESTER COUNTY

Brimfield Flea Markets,
held in May, July, and September, are like no other flea market or antiques show. Plan well in advance for lodging and expect inflated room prices or a long drive to an available room; (413) 245–9329.

Worcester Museum of Art,
An outstanding collection of paintings and decorative arts that many much larger cities would be proud to show. 55 Salisbury Street, Worcester; (508) 799–4406, www.worcesterart.org

More Places to Stay in Worcester County

Elias Carter House,
on the Common, Brimfield; (413) 245–0903; www.eliascarterhouse.com
A homey bed-and-breakfast, with summer rates at $95 except during Brimfield Flea Market weekends, when they jump to $200.

Commonwealth Cottage,
11 Summit Avenue, Sturbridge; (508) 347–7708; www.commonwealthcottage .com
A Queen Anne–style cottage on a hilltop, serving guests home-baked breads at breakfast and a civilized afternoon tea. Rooms begin at $95 (low season).

More Places to Eat in Worcester County

The Sunburst,
484 Main Street (US 20), Sturbridge; (508) 347–3097.
An upbeat place for breakfast (ham and eggs, omelets, hot muffins, French toast, granola) or lunch (soups, quiche, sandwiches) at reasonable prices.

Shorah's Ristorante,
27 Foster Street, Worcester; (508) 797–0007.
Don't be misled by the plain setting—the food is anything but plain, with imaginative dishes based on Italian tradition. Entrees are $13 to $17.

Oyster Cabin,
Route 146A, Uxbridge; (508) 278–4440.
Seafood reigns here, with an outstanding bouillabaisse and winning ways with the day's freshest catch. It's open Wednesday through Saturday 4:30 to 9:00 P.M. and Sunday 3:00 to 8:00 P.M.

Pioneer Valley

No one outside the Pioneer Valley seems to know where it is. The Pioneer Valley is actually the Connecticut River Valley; it follows the river's course the whole length of the state.

In its distance from Boston, this area may as well be another country. Residents know that Bostonians can't think of a good reason to come here. People here say "grinders" and "soda" instead of the Bostonian "submarines" and "tonic" and, unlike the Kennedys, pronounce their "*r*"s.

Still, it's hard to find another region in this state more markedly diverse. There's farmland here so isolated you wonder if anyone lives there at all. There are the large industrial cities of Springfield and Holyoke, ethnic rainbows. A centuries-old tradition of craftsmanship has drawn some 1,500 artists and craftspeople to live in the Pioneer Valley. Five of the state's best-known colleges are clustered here, and their thousands of students have kept the 1960s alive like a miniature Cambridge or Berkeley. For this unique blend of outlooks, the region is also nicknamed "the Happy Valley."

PIONEER VALLEY

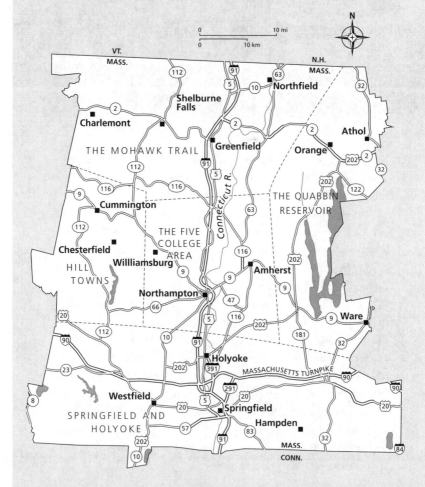

The Mohawk Trail

The **Mohawk Trail** (Route 2), originally an Indian footpath, today stretches 63 miles from Millers Falls to the New York border. A scenic delight to drive on, it passes through miles of farmland, apple orchards, and maple sugarhouses. Because of its brilliant fall foliage display, it's a popular tourist path for leaf-peeping and is often crowded in the fall. The first part of the Mohawk Trail passes through Franklin County in the northern part of the Pioneer Valley.

Despite the bumper-to-bumper traffic on the Mohawk Trail in the fall, lots of little nooks and crannies are tucked away to explore. Perhaps the least-known section of this scenic valley lies to the east of the river, in the not-so-gently rolling hills along the New Hampshire border, north of the Quabbin Reservoir. At Routes 10 and 63, **Northfield** lies along the Connecticut River, and a unique power plant/nature center uses its waters.

From Route 63, turn off at the **Northfield Mountain Recreation and Environmental Center,** established by Northeast Utilities (www.nu.com /northfield). A visitor center that holds interesting exhibits on ice harvesting and logging also explains the operation of the company's hydroelectric plant. In the exhibits in the visitor center or on a tour to the top of the mountain, you can see how the water is pumped from the river to the top of the mountain during off-peak times, then used to generate electricity for peak-hours use. You can't drive there yourself, but a bus can take you on the free tour. Call ahead for reservations; (800) 859–2960. Throughout the year, the center sponsors nature programs on everything from wild animals and plants to wilderness survival and astronomy. For a list of these and their fees, call the number above. You'll find some of the area's best cross-country skiing on Northfield Mountain trails; also here are a picnic area, campgrounds, and nature trails. One of these leads to a century-old quarry, and the Rose Ledge Trail leads to a scenic overlook above the river, about a forty-five-minute climb.

But the highlight of a visit to this area is a scenic 12-mile ride along the Connecticut River on the **Quinnetukut II,** an open-air riverboat with wooden benches. The ride is splendid on a sunny day, with the sunlight sparkling on the waves and the breeze in your face. The wide expanse of river is flanked

AUTHORS' FAVORITES IN PIONEER VALLEY

"The Quad" Springfield Museums	The Bridge of Flowers, Shelburne Falls
Historic Deerfield	

by unbroken green forests of pine and hardwoods, turning to rock cliffs imprinted with low-growing plants and mosses and, later, to marsh grasses. You pass under the **French King Bridge,** a graceful iron structure spanning 750 feet, built in 1932. You might spot a bald eagle among the many migratory birds and will certainly see geese and ducks. You should make reservations for the boat's three daily trips, Wednesday through Sunday, from mid-June through Columbus Day. For reservations and boat tour information, contact Northeast Utilities, (800) 859–2960. The boat ride costs $10.00 for adults, $9.00 for seniors, and $5.00 for children ages fourteen and under.

Downtown Northfield, sprawled out along Route 63, is home to the former campus of nearby Northfield–Mount Hermon School, a prestigious school founded by evangelist Dwight Moody, who ran summer religious conferences in Northfield. A follower of Moody built an extravagantly ornate house out in the woods to stay in only two weeks each summer during the meetings. The school has moved, but until the old campus is sold, it is a lovely place for a stroll.

hostelterritory

The first American Youth Hostel was opened in Northfield in 1934 by Monroe and Isabel Smith, who founded the U.S. organization. A membership card was $1.00 for those under age twenty-five, $2.00 for those older, and $3.00 for a family.

Inside **Northfield Antiques** (413–498–5825), at 37 Main Street, it's tough to move around because this big old barn is so stuffed with antique tools, collectibles, and furniture.

South along the river is **Barton's Cove,** also part of the Northfield Mountain project, with a campground shaded in tall pines and several carry-in sites for those who prefer to camp in quiet seclusion. For visitors who arrive by boat, Munns Ferry offers riverside campsites. Reservations for these sites, which cost $15 a night and have a two-night maximum stay, should be made in advance through Barton Cove Campground at (413) 863–9300. Campsites at Barton Cove are $15, and the area, which has picnic sites and nature trails, is open for day use from 8:00 A.M. to 8:00 P.M. A canoe and kayak rental and shuttle service is also available at the campground, so you can travel by water between the two facilities and arrange for a ride back upstream.

If you rode on the *Quinnetukut II,* you probably noticed a dam along the river. Just below the dam is the **Turners Falls Fishway** (800–859–2960), where fish ladders built by Northeast Utilities help anadromous fish make it back upriver to spawn. (Anadromous fish are fish born in freshwater that swim downstream to feed and grow in the ocean before returning upstream to reproduce; examples are shad and salmon.) The fish have been in great decline on the Connecticut River, and the fish ladders are helping to increase the population.

ANNUAL EVENTS IN PIONEER VALLEY

MID-MARCH

Central Massachusetts has two major St. Patrick's Day parades, usually held on different days. Worcester's begins on Park Avenue at Mill Street and includes twenty-five floats and twenty marching bands; (508) 753-7197. The second largest St. Patrick's Day parade in the United States is in Holyoke, beginning at the K-Mart Plaza on U.S. Route 5; (413) 534-3376.

MID-JULY

Green River Festival, Greenfield Community College, presents folk, country, and ethnic music; (413) 586-8686.

JULY–AUGUST

Summit House Concerts, Skinner State Park, Route 47, Hadley, presents Thursday evening concerts of Dixieland, folk, "big band," and barbershop music; (413) 538-9914.

MID-SEPTEMBER

The Big E, West Springfield, is the all–New England agricultural fair/exposition; (413) 787-0271.

EARLY OCTOBER

Zoar Outdoors Annual Used Equipment Sale, Route 2, Charlemont, with the company's own used kayaks, rafts, and canoes, plus those consigned by other owners; (800) 532-7483.

LATE NOVEMBER

Annual 17th Century Celebration, Historic Deerfield, includes tours, demonstrations, and crafts, as well as period music; (413) 774-5581.

From mid-May through mid-June, you can watch the fish through viewing windows as they fight the current on their way upriver to spawn; the hours are 9:00 A.M. to 5:00 P.M. Wednesday through Sunday. Along the riverbank is a small, grassy picnic area with a serene view of the river. You might pick up a lunch at the *Shady Glen Diner,* at 7 Avenue A in downtown Turners Falls, just north of Greenfield, near Interstate 91 and Route 2 (413–863–9636). They are open Monday through Saturday from 5:00 A.M. to 9:00 P.M. and, with its new owners, Sunday mornings.

Before heading west on Route 2 from Greenfield, make a detour south along Route 5. Parallel to I-91, which relieves it of most through-traffic, Route 5 travels through flat riverbottom farmlands where you will see stands selling the season's freshest produce. These grow thicker south of Deerfield, but your destination here should be *Historic Deerfield.* Though this is a well-known tourist attraction, it's still a special place to visit. The faithfulness and purity of its surroundings give a powerful sense of the past. The original Deerfield was a farming community founded in 1669. Twelve of its eighteenth- and nineteenth-century houses have been preserved and opened as house museums. The clapboard houses with mullioned windows and imposing Connecticut Valley doors stand serenely in oases of green lawns, neatly contained by wooden fences. When you look in the distance, you see nothing but cornfields, just as you would have centuries ago. Cars look out of place driving along the main street—called simply "The Street"—where no trace of modernity intrudes. Families still live cheek by jowl with the house museums on The Street and still use the old post office and church.

Each house offers its own treasures—remarkable collections of American decorative arts. The **_Stebbins House,_** the first brick house built in the county, features a carved freestanding staircase, painted ceiling garlands, Chinese export porcelain, tasseled swag draperies, and hand-painted French murals showing the voyages of Captain Cook in the Sandwich Islands. Another house holds dozens of glass cases full of exquisitely repoussé and engraved silver, from the seventeenth century on up. Besides coffeepots and candlesticks, there's a pagoda-shaped, filigreed epergne so beautiful it could be a piece of sculpture.

In the fall of 1998, Historic Deerfield opened a new, state-of-the-art building to house the overflow collections and mount creative exhibitions in other-than-historic house settings. This is a radical departure from the town's past policies and gives as many as 5,000 pieces not normally on display a chance to be shown. The exhibit building's unusual stagelike design is intended to show not only the objects but also the way in which early New Englanders perceived their value and importance.

Historic Deerfield

Historic Deerfield also includes a museum shop that sells some nice reproductions, books, and handicrafts. Historic Deerfield is open daily April through December from 9:30 A.M. to 4:30 P.M. A ticket to all twelve houses costs $14.00 for adults and $5.00 for children up to age seventeen; (413) 774–5581; www .historic-deerfield.org.

In the village, and part of the National Historic District, is the restored **Deerfield Inn,** built in 1884. Furnished in antiques and reproductions of furnishings appropriate to various periods of Deerfield's history, the inn gives visitors to the town a chance to complete the sensation of moving back in time. The restaurant is far from old-fashioned, however, with creative seasonal entrees and a very good wine and beer list, featuring the products of a number of New England microbreweries. To reserve a room at the inn, which ranges from $230 to $280 for a double during peak season, call (413) 774–5587.

History isn't the only draw in Deerfield: **Magic Wings Butterfly Conservatory and Gardens,** in South Deerfield, is another reason to visit this Connecticut Valley town. Step inside this 8,000-square-foot glass conservatory to find a world alive with butterflies and moths, fluttering and resting on the tropical plants and trees. In the winter, when it's frosty or worse outside, this is like a quick trip to the tropics, at 80 degrees, with 3,000-odd butterflies and lush green all around. A gift shop, restaurant, and outdoor gardens planted with species that attract native butterflies complete the complex, which is open daily Memorial Day through Labor Day 9:00 A.M. to 6:00 P.M. and early September through late May 9:00 A.M. to 5:00 P.M. The last admission is thirty minutes before closing. 281 Greenfield Road (Routes 5 and 10), South Deerfield; (413) 665–2805; www.magic wings.com.

Another short detour off the Mohawk Trail, up Routes 5 and 10, will bring you to an excellent restaurant in Bernardston, the **Four Leaf Clover Restaurant** (413–648–9514). A country place full of good cheer, this little restaurant, founded in 1949, has wooden booths and excellently priced homemade food. Lunches feature generous hot and cold sandwiches, as well as salads. At dinner, you can get chicken potpie, seafood, or veal cutlets, among the other classic dishes. Top it all off with homemade puddings and pies or a sundae. Be prepared to wait in line on a Saturday night, but main courses will only cost you $8.00 to $15.00.

Instead of returning to Greenfield, you can continue up Route 5, where you will pass **Carriage Barn Antiques.** Just as you think you have seen all the furniture in the barn, you notice another building. Be sure to explore them all, not only for the chance to see some very nice antiques but also for the reasonable price tags on them, unusual for this antiques-conscious region.

Before the road crosses the border into Vermont, you'll come to an unnumbered road to your left, marked **Brook Road.** If you're really serious about see-

Free Love in the Hills

If you think life is dull in these little villages, read on. Late in the 1700s, William Dorrell moved to the hilly town of Leyden and began to preach a doctrine based on free love and the sanctity of life—animal as well as human. He attracted a group of followers who embraced his philosophy and practiced his new religion. The people of Leyden were a tolerant lot and ignored his unusual doctrine until his followers began to demonstrate their religion publicly, in ways their neighbors found profoundly shocking. A town elder named Ezekiel Foster put an end to Dorrell's preaching once and for all, but Dorrell continued to live in the community, presumably a chastened man, until his death at age 94.

ing off-the-beaten-path Massachusetts, take it. You may get lost, but you can't get too far without coming upon Route 112, crossing the Vermont border, or finding yourself back in Greenfield. To add to your sense of adventure, the road isn't even on the state's "Official Transportation Map" (which is about as poor an excuse for a road map as we've seen outside the Third World).

Brook Road begins by climbing through the woods, with a rocky ledge on its north side and a brook to its south and a few pullouts that would make nice spots for a picnic on a hot summer day. When you reach a crossroad, after the road becomes gravel at the Vermont line, turn left and you'll be back in Massachusetts—and on a paved road. Look for Zimmerman Hill Road, which takes you to the unusual town of **Leyden Center,** perched on a very small hilltop.

Bear right at the church and head downhill until you reach a T, where you should go right. Go left at the fork and follow the signs to Colrain. At the foot of a steep hill, go right, then left at a three-corners. All the while, you will be traveling past hill farms with pastures of grazing cattle, red barns, and hillside orchards. In late summer you may find peaches for sale beside the road. When you reach the first wide road you've seen during this journey, go right and you will literally drop into the town of Colrain.

A left turn above Colrain will take you to **Pine Hill Orchards,** a farm stand, and **West County Winery,** which specializes in fruit wines from locally grown apples, blueberries, and peaches, and in hard cider; (413) 624–3481. In the cafe, you can have sandwiches, apple pie, or shortcake of the season's fresh fruit. Outdoors your children will enjoy meeting the array of animals and birds, which includes goats, rabbits, ducks, and geese.

On Lyonsville Road is a tiny covered bridge, one of only three original nineteenth-century covered bridges left in Massachusetts. Restoration of the bridge was done using hundred-year-old methods—teams of pulling oxen hauled it from its footings. Another, the **Arthur Smith Covered Bridge,** sits unrestored beside the river, visible from Route 112, which you should take into Shelburne Falls to connect with the Mohawk Trail.

If, instead of going on this adventure through the hill borderlands, you leave Greenfield on Route 2, the Mohawk Trail, you will begin to climb almost immediately. About halfway up this long hill is **Old Greenfield Village,** a new museum of old things, collected with remarkable foresight by Waine Morse. In 1962 Morse began buying not just an item here and there but entire shops as craftspeople and artisans retired or old properties were sold. He began con-structing buildings to house them, often out of old timber and fixtures—a door from here, a set of windows from there—until he now has a total of fourteen buildings housing a complete village of shops, with a church and schoolhouse.

The most remarkable thing about this museum, apart from its being the work of one person, is the range of things you will find here, from common everyday items to the most comprehensive collection anywhere of taps and dies, an industry that made Greenfield the thread-cutting capital of the world. The general store looks much more real, with its stacks of wooden crates and its glass cabinet full of tobacco—another local product—than those clean-countered replicas in most museum villages. In the original pharmacy, you really expect a bewhiskered pharmacist in his rumpled white jacket to step out from behind the rows of glass bottles. It's the kind of place you could poke around in all day, which you are welcome to do; each building has a recorded narrative and often signs and diagrams to show how things worked. Admission is $5.00 for adults, $4.00 for seniors, and $3.00 for children ages six through sixteen, and the museum is open from May 15 through October 15 from 10:00 A.M. to 4:00 P.M. Saturday and holidays, and from 12:00 to 4:00 P.M. Sunday. The museum is at 386 Mohawk Trail; (413) 774–7138.

Just to the south of the Mohawk Trail is the town of **Shelburne Falls,** with several interesting places to visit. The village is blessed with really nice shops, galleries, and restaurants, along with two strikingly unusual attractions. The first is the **Bridge of Flowers,** a graceful, five-arch span over the Deerfield River. Three seasons of the year, beautiful blooming plants line both sides of this old bridge, making it a wonderful spot for a stroll. More than five hundred species bloom here, including crocuses and other spring bulbs, chrysanthemums, del-phinium, foxglove, and wisteria. It's also pleasant to look at from the river-banks, and the bridge is lighted at night; (413) 625–2544.

Across the street from the Bridge of Flowers is a great place to stock up on picnic fixings: **McCusker's Market and Deli** (413–625–9411). Freshly made pasta and tabouli salads are specialties, as are gourmet coffees and teas and homemade ice cream.

Recycling on a Major Scale

The Bridge of Flowers has an interesting history, which involves Colrain. In 1896, Shelburne Falls had a trolley line and was a station on the Boston & Maine Railroad. The town of Colrain, for reasons not quite clear, had become a major center for washing the oils out of cotton grown in the South and transported to Shelburne Falls by train. Because Colrain is so much higher in altitude than Shelburne Falls, it was impossible to carry the cotton there by train, so a trolley line was built from the B&M railyard to the mills in Colrain, and a bridge was built beside the iron road bridge to carry the trolley line over the river. It also carried a water main—as it still does.

Until 1926 the cotton moved back and forth on trolley cars, which also carried apples, cider, coal, oil, and passengers, although it was primarily a freight line. In 1927 the line was abandoned after trucks became more efficient, and all the cars were burned—except one, which was bought by a local farmer as a pre-fab chicken coop. The bridge, too narrow for automobile traffic, soon became an eyesore but was purchased by the Fire District because of the water supply it provided. In 1929, Mr. and Mrs. Walter Burnham began the effort to turn the bridge into a public garden, which the Women's Club agreed to maintain. The bridge has become a source of pride to the whole community, and when the structure needed major restoration in the 1970s, community groups and businesses all contributed.

The other truly unusual sight in Shelburne Falls is that of the *glacial potholes.* These are round holes carved into stone millions of years ago by the glacial action of water swirling rocks along the ground. Besides being an interesting natural phenomenon, Shelburne Falls's glacial potholes make great swimming holes. The potholes vary from a few inches to almost 40 feet in diameter, scattered along the riverbed with little waterfalls here and there. The rock surface is a moonscape of smooth curves, perfect for sunning. To get to the potholes, walk down the steps behind Mole Hollow Candles on Deerfield Avenue.

The *Salmon Falls Artisans Showroom* (413–625–9833), 1 block from the Bridge of Flowers, on Ashfield Street, is housed in an old three-story granary that nicely showcases the high-quality work of more than 150 regional artists and craftspeople. Wares include paintings, jewelry, pottery, weaving, sculpture, and furniture. The showroom is open daily April through December and closed Monday and Tuesday in winter.

The *Shelburne Falls Trolley Museum,* past the Salmon Falls Artisans Showroom on the hill overlooking the river, is devoted to restoring the one remaining car from the Colrain trolley line, rescued after sixty-five years' service as a chicken coop. Some of the basic structure of the car was in surprisingly good shape, other parts nearly irreparable. For a utilitarian car, it has a lot of fine detail, including brass fittings and mahogany paneling, which volunteers have painstakingly repaired and restored. In the building are photographs of the car as found and of the restoration process, as well as other material relating to railroads and trolleys in the area. The museum is open Saturday, Sunday, and holidays May through November, 11:00 A.M. to 5:00 P.M., or by chance or appointment. In July and August it is also open Mondays from 1:00 to 5:00 P.M.; (413) 625–9443; www.sftm.org. You can now ride the restored Trolley Car #10 in the old freight yard, which includes a historical talk; $2.50 for adults, $1.25 for children.

As you travel the Mohawk Trail, you'll see lots of signs for maple sugar farms. One of the best to visit is *Gould's Maple Farm* (413–625–6170), 7 miles west of I-91. Gould's has been making maple syrup for more than thirty years and lets visitors watch the process each spring. A shed behind the 1827 barn holds the old-fashioned, wood-fired evaporators that boil down the maple sap in March. You can have "sugar on snow," a traditional New England treat, and buy homemade syrup and maple-sugar candy. The biggest treat, though, is breakfast in the Gould Sugar House. The country-style dining room could not be more rustic, with oxbows hanging from the rafters, wooden picnic tables covered with red-and-white-checkered tablecloths, an old woodstove, and the smell of maple syrup hanging warmly in the air. Feast on homemade pancakes, corn fritters, and waffles, all served with the sweet golden liquid. Large windows offer spectacular vistas of the surrounding forests. Gould's is open daily March and April (sugaring season) and September and October (leaf-peeping season).

In *Charlemont, Zoar Outdoors,* handily facing the Mohawk Trail (Route 2) on one side and the Deerfield River on the other, rents kayaks, gives kayak lessons, and offers guided kayak and river-rafting trips. Two-day clinics start at $245 with graded sessions designed for beginners as well as those who need to polish their paddling skills. Zoar Gap, on the Deerfield River, is ideal for beginning and intermediate rafters, with class II and III rapids. Trips include all equipment and a riverbank picnic lunch, for $79 midweek, $87 weekends. Check the Web site at www.zoaroutdoor.com or call (800) 532–7483.

Hill Towns

Driving through the "hill towns" of Franklin County is pure pleasure. These tiny villages are some of the most rural and traditional in all of New England. In particular, take Route 112 south from Route 9 through *the Worthingtons:* Worthington Corners, Worthington Center, and South Worthington. As it heads south from Route 9, Route 112 is barely one lane wide and is lined with thick-trunked trees that grow right out to the edge of the road. Sheep graze, and farmers harrow their fields. You'll pass a pick-your-own blueberry farm, Cumworth Farm. At Worthington Corners there's an old-fashioned general store, the Worthington Corners Grocery.

A turnoff from Route 112 leads you to the **William Cullen Bryant Homestead** (413–634–2244) in Cummington, boyhood and country home of the famous poet and *New York Evening Post* editor. This home was a splendid retreat for Bryant, and he derived much inspiration for his poetry here. Handsome, tall maples line the long drive up to the rambling, twenty-three-room white house with open-air porches and gambrel roof. The house commands superb views of the countryside and is at such a high remove that it seems to float in its own green sea. In Bryant's day, the homestead was very much a working farm, with productive orchards and fields. The house is filled with Bryant's belongings and with souvenirs of his travels around the world. Among them are his Empire canopied, four-poster maple bed, a fit bed for a poet. His straw hat for berry picking still rests on a corner of his oak desk in the study, which has a view of the Hampshire Hills in the distance. The Bryant Homestead is open from Friday to Sunday and holidays late June through Labor Day and only on weekends between Labor Day and Columbus Day; hours are 1:00 to 5:00 P.M. Admission is $5.00 for adults and $2.50 for children. The grounds are open year-round, free of charge.

The most rugged spot in the hill towns is **Chesterfield Gorge.** A deep canyon carved into sheer granite cliffs, the gorge courses with tumbling white water. Looking down into its swirling depths is a dizzying experience. You can also see the crumbling stone remnants of a bridge over the gorge, built in 1739, a part of the Boston-to-Albany Post Road. Thick forests of pine and hemlock shelter picnic tables here and there. The gorge is a Trustees of Reservations property; call (413) 684–0148 or (413) 298–3239 for information. There is a $2.00 fee for adult visitors.

The Five-College Area

Naturally enough, there are five college campuses here: Mount Holyoke, Smith, Hampshire, Amherst, and the University of Massachusetts. The campuses all have interesting museums, and the lively student life means there are plenty of restaurants, shops, and arts events. You can start in the small towns north of Amherst and Northampton and work your way south through the Connecticut River Valley, passing by farmland and old tobacco barns.

In a bookstore don't you always want to sit down and read? At the **Montague Book Mill,** you can. This unique spot is a book lover's paradise. It's housed in an 1834 grain mill overlooking the Sawmill River, a building that has also done duty as a manufacturer of industrial machinery. The mill's old wooden floors, massive ceiling beams, and floor-to-ceiling windows have been retained, and now they hold three floors of used and discount books on every conceivable subject. Comfortable old chairs have been placed in reading nooks overlooking the river and a waterfall. A cafe serves coffee, baked goods, soups, and sandwiches, as does an outdoor deck in season. The Book Mill hosts jazz, folk, and classical-music concerts in its basement. Off Route 63 on Greenfield Road in Montague Center, the Book Mill is open daily from 10:00 A.M. to 6:00 P.M., until 8:00 P.M. Thursday through Saturday. Call (413) 367–9206.

For a truly wild ride, drive on the aptly named ***Rattlesnake Gutter Road.*** To get there, follow the sign for Rattlesnake Gutter Road at the intersection of Dudleyville, North Leverett, and Church Roads in ***North Leverett.*** Rattlesnake Gutter Road is a dirt road that climbs more than 1.5 miles through a steep, densely wooded ravine. The road falls away sharply on either side, almost 100 feet down. Tangles of massive boulders and the huge, moss-covered trunks of fallen trees line the sides of the ravine. The temperature drops noticeably as you drive in the dark shadow of looming pines.

You might think a small farming town an unlikely place for a major monument to world peace. But in the woods of North Leverett stands the three-story ***Peace Pagoda,*** built by Buddhist monks and nuns. Its white dome has a gold statue with a shrine underneath on each of three sides, and there are stairs for a closer view. The grounds hold a small landscaped pond with goldfish. The Buddhists are building a large temple to serve as an altar and resi-

dence for the pagoda's caretakers. From the height of this hill, you can see for miles, as far as the Berkshire Hills. To get to the Peace Pagoda, from Moore's Corners in the center of North Leverett, go about 2 miles on North Leverett Road. Opposite the North Leverett Baptist Church, turn left onto Cave Hill Road. Go 0.9 of a mile until you see a tiny white sign for the Peace Pagoda, then turn left onto an unmarked dirt road that leads to a small parking area.

Pig Out in Style announces the billboard outside ***Bub's Bar-B-Q*** on Route 116 in Sunderland. This low-lying shack serves some of the best southern-style

Peace Pagoda, North Leverett

barbecue you'll find anywhere in New England: barbecued chicken, ribs, pulled pork, and burgers, with a secret sauce and an "unlimited" menu of side dishes, including hickory-smoked potatoes, collard greens, spicy dirty rice, ranch beans, orange-glazed sweet potatoes, black-eyed-pea salad, dill potato salad, and bread and butter. Combo dinners range from $10.95 to $14.95. Picnic tables serve as seating, and rolls of paper towels on each one serve as napkins. Bub's is open daily mid-afternoon to mid-evening plus for lunch on weekends. It's closed Mondays Labor Day to Memorial Day; www.bubsbbq.com.

"Because I could not stop for Death, / He kindly stopped for me— / The Carriage held but just Ourselves / And Immortality." These lines were written by "the Belle of Amherst"—poet Emily Dickinson, who spent her whole life here. At the **Emily Dickinson Museum: The Homestead and The Evergreens,** you can see where she lived and worked. The brick mansion with white trim is so heavily shaded by thick-growing trees that it looks as secretive as Emily herself. The poet lived a strange, reclusive life, spending most of her time at home. In her later years she dressed all in white and never left the house. Still, she wrote powerfully of life and death, love and nature. Unknown and virtually unpublished in her lifetime, she became one of America's most famous poets after her death.

Although most of the house is an Amherst College faculty home, you can see several rooms. In the poet's spare, simple bedroom are the sleigh bed she slept in and one of the white dresses she wore. The house is at 280 Main Street. Tours now include the Evergreens, the home of Dickinson's brother's family, and the grounds of the homes. The museum is open for guided tours only, and it's a good idea to call ahead to confirm the schedule. Summer hours are Wednesday through Saturday 10:00 A.M. to 5:00 P.M., Sunday 1:00 to 5:00 P.M. (last tour starting at 4:00 P.M.); the rest of the year, hours and days are reduced. Closed mid-December through February. Call (413) 542–8161 or visit www.emilydickinsonmuseum.org. Admission is $8.00 for adults, $7.00 for seniors and college students, and $5.00 for children ages six through eighteen.

Northampton's Main Street bustles with activity day and night, and this is where you'll find yourself spending most of your time.

At the **Smith College Museum of Art,** on Elm Street at Bedford Terrace, you'll find more than 20,000 works, spanning human artistry from the shadows of antiquity to the present. American and European painting of the nineteenth and twentieth centuries are particularly strong. Gallery talks by art experts, guided tours of the collections, lectures, films, and chamber music concerts keep the museum's schedule filled with art-related activities. The museum is open Tuesday through Saturday from 10:00 A.M. to 4:00 P.M. and Sunday from 12:00 to 4:00 P.M. Admission is $5.00 for adults, $4.00 for seniors, $3.00 for students, and $2.00 for children ages six to twelve; (413) 585–2760. Current exhibit information is available at www.smith.edu/artmuseum.

Right next door to the museum, at 150 Main Street, ***Thorne's Market-place*** (413–584–5582; www.thornesmarketplace.com) is where everybody goes, sooner or later. A century-old office building that's been made over into four floors of boutiques, the Thorne's complex still looks interestingly old. Here, you'll find half the population of Northampton, as well as gourmet kitchen items, arts and crafts, clothes, toys, and home goods.

Main Street is so loaded with restaurants that it's hard to choose among them. ***Spoleto*** concentrates on fine Italian cuisine. The menu includes pasta, seafood, meats, and vegetarian entrees. Offerings might include fettuccine with wild mushrooms and chicken or bistro chicken rollatini with Tuscan sausage and broccoli rabe in a tomato, fennel, wild mushroom marsala sauce. A phyllo ravioli appetizer is filled with smoked chicken, spinach, and goat cheese, which create a unique combination of flavors. Most entrees are $15 to $20. Spoleto is open for dinner every evening (reservations suggested Sunday through Thursday) and for brunch on Sunday, at 50 Main Street, Northampton; (413) 586–6313.

Paul and Elizabeth's, in Thorne's Market (413–584–4832), is veggie paradise, although they also serve daily specials with organic meat and several with fish, too. Their soups are heavenly, and a big bowl of soup with one or two of their fluffy, wheaty rolls makes a highly satisfying meal. They cook vegetarian dishes the right way—they're filling and flavorful, not drenched in cheese. The restaurant's decor is equally pleasing, with exposed brick and old wood, stained-glass panels and artisan ceramics as decoration on the walls.

Calvin Coolidge was an Amherst grad and lived many years in Northampton, up until his death in 1933. Before becoming president, he practiced law and served as Northampton mayor and Massachusetts governor. A collection of his personal mementos, family photos, and souvenirs of office is exhibited in the ***Calvin Coolidge Memorial Room*** in the Forbes Library. Amid these family memorabilia, "Silent Cal" seems a little more human. Although the official White House oil portraits of Coolidge and his wife hang on the wall, there are also many black-and-white photos of the Coolidges, who had two sons, one of whom died very young. Also in the collection is a full Indian feather headdress that a descendant of Sitting Bull gave to Coolidge in the Black Hills of South Dakota, where Coolidge kept a summer White House. Although many constituents thought he looked pretty funny in the headdress, Coolidge was not too proud to be photographed wearing it. The library is located at 20 West Street; the memorial room is open variable hours depending on staffing; call to make an appointment: (413) 587–1014.

While all the campuses have their attractions, one of the nicest places to visit is the *Lyman Plant House* at Smith College in Northampton. It gives you a real lift no matter what the season to walk into these labyrinthine greenhouses and smell the potting soil and growing things. Besides scads of common plants like begonias and African violets, the thirteen greenhouses hold tropical plants from Africa, cacti from the Peruvian desert, and tree ferns from Tasmania—3,500 species in all. Outdoor gardens and an arboretum surround the 1890s greenhouses. They're open daily from 8:30 A.M. to 4:00 P.M.; call (413) 585–2740.

The *Arcadia Nature Center and Wildlife Sanctuary* is a pleasant place to spend a morning or an afternoon. Located on an ancient oxbow of the Connecticut River, it has trails leading through floodplain forest, meadowland, and marsh, with an observation tower overlooking it. All kinds of programs are offered, including canoe excursions on the Connecticut River, hawk watches, and wildflower walks. The sanctuary is at 127 Combs Road in Easthampton, south of Northampton on Route 10. Admission is $4.00 for adults and $3.00 for children ages three through twelve. The sanctuary is open Monday through Friday 9:00 A.M. to 3:00 P.M.; trails open dawn to dusk daily. Call (413) 584–3009.

A favored student eatery (because it's so cheap) is the *Miss Florence Diner* on North Main Street (west of Northampton on Route 9) in Florence. This is an authentic vintage diner, with bright yellow sides lettered in red art deco style, green awnings, and glass-block corners. Yankee pot roast, meat loaf, or baked stuffed peppers usually won't set you back much more than $5.00.

The town of *Williamsburg,* whose white nineteenth-century buildings range attractively along Route 9, has two points of interest. The first you'll come to is the *Williamsburg General Store.* This nineteenth-century store, in a historic wooden building with a columned porch, lives up to a general store's expectation of being a purveyor of almost everything. In its two cramped rooms, there's barely room for the merchandise, let alone the customers. The store sells everything from dozens of kitchen gadgets to candy and baked goods, children's books, Christmas items, soaps and shampoos, candles, and jewelry. It's a fun place to browse and shop.

Continuing west on Route 9 brings you to the *Williamsburg Blacksmiths,* where wrought iron has been crafted since the late 1800s in the same building. A small showroom sells its wares: hooks and hinges, fireplace tools, lamp stands, even bedsteads, as well as some pewter, tin, and brass pieces. The shop gives blacksmithing demonstrations on weekends near Columbus Day. Call (413) 268–7341.

The Quabbin Reservoir

If you head east out of Amherst on Route 9, the road will bring you to the **Quabbin Reservoir,** a 55,000-acre watershed that supplies greater Boston's drinking water. This vast tract also offers splendid recreation: fishing, hiking from most of its fifty-two gates, biking, and picnicking. There's a spectacular array of wildlife in its thick woods, from white-tailed deer and beaver to wild turkeys and hawks. The Quabbin is also the best place in Massachusetts to see bald eagles, which were reestablished here as a nesting species in the state, as were wild loons.

A sign on Route 9 marks **Quabbin Park,** a small peninsula of the reservoir that has a lookout tower, a dam, and a visitor center. In the visitor center, a colored board shows the serpentine journey the water takes from the Quabbin to Boston. To create the reservoir, four towns in the Swift River Valley were flooded in 1939; on display are aerial photos taken of those towns in 1930. A video presents oral histories of former town residents. (Mementos from the four towns are preserved up the road a piece at the Swift River Valley Historical Society, which is discussed later in this chapter.) The **Quabbin Park Cemetery** is where all the graves of the Swift River Valley were moved, some dating back to colonial times. The visitor center also has trail maps, as well as books and brochures on the Quabbin. Located at 485 Ware Road in Belchertown, the visitor center is open daily year-round, from 9:00 A.M. to 4:30 P.M.; (413) 323–7221.

Route 9 intersects U.S. Route 202, which winds around the western half of the reservoir and offers several interesting stops along the way. Off US 202 is **Hamilton Orchards** in New Salem (978–544–6867), a family operation since the 1920s. There are all kinds of treats and activities here. You can pick your own apples, raspberries, and blueberries or watch the making of cider or maple syrup in season. A unique "doughnut robot" turns out cider doughnuts by the dozens. In the barn and shop, the irresistible smells of warm apple pie and turnovers waft through the air. There are free apples for "kids of all ages" and a cafeteria serving apple dumplings, baked beans, hot dogs, and sundaes. The cafe is a cheery, hearty place, with a woodstove, apple-print tablecloths, and a wall of windows looking out on a clean sweep of mountain and forest. A nature trail and small animals for children to pet round out the farm, which is open only on weekends through the harvest season.

If a visit to the Quabbin Reservoir whetted your curiosity about the four towns flooded to create it, you can find out about them at the **Swift River Valley Historical Society** (978–544–6882), on Elm Street off US 202. Three small buildings cluster together in a clearing: a white, early-nineteenth-century house, a church, and a red barn, all holding memorabilia from the four towns—Greenwich, Dana, Prescott, and Enfield. The church originally stood in North Prescott.

The four towns were officially declared out of existence in 1938. All 2,500 residents had to leave, and their homes were razed or relocated, businesses torn down, and cemeteries dug up. Nothing remained but old lanes and cellar holes. Among items saved by the historical society are a handwoven palm-leaf hat made in Dana, hatmaking having been one of its principal industries, in addition to wedding gowns, lace handkerchiefs, cameos, and jewelry. The historical-society buildings are open Wednesday and Sunday in July and August and only on Sunday from September to mid-October. Hours are 2:00 to 4:00 P.M., and admission is $2.00. We recommend you call ahead to confirm hours.

In the nineteenth century, the town of **Orange** was a hive of industry. Like a miniature Lowell, it was laced with canals and brick factories and mills. Many mementos of this industrial past are kept at the **Orange Historical Society,** at 41 North Main Street. The museum is in a large Victorian home that seems to ramble on forever. It was built in 1867 for Stephen French, cofounder of the first sewing-machine company, the New Home Sewing Machine Company of Orange. A handful of New Home sewing machines, elaborately painted and housed in solid oak cabinets, are on exhibit.

By 1832, Orange had a wooden-pail factory, a carding mill, a sawmill, a grist-mill, a blacksmith, tanneries, a wheelwright and carriage shop, and a scythe factory. Orange is also where Minute Tapioca was invented, in 1894. The museum has a coffee grinder that was used in the first production of tapioca and has pictures of the tapioca plant and vintage ads for the product. At the turn of the twentieth century, Orange made Grout Steam Cars, steam-powered vehicles that started with a match and won prizes for hill climbing, speed, and endurance all over the world; on display at the museum is a 1904 Grout Steam Car.

Besides these hallmarks of industry, the museum holds large and varied collections of decorative arts and household memorabilia too numerous to list completely. They include china, pewter, and porcelain; dolls and dollhouses; antique iron cookware; hats, shoes, and jewelry; and military memorabilia. A barn houses antique fire vehicles, old plows and farm tools, and a 1915 World War I caisson. The museum is open from 2:00 to 4:00 P.M. Sunday and Wednesday, June through August; admission is $2.00. For information call (978) 544–6286.

On US 202 in Orange, the **202 Grill and Restaurant** is an attractive, family-owned spot that welcomes families. Daily lunch specials are inexpensive, and they serve everything from sandwiches and burgers to a complete dinner. Ask for your sandwich on homemade oatmeal or buttermilk bread or on rosemary focaccia. The 202 is open seven days a week 6:00 A.M. to 9:00 P.M., (978) 544–0990.

Routes 2 and 2A lead east to the workaday town of **Athol.** Leave Athol heading northeast, following Crescent Street to Chestnut Hill Road, on the way to Royalston, and you will eventually cross a stone bridge and see the trail leading to **Doane's Falls.** If the water here only knew it was headed for the endless eddies in Tully Dam below, it might not be in such a hurry to rush over the series of abrupt ledges that make up this dramatic 200-foot waterfall. As you head down the trail alongside the falls, you will pass the foundation stones of mills that used power from the rushing waters to grind grain, saw lumber, process cloth, and make wooden buckets from 1753 into the 1800s. Be careful here any time but especially in wet weather or in the spring. The falls have been left in their natural state, without fences and restraining rails, by the Trustees of Reservations, which owns the property.

The unnumbered road leads on uphill to the lovely village of **Royalston,** a cluster of stately old homes and meeting houses around a wide green. From Route 68, between the village and its intersection with Route 32, Falls Road heads north, diminishing as it goes. Those without four-wheel drive should stop at the end of the town-maintained road (a sign marks this point) because a serious washout is ahead, and on a hill where backing out or parking is quite difficult. Follow the road on foot to the trailhead for **Royalston Falls,** about fifteen to twenty minutes from your car. The trail through the woods is another half-mile; you will hear the falls on its 70-foot drop before you see it. This falls has a fence along its precipitous brink. You can also reach the falls from Route 32, north of its intersection with Route 68, from the Newton Cemetery. The sign for this trail is all but hidden on the east side of the winding road, and although the walk to the falls is shorter from here, the climb back out will make you wish for the longer, but kinder and gentler, route from the other side.

Between Doane's Falls and Route 32 are the waters of the impoundment for Tully Dam and the camping area and recreation area of the U.S. Army Corps of Engineers at **Tully Lake.** Created by the damming of the Tully River and its tributaries, the project has protected the city of Athol from serious flooding since 1947. In the spring of 1987 alone, the dam prevented more than $3 million in damages downstream. The added benefit is a fine recreational area for the public to enjoy.

A picnic area is on the east side of Route 32 north of the dam, with fireplaces and a put-in for boats, canoes, and kayaks, which can be rented on-site. To get to the camping area, which is on the other side of the lake, take Doane Hill Road from Athol Road (Chestnut Hill Road in Athol) or from Route 32 on the west side of the lake. Camping is at twenty-four primitive walk-in sites.

A hiking trail a short distance east of the campground road runs from Doane Hill Road north along the impounded waters of the Tully River to Spirit

Falls. This trail is part of the 18-mile **Tully Trail** that starts here on Doane Hill Road and travels north past Spirit Falls and into Royalston to Royalston Falls. You'll have to leave a car at the end of the trail or have someone meet you there, since it's linear, not a loop. Another nice walk is the 4.3-mile **Tully Lake Trail**, a walk in the woods all the way around the lake. Pick up a trail map at the recreation area. Tully Lake Park Office is at 2 Athol-Richmond Road (Route 32), Athol; (978) 249–9150; www.nae.usace.army.mil/recreati/tul/tulhome.htm. Tully Lake Campground is managed by the Trustees of Reservations, (978) 249–4957 in season, or (978) 248–9455.

Springfield and Holyoke

I-91 goes bombing right through the heart of these two busy cities. It's hard to find your way around here, but do take the trouble, because you'll be well rewarded. For travel information contact the Greater Springfield Convention and Visitors Bureau, 34 Boland Way at Baystate West, Springfield 01103; (413) 787–1548; www.valleyvisitor.com.

The **Hadley Farm Museum** is a delightful assemblage of the implements and daily objects of early rural living. From a well-preserved Concord Coach and fully equipped peddler's wagon to cranberry rakes and a tool used to remove apples from the throats of cows, every detail of farm and small town life is here. The barn in which all this is displayed, a three-story estate barn built in 1782, is as interesting as its contents. Many of the implements highlight the early agriculture of the valley—a broom-making machine recalls the town's prominence as a grower of broomcorn. You can browse through the museum at your own pace Wednesday through Saturday 11:00 A.M. to 4:00 P.M. or Sunday 1:00 to 4:00 P.M., May through October. Admission is free, but donations of $2.00 per person are welcome. It's at 147 Russell Street (Route 9), Hadley; (413) 584–3120.

The world's only "dinosaur quarry," **Nash Dinosaur Land**, is in South Hadley, just outside Holyoke. Although scientists recoil in horror at the idea, entrepreneur Carlton Nash made a fifty-year business of selling real, two-hundred-million-year-old dinosaur tracks found here by a local farmer in 1802. Nash sold the tracks to such celebrities as the late General George S. Patton, at prices varying according to size and rarity, up to thousands of dollars. What do you do with dinosaur tracks? Use them as paperweights, edge your pool or garden with them, keep them as conversation pieces. Now run by Carlton's son, Cornell, the charmingly dated Nash Dinosaur Land is gradually being updated to the point of even being educational. It is on Route 116 and open approximately Memorial Day "until the snow gets us," daily. It's best to call ahead if you'll be going out of your way; (413) 467–9566. Adults $3.00; children $1.50. The quarry and the museum are closed between Christmas and March.

The next stop is **Holyoke Heritage State Park** (413–534–1723), which colorfully chronicles the industrial history of **Holyoke.** In the nineteenth century, the city built a three-level canal system 4.5 miles long to channel Connecticut River water, first to its cotton mills and later to its paper mills. Holyoke once had so many paper mills—some two dozen—that it was known as "Paper City" and made a great deal of the world's fine writing papers. You'll find lots of memorabilia of city residents, papermaking machinery, and a slide show about the industrial and social history of Holyoke. A train with vintage 1920s passenger cars occasionally runs through the park and through town. (Call for the schedule.) A children's museum and merry-go-round make the park kid-friendly. The landscaped grounds, which overlook a canal and several century-old redbrick mill buildings, are also a fine spot for a picnic. The park is located at 221 Appleton Street. Visitor center hours are 10:00 A.M. to 4:00 P.M. Tuesday through Sunday.

yikes!dinosaurs!

The Connecticut Valley has yielded some of the most interesting of New England's prehistoric animal finds. The first of which was in 1865, when a worker noticed strange three-toed imprints in sandstone slabs quarried in Montague, which he was laying for a walkway.

A site in Gill and a third near Turners Falls added more, and further finds were made later in Northampton. In addition to Nash's, dino-searchers will want to visit the Springfield Science Museum, which has a life-size replica of Tyrannosaurus rex and a dinosaur footprint the kids can climb into; (413) 263–6800.

Adjacent to the park is the **Volleyball Hall of Fame** (413–536–0926), a tribute to the fact that volleyball was invented in Holyoke in 1895. Boldly painted, contemporary exhibits explain that volleyball was invented by a local YMCA physical-education director who used a tennis net and the inside of a basketball and called his new game "mintonette." The museum, at 444 Dwight Street, is open Tuesday through Sunday from noon to 4:30 P.M. Admission is $3.50 for adults, $2.50 for seniors and children ages six through seventeen.

A bright jewel that you should not overlook in Holyoke is the **Wistariaburst Museum,** an elegant Victorian mansion that was the home of a wealthy silk manufacturer, William Skinner, and his family. Lavishly decorated with stained glass, parquet floors, coffered ceilings, and a marble lobby, the home also holds many period furnishings and paintings. A Renaissance-style music hall is a frequent venue for concerts, as this fine mansion serves as a cultural center for the city.

Also on the grounds are landscaped gardens and a carriage house containing North American Indian and natural-history exhibits. Wistariahurst is at 238 Cabot Street in Holyoke; call (413) 322–5660. Admission is $5.00 for adults, $3.00 for seniors, and free for children under age twelve with an adult. Hours are from noon to 4:00 P.M. Saturday through Monday.

The cultural centerpiece of downtown **Springfield** comprises four important museums, all handily arranged in a cluster off State Street and Chestnut Avenue and called the **Springfield Museum Quadrangle.** There are not one but two major art museums. The **George Walter Vincent Smith Art Museum** houses the collection of the Victorian gentleman it's named after, who collected what he liked: Japanese arms, Chinese cloisonné, and Oriental jades, textiles, and ceramics. The **Museum of Fine Arts** holds twenty centuries of art, including impressionist, expressionist, and early European paintings, and works by Helen Frankenthaler and Georgia O'Keeffe. More fun for children is the **Science Museum,** which invites children to touch many exhibits and also has a planetarium. At the **Connecticut Valley Historical Museum** you can see many fine decorative artworks made by Connecticut River Valley residents, including pewter, silver, furniture, and the work of itinerant portrait painters. Early valley life is illustrated by a colonial kitchen, a Federal dining room, and two nineteenth-century tavern rooms brought here. Hours to all but the Science Museum are rather limited due to budget cuts—Tuesday through Sunday, 11:00 A.M. to 4:00 P.M.; the Science Museum is open the same days, 10:00 A.M. to 5:00 P.M. These limited hours make it a real race to see the art museums on the same day as the Historical Museum or Science Museum. We'd rank the Smith collections as the most intriguing, if you have to choose. Admission is $10.00 for adults, $7.00 for seniors and college students with an ID, and $5.00 for children ages six to seventeen. For information call the Springfield Library and Museums Association at (413) 263–6800 or (800) 625–7338; www.springfieldmuseums.org.

The imaginative storyteller Theodor Seuss Geisel grew up in Springfield, and the inspiration for his famous Mulberry Street was the actual street of that name. You, too, can see it on Mulberry Street, and you can visit the **Dr. Seuss National Memorial,** at the Quadrangle. This sculpture park captures the wonderful absurdities of this gifted children's author in a series of bronze statues of his creations, one of which is 14 feet tall; www.catinthehat.org.

In the late nineteenth century, Springfield had so many fine Victorian homes set on tree-lined streets that it earned the nickname "City of Homes." Hundreds of these houses still stand, and two areas are now historic districts. One of them, the **McKnight District,** has almost 900 Victorian houses built between 1870 and 1900. Huge, rambling affairs, they have wide porches and, often, carriage houses and stables. The McKnight District centers on Worthington Street.

The **Student Prince and Fort Restaurant,** at 8 Fort Street (413–734–7475), has been a much-loved local institution since 1935. Its Old World German feeling is created by stained-glass windows, wood-paneled booths, and a priceless collection of some 1,500 antique beer steins lining the shelves of its dining-room walls. Some steins are one of a kind; one once belonged to a Russian czar. The stained-glass windows show classic scenes of Springfield and Germany.

The German and American menu lists such specialties as oxtail soup, hasenpfeffer, jaeger schnitzel, and sauerbraten. You'll find all kinds of German beers on draft, as well as many wines and European liqueurs. To add to the fun, the restaurant throws festivals several times a year. In February, a Game Fest features pheasant, buffalo, venison, and bear. A May Wine Fest and an Oktoberfest are also popular. And at Christmastime, the Fort puts up decorations and brings in carolers.

Even if you're not a military buff, you'll find the **Springfield Armory National Historic Site** an interesting place. George Washington chose Springfield as the site for a national arsenal in 1794. The small arms and weapons made there played a major role in American wars thereafter. On and around the armory green stand a number of original buildings, including the Main Arsenal, the Commanding Officer's Quarters, and the Master Armorer's House.

The weapons housed in the Main Arsenal form the world's largest collection of small arms. Here you can see the Springfield rifle used in World War I and the famous M-1 rifle used by millions of servicemen in World War II. The armory is located at One Armory Square and is open in summer Tuesday through Sunday from 10:00 A.M. to 5:00 P.M.; the rest of the year it is closed on Sunday. Call (413) 734–8551. There is no charge for admission.

Springfield is also the birthplace of the motorcycle—invented in 1901 when bicycle-racing champion George Hendee teamed up with C. Oscar Hedstrom to open the Indian Motocycle Manufacturing Company (they dropped the *r* as an advertising ploy). The famous Indian Motocycle the company produced was known worldwide for quality and beauty. In World War I, more than half the army motorcycles in use were Indians. In its heyday, the company also made airplane engines, bicycles, and outboard motors. You can see a large collection of Indian Motocycles, toy motorcycles, and memorabilia at the **Indian Motocycle Museum,** at 33 Hendee Street (413–737–2624). An annual Indian Day rally attracts proud Indian owners from all over the country. The museum is open from 10:00 A.M. to 5:00 P.M. daily; admission is $5.00 for adults. Children up to age twelve are admitted free.

Although not so well known as Old Sturbridge Village, the ***Storrowton Village Museum*** was established much earlier. It is a collection of nine eighteenth- and nineteenth-century buildings brought here in the 1920s from all over New England and arranged like the heart of an old New England village. Besides a meetinghouse and church, you'll find a blacksmith shop, tavern, and school. Storrowton Village is on the grounds of the Eastern States Exposition, off Memorial Avenue in West Springfield; (413) 787–0136; www.thebige.com. Admission is $5.00 for adults and $3.00 for children. Tours are given from 11:00 A.M. to 3:00 P.M. Tuesday through Saturday, from mid-June through Labor Day.

Author Thornton Burgess, who wrote tales of Peter Rabbit and *Old Mother West Wind,* once lived in ***Hampden,*** southeast of Springfield. His former home can be toured and is now part of ***Laughing Brook Education Center and Wildlife Sanctuary.*** Several miles of hiking trails take you through woodlands and fields, past streams and a pond. Unfortunately, visitors seeking the northeastern species habitats exhibits will be disappointed; the Audubon Society has reduced them to a nature trail. The sanctuary is located at 789 Main Street in Hampden. Trails are open year-round Tuesday through Sunday, and Monday holidays, dawn to dusk. The Education Center is open Saturday, Sunday, and Monday holidays 12:30 to 4:00 P.M. You can tour Burgess House May through September on the third Saturday of the month from 12:30 to 4:00 P.M., or by appointment. Admission is $3.00 for adults and $2.00 for children and seniors. Call (413) 566–8034.

WORTH SEEING IN PIONEER VALLEY

Naismith Memorial Basketball Hall of Fame,
1000 West Columbus Avenue,
Springfield;
(413) 781–6500;
www.hoophall.com
A high-tech museum that's fun even if you're not a fan.

Memorial Hall Museum,
8 Memorial Street (on the campus of Deerfield Academy),
Deerfield;
(413) 774–3768.
Includes the famed door with tomahawk marks in it from the Deerfield Massacre.

More Places to Stay in Pioneer Valley

Allen House Inn,
599 Main Street,
Amherst;
(413) 253–5000.
A Victorian bed-and-breakfast decorated in Eastlake and William Morris styles, within walking distance of the center of Amherst; rates are $75 to $175.

The Lord Jeffrey Inn,
on the Common,
Amherst;
(413) 253–2576 or
(800) 742–0358;
www.lordjeffreyinn.com
A classic upscale New England inn, with rates starting below $100.

The Johnson Homestead Bed-and-Breakfast,
79 Buckland Road,
Shelburne Falls;
(413) 625–6603.
A late 1800s home, 1½ miles off Route 112, with rooms at $75 to $110, including a full country breakfast.

More Places to Eat in Pioneer Valley

!Cha Cha Cha!,
134 Main Street,
Northampton;
(413) 586–7311.
South-of-the-border favorites, plus vegetarian selections ($5.00 to $8.00), open from 11:30 A.M. to 10:00 P.M. Monday through Saturday and Sunday from noon to 9:00 P.M.

Sylvester's Restaurant & Bakery,
111 Pleasant Street,
Northampton;
(413) 586–5343.
Good hearty breakfasts and lunches at reasonable prices and a friendly staff.

The Lord Jeffrey Inn,
on the Common,
Amherst;
(413) 253–2576.
Continental classics here may include veal Madeira, braised pork tenderloin in Pernod, or chicken Dijon, many under $20.

Countree Living,
63 French King's Highway,
Millers Falls;
(413) 659–2624.
Along with old favorites—prime rib, baked stuffed shrimp, and grilled chicken—are more unusual offerings, such as fresh swordfish piccata and baked haddock topped with Maine lobster meat. Most entrees are $13 to $20. Open for lunch and dinner Tuesday through Sunday and for breakfast on weekends.

TO LEARN MORE ABOUT PIONEER VALLEY

Franklin County Chamber of Commerce,
for travel information on the Mohawk Trail and Franklin County areas,
P.O. Box 790,
395 Main Street,
Greenfield 01302;
(413) 773–5463, or (413) 773–9393 (for the visitor center);
www.co.franklin.ma.us

The Berkshires

If the crowded, manicured lawns and black tie of Tanglewood are not your style, don't despair. That kind of mannered existence centers in the Stockbridge and Lenox area of the Berkshires, where most tourists head. The rest of the Berkshires, north and south, is hidden territory, friendly and casual.

The countryside of the southern Berkshires is about as bucolic as it gets. Country roads disappear into the trees; small villages with white-steepled churches appear at rare intervals among the fields and meadows of rural farmland. Not a few artists and craftspeople have chosen this lovely hinterland for their home.

Almost no one thinks of heading north from Tanglewood. But if you do, you'll find some splendid natural wonders and old mill towns with a patina of industrial history. And your travels there will be wonderfully uncrowded.

Still, the central Berkshires is no place to sneeze at. It's here that world-famous cultural sophistication and scenic beauty come together in a unique amalgam, an amalgam you won't find anywhere else in the state. Acres of greenery and stately mountains embrace dance and theater festivals and the summer home of the Boston Symphony Orchestra. The inspiring beauty of the mountains attracted Nathaniel Hawthorne,

THE BERKSHIRES

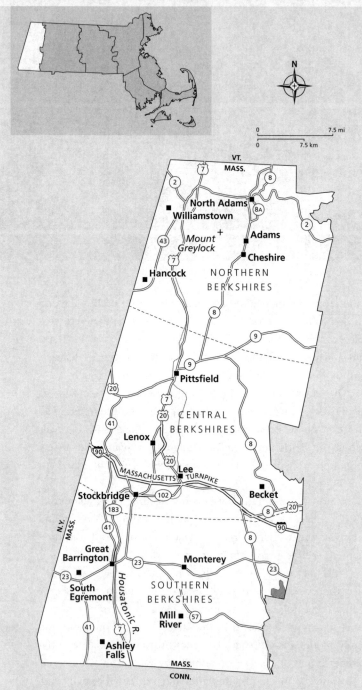

N

0   7.5 mi
0   7.5 km

VT.
MASS.

North Adams
Williamstown

Mount
Greylock

Adams

Cheshire

Hancock

NORTHERN
BERKSHIRES

Pittsfield

CENTRAL
BERKSHIRES

Lenox

Lee

MASSACHUSETTS TURNPIKE

Stockbridge

Becket

N.Y.
MASS.

Great
Barrington

Monterey

South
Egremont

SOUTHERN
BERKSHIRES

Mill
River

Housatonic R.

Ashley
Falls

MASS.
CONN.

Herman Melville, Edith Wharton, William Cullen Bryant, and Henry James. They in turn attracted the wealthy, who found it chic to build enormous summer "cottages" here in the Gilded Age.

Southern Berkshires

Winding country roads make it impossible not to double back on your tracks around here, but you won't mind in this scenic New England of yesteryear, composed of farms, ponds, meadows of Queen Anne's lace, and pastures full of cows. Follow the narrow Tyringham-Monterey Road from Route 102 in Lee, and you'll come to a little thatched cottage, densely shadowed by a grove of trees, that looks for all the world exactly like the fairy-tale house of Hansel and Gretel. Grottoes of stone reach up the walls to the rolling curves of its roof. *Santarella* belonged to the late sculptor Sir Henry Kitson, who used it as his studio. Kitson sculpted the *Minute Man* at Lexington and also the *Pilgrim Maid* at Plymouth. Behind the cottage are two improbable round tower structures with witch-hat roofs. No longer open to the public inside, a quick peek is still allowed—or indulge in a vacation rental and live there yourself (413–243–2819 for information).

North of Monterey, *Tyringham* is a pretty town with a number of very old homes and farmhouses dating from the mid-1700s. But be very careful to travel well under the posted speed limit as you go through the village, since there is usually an officer waiting at this notorious speed trap.

A little farther south on the Tyringham-Monterey Road, you come to a dirt road on the right called Art School Road. It leads to the historic *Bidwell House,* high on a hill in the forest. In a region not overflowing with historic houses, this one is a real jewel.

Santarella

AUTHORS' FAVORITES IN THE BERKSHIRES

Naumkeag	Hancock Shaker Village
Chesterwood	Bash Bish Falls

The Reverend Adonijah Bidwell built the house around 1750, soon after he came to Monterey to set up a church. The luxury of this white Georgian saltbox house is quite a surprise to those of us expecting ascetic surroundings. Son of a wealthy merchant, Reverend Bidwell furnished his house with nothing but the best: elegantly carved paneling, beautiful colors of cranberry and blue, and two beehive ovens. Among the fine goods are imported gold and embroidered fabrics, patterned carpets, canopied four-posters, redware, pewter, English delft china, and six punch bowls. Listed on the National Register of Historic Places, the house was opened to the public in 1990. Hours are 11:00 A.M. to 4:00 P.M. Thursday through Monday, Memorial Day through mid-October. Admission is $6.00 for adults, $5.00 for seniors and students, and $2.00 for those seventeen and under. Call (413) 528–6888 for information.

Also on Art School Road you'll find *Joyous Spring Pottery,* a unique, one-man gallery. Many pairs of visitors' shoes sit on the deck outside the glass doors, removed in honor of the Japanese-style salon. Owner Michael Marcus works in a most unusual vein, an ancient Japanese technique called *yakishime,* which he studied in Japan; only a handful of craftspeople in this country know it. Rather than using glazes, this method lets molten ash from a wood-fired kiln create random patterns in tans, browns, pale yellows, and siennas. Marcus built his own Japanese-style, multichambered kiln to get these results. His showroom is filled with many curved and rounded pieces based on such traditional forms as sake bottles, sushi plates, and tea ceremony pieces. Although this pottery is expensive, it's also exquisite. The gallery is open from 10:00 A.M. to 5:00 P.M. daily in summer and by appointment from November to Memorial Day; call (413) 528–4115.

A few miles down the road, a right-hand fork off the Tyringham-Monterey Road turns into the Monterey Road, which, naturally enough, brings you into tiny *Monterey.* The center of town, on Route 23, is the *Monterey General Store,* right next door to the post office. The store's white-columned porch shelters two wooden benches and a sign listing the goods of 1780, when the store was established: spices, molasses, beeswax, hops, tinware, burlap, awls, castor oil, seeds, and rock candy, among others. Inside is more modern merchandise, as well as a small coffee shop that is a popular gathering place for socializing.

One of the best goat cheeses is produced right in Monterey: Monterey Chèvre, made at **Rawson Brook Farm** (413–528–2138). Wayne Dunlop and Susan Sellew like living off the land in a simple way on a farm. They keep a herd of French and American Alpine goats, with their names printed on green collar tags—Vanilla, Azaline, Anisette, and Mocha, for example. You are welcome to visit the farm and see the pretty goats out in the fields. You can watch them being milked in the "milk parlor" from April 1 through November 1, around 5:00 P.M. Five kinds of chèvre are sold from a tall, steel refrigerator in the milking parlor: plain chèvre, chèvre with chives and garlic, chèvre with no salt, chèvre with thyme and olive oil, and peppered logs of chèvre.

To reach Rawson Brook Farm, follow the signs just past the general store, taking the first right off Route 23 heading east. Because Wayne and Susan live there, you can visit the farm almost anytime, but they ask that you not be unreasonable about this.

Head back out to Route 23 west and go a little more than 2 miles to see a unique little restaurant, the **Roadside Store and Cafe,** with two gas pumps out front. The tiny dining room, with its old wooden tables and butcher-block

ANNUAL EVENTS IN THE BERKSHIRES

MID-JULY

Berkshire Choral Festival,
Berkshire School, Route 41, Sheffield, presents a variety of music including Broadway show tunes and works by Handel and Beethoven;
(413) 229–8526 or (413) 229–1999;
www.chorus.org

EARLY AUGUST

Flower Show,
Berkshire Botanical Garden, Stockbridge;
(413) 298–3926.

LATE SEPTEMBER

Autumn Fair,
Hancock Shaker Village, Hancock, celebrating the season with Shaker skills and traditions;
(413) 443–0188.

DECEMBER 26

Holiday House Tour,
Lenox, with eight historic inns and homes open to the public on a self-guided tour;
(413) 637–3646.

DECEMBER 31

First Night festivities,
in Pittsfield ring in the New Year with a parade, music, and fireworks;
(413) 443–6501.

counter, is always crowded. A favorite haunt of locals, bicyclists, and fishermen, the Roadside Store is owned and operated by the Gould Farm Community, a working farm for people with psychiatric problems. The "guests," as they are called, live and work on the farm and wait on tables in the restaurant to gain work experience. On the breakfast menu are buckwheat pancakes that hang over the edges of a 10-inch plate, French toast (made with the farm's home-made bread and served with its own maple syrup), omelets, and lots of baked goods. For lunch, there are burgers and sandwiches. The store is open from 7:30 A.M. to 1:30 P.M. Thursday through Tuesday; call (413) 528–2633.

In the lovely little village of **New Marlborough,** south of Monterey on Route 57, is the **Old Inn on the Green** and **Gedney Farm,** Village Green; (413) 229–3131. Both on the same property, one is a former stagecoach inn and general store, the other a Percheron barn. The barn's high ceilings make the perfect setting for dramatic decor, while the inn is furnished traditionally in antiques and oriental rugs. Some of the inn's rooms have fireplaces.

West of New Marlborough, tiny **Mill River** takes its name from the many paper mills here in the mid-1800s. It's no longer an industrial center; now it's just a charming village with an antique general store and town hall.

If you're in need of a quiet respite, you'll find it not far from the village. About 1 mile south of the bridge into Mill River, on the Clayton–Mill River Road, there's a sign saying **UMPACHENE FALLS.** A dirt road leads to a rushing river by a small park. The falls lie a short walk away under a mantle of pines. Large boulders offer nice vantage points to gaze at the falls and listen to the play of water falling from terrace to terrace over its half-mile course. In the pool below, small children swim in hot weather.

The southwest corner of the southern Berkshires embraces two lovely spots, **Bartholomew's Cobble** and the historic **Colonel John Ashley House,** adjoining properties of the Trustees of Reservations (413–229–8600 or 413–298–3239) in **Ashley Falls.**

The word *cobble* means rocky-topped hill—and it's a remarkable natural phenomenon. Bartholomew's Cobble is only the second National Natural Landmark to be so designated in Massachusetts (the first was Gay Head Cliffs on Martha's Vineyard). The two marble outcroppings here were formed 500 million years ago from recrystallized limestone. The limy soil nurtured many unusual ferns and other rock-dwelling plants, including maidenhair spleenwort, columbine, and harebells. Besides some fifty-three kinds of ferns, there are almost five hundred species of wildflowers and one hundred species of trees.

This sylvan setting is a wonderful place to walk, with about 6 miles of trails. The very short Eaton Trail up the cobble can be climbed in a few minutes, rewarding the climber with a peaceful view of the Housatonic River Valley and grazing cows on green meadows. Take time to visit the rustic little museum holding animal and plant specimens, along with Indian relics.

Bartholomew's Cobble's museum and visitor center are open from 9:00 A.M. to 4:30 P.M. daily; closed Sunday and Monday December through March. Admission is $4.00 for adults and $1.00 for children. The trails are open sunrise to sunset, year-round.

In colonial days, Bartholomew's Cobble was owned by Colonel John Ashley, a wealthy merchant and lawyer and the leading citizen of Sheffield. His two-story wood-frame house, built in 1735, is the oldest in Berkshire County.

As you step into the cool, dim interior of the Ashley House, the years fall away to that much more primitive time. Colonel Ashley imported craftsmen from far and wide to create intricately carved paneling and moldings, boxed ceiling beams, and, in his study, an exquisite, sunburst-topped cupboard. There's a fine collection of redware and Benningtonware in the buttery.

In his study, Colonel Ashley and a committee drafted the Sheffield Declaration of 1773, which prefigured the Declaration of Independence. It also inspired an Ashley family slave called Mum Bett to seek her freedom. With Colonel Ashley's help, she became the first freed slave in Massachusetts. The Ashley House adjoins Bartholomew's Cobble, off Route 7A in Ashley Falls, and is well marked by signs. It's open from 1:00 to 5:00 P.M. Saturday, Sunday, and holidays, from the last weekend in June through Columbus Day. Tickets cost $5.00 for adults and $3.00 for children.

Make your way west on Salisbury Road to Route 41 south to find a great base for further explorations. Housed in a renovated nineteenth-century barn, **Race Brook Lodge**—864 South Undermountain Road, Sheffield—calls itself a "chintz-free zone." The original hand-hewn beams define all its rooms, which are finished with stenciled walls and country-style comforters, rugs, and furniture. The whole effect is comfortable and casual, and rooms are quiet and private, tucked into various corners of the barn. The inn sits at the foot of Race Mountain next to a small brook, which you can hear from your window at night. One appeal of staying here is that you can hike up along the brook and pick up the Appalachian Trail where it traverses the ridge of Race Mountain. The ridge offers unparalleled views of both the Housatonic River Valley and the Hudson River. About forty-five minutes from the back door of the lodge is Race Brook Falls, a secluded spot, and the top of the ridge is about a 2.5-mile climb. The owners of Race Brook Lodge, a congenial couple who spend time with their guests, can give you information on the trails, and will loan you snowshoes for your winter hikes. Cyclists should look here for an excellent Berkshires biking map. Call (888) 725–6343 or (413) 229–2916.

Just north of Route 41, strung out along narrow and winding Route 23, **South Egremont** is like a little village lost in time. The whole downtown, including a pretty white church and town hall, is a National Historic District.

The nineteenth century lives on at the **_Gaslight Store_** (413–528–0870), where you can still buy an egg cream and purchase penny candy for a penny. An egg cream has neither egg nor cream in it but tastes delicious all the same. Like an ice-cream soda without ice cream, it's made with syrup, seltzer, and milk. The owner makes no profit on his penny candy but prices it that way anyway to keep tradition alive.

The store has been there for 150 years and still has the original marble ice-cream counter. On shelves stand antique boxes of Rinso and Ivory Snow, Royal baking powder, and Lydia Pinkham tablets, along with old-fashioned glassware. Ice-cream-parlor chairs with heart-shaped backs add to the vintage feeling, as do the red-and-white-checkered tablecloths. An antique cash register in beautiful repoussé bronze sits ready to ring up purchases.

Several doors away, **_Mom's Country Cafe_** (413–528–2414) offers down-home cheer exuded by friendly waitresses, homemade food, lace curtains, and tables made out of old sewing machine tables. Breakfast is served all day.

In distinct contrast to its rustic surroundings, **_John Andrew's_** is a gourmet restaurant to equal any in the big city. On Route 23 about 2 miles south of the Route 41 intersection, John Andrew's is a real surprise. Housed in a white colonial house, it looks cutting-edge contemporary on the inside. An artist designed its interior with deep pink sponge-painted walls, which make the dining room feel warm, and chic black wall sconces. The young and talented chef changes his eclectic menu every couple of months. You might start with an appetizer of whole roasted garlic with peasant bread, goat cheese, sundried tomatoes, and black olives, then move on to a green salad with baked buffalo mozzarella. An entree might feature tortellini with artichokes, spinach, and mascarpone; or perhaps a risotto with wild rice, portobello mushroom, potato, and grilled radicchio. Desserts are luxurious: white-chocolate raspberry tart or strawberry napoleon with crème anglaise, for example. For reservations (which are strongly advised on weekends), call (413) 528–3469.

Tucked into the very southwest corner of the state, bordering on New York, is the wildest countryside you'll encounter in the southern Berkshires. A narrow, rutted road with dizzying switchbacks dips and swoops up and down Mount Washington, winding through a towering dark forest. Long before you get to the spectacular 80-foot waterfall that barrels down the mountainside— **_Bash Bish Falls_**—you'll swear you're lost in the wilderness.

Indian legend has it that a beautiful Indian maiden, White Swan, hurled herself into the falls to her death. Two paths lead down to the falls. One is so unbelievably steep that it looks as though only world-champion rock climbers should attempt it; the other, a wide gravel path, descends to a point just above the falls. From Route 23, take Route 41 south and then make an immediate right onto Mount Washington Road. Follow signs first for Mount Washington State Forest and then for Bash Bish Falls. Call (413) 528–0330 for information.

Busy **Great Barrington** brims with restaurants, some of the nicest of them on **Railroad Street,** just off U.S. Route 7 downtown, a little enclave that also mixes in several intriguing boutiques. Among the eateries here is **Martin's** at number 49 (413–528–5455), offering all-day breakfast, blackboard specials, and homemade muffins, soups, and desserts. Open from 6:00 A.M. to 3:00 P.M. daily. Around the corner from Railroad Street, at 10 Castle Street, is the **Castle Street Cafe** (413–528–5244), a citified cafe whose sophisticated chef makes such ambitious dishes as grilled Cornish game hen marinated in garlic and herbs, and roast duck with black currants and cassis, as well as other American and continental fare. They are open for dinner only.

Our favorite of these is the **Helsinki Cafe,** hidden in the back of a building that faces onto Main Street. Cozy, noisy, and very Finnish, the cafe makes a fine art of tea, with an excellent selection and proper brewing. The food is not necessarily Scandinavian (not unlike food in Helsinki restaurants) and blends Nordic flavors with those of Eastern Europe. Think sausage platters with local sauerkraut and latkes, or tea-and-horseradish–seasoned seared salmon with dill sauce and potato strudel. Entrees are priced from $15 to $20, and daily specials include soup or salad. At lunch the menu offers sandwiches, wursts, and gravlax. Club Helsinki, adjoining the cafe, presents a year-round series of recognized artists in a small music-hall setting; (413) 528–3394.

Central Berkshires

On your way to Stockbridge, you'll see **Monument Mountain Reservation** on US 7, about 2.5 miles south of town. This mountain was the scene of what has been called the world's most famous literary picnic. Herman Melville, Nathaniel Hawthorne, and Oliver Wendell Holmes climbed it on an August day in 1850. Dressed in their frock coats, they admired the view, lunched among the rocks, and toasted William Cullen Bryant. This craggy mountain rises some 1,700 feet to wonderful scenic views. At the entrance are picnic tables shaded by pines.

In **Stockbridge,** hordes of tourists clump about the porch of the **Red Lion Inn** and congregate around the shops on Main Street. It's worth a step inside the Red Lion Inn to see its colonial-looking lobby and a grand collection of Staffordshire china lining the edge of the ceiling. Originally built as a stagecoach stop in 1773, the inn is one of the few continuously operating in New England since before 1800 and hosted five presidents in its day. It was rebuilt after a fire in 1896.

Staying at the Red Lion Inn is expensive (rooms begin at about $170 in summer, $110 in winter), as is dining there. But tucked downstairs, the *Lion's Den* pub is a cozy and inexpensive spot to grab a bite. In dramatic red-and-white surroundings, with a pressed-tin ceiling, wainscoting, and Tiffany lamps, the restaurant offers a pub menu of homemade soups and sandwiches and such daily specials as meat loaf and shepherd's pie. Call (413) 298-5545.

Right on Main Street are two attractions that most people don't pay any attention to. One is a tall stone tower, sort of Gothic-looking. It's the *Children's Chimes,* a carillon given to the town in 1878 by David Dudley Field Jr., in honor of his grandchildren. Field left money for the chimes to be played, by hand, from apple blossom time until frost.

The other site, located across the street in the town cemetery, is one of the country's most unusual family plots—the *Sedgwick Pie.* It's indeed shaped like a pie, with dozens of headstones and monuments in varying shapes and sizes placed in concentric rings, all facing toward the center. Legend has it that this design was intended to make sure the Sedgwicks saw only Sedgwicks when they woke up on Judgment Day, but that notion has been categorically denied by more than one Sedgwick. Generations of Sedgwicks have been buried in the pie, eschewing fancy coffins and wearing their pajamas. Be sure to look for the grave of Mum Bett, the slave who obtained her freedom in court with the help of an early Sedgwick. She went to work for the Sedgwick family after being freed and was so loved and admired by them that she was buried in their family plot. Her epitaph was written by one of the Sedgwick daughters. To learn the remarkable story of this former slave (yes, the North had them, too), read *More than Petticoats: Remarkable Massachusetts Women,* by Lura Seavey (The Globe Pequot Press). To see the pie, walk through the cemetery toward the right back corner.

Once you step away from Main Street, you can find many secluded areas in Stockbridge. One, the *Ice Glen,* is a great place for a walk on a hot day. The Ice Glen was carved out by a glacier that left massive boulders where the sun never reaches. It has been said that you can find ice crystals there even in summer, although it is more likely the rocks will be just moist. When you stand in front of these moss-covered stones, it's as cool as opening a refrigerator door. This mystical place used to be the site of Halloween bonfires and torch-light parades.

To reach the Ice Glen, turn onto Park Road off US 7 just south of down-town Stockbridge. Park at the end of the turnaround. Over the wooden foot-bridge, the right branch of the trail leads up to the Ice Glen, about a fifteen- to twenty-minute walk.

Just north of Main Street are yet two more inviting places. One of the most beautiful spots in town is the **Marian Center** monastery on Eden Hill, founded by an order that originated in Poland. A long drive leads up to grassy lawns surrounding the abbey and an exquisite stone chapel. The grounds are an inspiring place for a walk or picnic, and no one should miss seeing the chapel. Inside it are marvelous stained-glass windows of saints, frescoes, marble altars, gospel scenes, and a magnificent rose window. The craftsmanship of all these creations rivals that of the great cathedrals of Europe, and indeed the work was led by an Italian master stonecutter. Call (413) 298–3691.

The second inviting spot stands across from the Marian Center—**Naumkeag,** a turreted mansion designed in 1885 by Stanford White for lawyer and diplomat Joseph Choate, who served as ambassador to England. The twenty-six-room house is full of offbeat personality, as White intended it to be. Turrets and bay windows are asymmetrical and appear at odd places.

Inside and out, this Norman-style, shingled-and-gabled mansion radiates the extravagance of the Gilded Age. The spacious rooms have high ceilings and mahogany trim. A Waterford-crystal chandelier and silk-damask-patterned walls highlight the drawing room. Rare Chinese porcelains collected by Choate's daughter, Mabel, are on view, as are drawings and paintings by Choate's wife, who was an artist. An elegant, red-carpeted staircase with rope-turned balusters leads up to the seven bedrooms. President William McKinley stayed in the master guest bedroom when he visited the Choates.

On the veranda, you can admire the expansive views of the azure Berkshire Hills dropping off below you. The gardens are among the loveliest in America, graced with a topiary promenade, Venetian-style posts, a Chinese pagoda, and a linden walk archway. The most significant feature of the landscape design here is the multitiered staircase leading up a steep hillside between sheltering birches, with a fountain playing down its center. The way the garden has been designed to frame the view of the Berkshires make this among New England's finest landscaped gardens. On the upper level, near the entrance to the house, is a Japanese garden with a moon gate, added later. Naumkeag is located on Prospect Hill Road. The house and gardens are open daily Memorial through Columbus Day. Hours are 10:00 A.M. to 5:00 P.M. with the last tour beginning at 4:00 P.M. Adults and teens pay $10.00 and children ages six to twelve pay $3.00 for admission to the house and gardens—less for the gardens only. Call (413) 298–8146.

The much-loved illustrator and artist Norman Rockwell lived and painted for the last twenty-five years of his life in Stockbridge, where he was fond of using local people as models. A palatial new headquarters for the **Norman**

Rockwell Museum opened in 1993 to display the world's largest collection of his paintings. Housed in a white, New England–style building, the museum shows off early illustrations and drawings, as well as instantly recognizable *Saturday Evening Post* covers. The red studio that Rockwell fashioned out of a carriage barn has been moved to the thirty-six-acre grounds as well, so you can see his art library and easel. The attractive grounds offer scenic views of the Berkshire Hills and include a picnic spot. The museum is open daily 10:00 A.M. to 5:00 P.M. from May through October. From November through April, hours are 10:00 A.M. to 4:00 P.M. weekdays and 10:00 A.M. to 5:00 P.M. weekends and holidays. Admission in high season is $12.00 for adults, $7.00 for students with ID, and free for those eighteen and younger. For information call (413) 298–4100 or visit www.nrm.org. To get to the museum, head west on Route 102 out of town and go about half a mile south on Route 183.

About a half mile south of the Rockwell Museum on Route 183, you'll see signs for *Chesterwood,* the former summer estate of sculptor Daniel Chester French. French, who worked here for more than thirty years, was most famous for his statue of Abraham Lincoln for the Lincoln Memorial in Washington D.C., and the *Minute Man* in Concord. In his studio are the plaster "sketches" for Lincoln and for several others. This estate, on beautifully landscaped grounds, is still truly a country home, almost half a mile down a dirt road. A pair of 23-foot-tall doors and a modeling table that rolled outdoors on railroad tracks let the artist view his work in natural light and from the perspective it would later be viewed from. Chesterwood is open daily from 10:00 A.M. to 5:00 P.M. late May through October. Admission is $10.00 for adults, $5.00 for youth six through eighteen, and $9.00 for seniors; (413) 298–3579; www.chesterwood.org.

Before you leave Stockbridge, stop in at the *Berkshire Botanical Garden,* 2 miles west on Route 102. At the visitor center, you can get a self-guiding map to the gardens and greenhouses. Among the prettiest displays are a massive stand of daylilies in glowing pinks, yellows, and oranges; a primrose walk; a rose garden; and a small pond thickly growing with pond lilies and cattails. Also here are a diminutive herb garden, wildflowers, and many trees and shrubs. The gardens are a nice place to spend an afternoon or have a picnic. The center and gardens are open May through October from 10:00 A.M. to 5:00 P.M. Admission is $7.00 for adults, $5.00 for seniors and students, and free for children under twelve. (Greenhouses stay open year-round, and admission is free in winter.) Call (413) 298–3926.

If you keep going west on Route 102, you'll end up on the main street of *West Stockbridge,* a small village that is always less crowded than Stockbridge and is much more quaint. West Stockbridge still has its library and town clerk's office in a white house dating back to 1774. A cluster of crafts shops, art galleries, antiques stores, clothing boutiques, and restaurants lines both sides of the street, going back several blocks.

East of Stockbridge along Route 102 lies **Lee,** a town often bypassed by those on their way to Lenox or Stockbridge. An unusual bed-and-breakfast is to be found here out in the country. **Devonfield** is a Federal-era mansion that served in 1942 as the summer home of Queen Wilhelmina of the Netherlands and the Princess Beatrix, now queen. The inn's rolling green grounds encompass acres of lawn, a swimming pool, tennis courts, a flagstone terrace, stands of white birch, and views of the Berkshires. The house is spacious, elegant, and welcoming, retaining such touches as wide, oak-pegged floors, black iron hardware, and 2-inch-thick doors. A number of the very large rooms have gorgeously patterned wallpapers, working fireplaces, canopied four-

capitalrock!

Marble and limestone are common throughout this area and were quarried in several places. Especially fine building stone came from quarries in nearby Lee, which supplied the marble for the wings of the Capitol building in Washington, D.C., in 1861 and 1862. Stone for the City Hall in Philadelphia also came from this quarry. A nearby mill cut thousands of stones for veterans buried in Arlington National Cemetery.

posters, and window seats with views of the grounds. The living room and dining room are large enough for many guests to spread out without crowding each other. Breakfast is a three-course affair of fruits and juices, homemade muffins, and a cooked entree, perhaps blueberry pancakes. Although this is a beautifully appointed manor house, there is nothing stiff or formal in its atmosphere. After ten minutes you feel as though it is your own home. Winter packages make it a fine place to escape to. Rooms begin at $180, the penthouse and guesthouse at over $250 off-season. Reserve by calling (413) 243-3298 or (800) 664-0880.

Norman Rockwell fans should stop in at **Joe's Diner,** 85 Center Street, Lee; (413) 243-9756. They will recognize it at once as the scene of the endearing *Saturday Evening Post* cover "The Runaway." Joe Sorrentino is the friendly man behind the counter in the painting, and you can see a copy of it on the wall. You may also see him at the counter: Though he sold the diner a few years ago to retire, he can't bear to be away too long. It's hard to spend more than $5.00 for breakfast, and sandwiches run from $1.25, maxing out at less than $3.00 for a roast beef grinder. Each day brings its diner specials, most priced around $5.00. Look for roast beef on Monday, turkey or meatloaf on Tuesday, fresh roast pork on Wednesday, corned beef or kielbasa on Thursday, a long list of seafood on Friday, and baked ham on Saturday. Joe's opens at 5:30 A.M. and closes at 8:30 P.M. Monday through Friday and at 6:30 P.M. on Saturday; closed Sunday.

Main Street in Lee holds a number of eateries. If you like Mexican food—a rare find in these parts—head for the **Cactus Cafe** (413–243–4300), a convivial spot all done up in pink and green, with serapes and sombreros on the wall. Its wide windows look out on Main Street. Diners can order a full range of traditional choices: enchiladas, chiles rellenos, fajitas, guacamole, and an excellent flan for dessert.

Lovely **Lenox** was once a nucleus of millionaires' mansions, helping to win the Berkshires its nickname of "the Inland Newport." Novelist Edith Wharton had her home at The Mount, now open to the public and the setting for Shakespeare and Company productions of the bard's plays.

Today Lenox is a verdant place, still a favorite of the well-heeled. Fine shops and restaurants stand ready to serve them. Every summer, thousands throng the lawns of nearby Tanglewood to hear the Boston Symphony Orchestra.

Just outside Tanglewood, Hawthorne Street intersects with Lake Road, which winds along the **Stockbridge Bowl.** This large lake, ringed with forests and mountains, is so blue and beautiful that it will remind you of a Swiss lake.

At 92 Hawthorne Street in Lenox is the **Frelinghuysen-Morris House and Studio,** once the home and studios of Suzy Frelinghuysen and George L. K. Morris, leading abstract artists of the 1930s and 1940s. Their residence, opened as a museum in 1998, is a stunning creation of architect John Butler Swann in the Bauhaus style and contains the original furniture designed for the house, as well as murals by the owners. In addition to the art of Frelinghuysen and Morris, the collections include works by Picasso, Braque, Leger, and Gris. There are hourly guided tours late June through Labor Day, Thursday through Sunday 10:00 A.M. to 4:00 P.M., and September through Columbus Day, Thursday through Saturday. Admission is $10.00 per adult and $3.00 per child. From Route 183 south of Tanglewood, take Hawthorne Road and in less than a mile turn left onto Hawthorne Street; (413) 637–0166; www.frelinghuysen.org.

The most entertaining thing about the **Pleasant Valley Wildlife Sanctuary** has to be the beaver dams and

justalittleplace inthehills

To qualify as a "Berkshire Cottage," a summer home must have at least thirty rooms and be surrounded by more than twenty acres of estate lands. But that was the bare minimum. Shaddow Brook, the largest before it burned down in 1956, had a nice even one hundred rooms and sat on upwards of 700 acres. More than ninety summer estates qualified for the title, including Naumkeag, Chesterwood, The Mount, and Arrowhead, all open today as museums. When noted actress Fanny Kemble suggested a benefit for the village poor, she was told, "But we have no poor."

lodges you can see in two ponds. Besides nature's oldest engineers, the 7 miles of trails also show off uplands and meadows, a hemlock gorge, a hummingbird garden, and a limestone cobble. There are also a natural-history museum and lots of special programs, including bird and wildflower walks. The sanctuary is located at 472 West Mountain Road. To get there, follow US 7 and 20 north till you see the blue-and-white Audubon sign on the left, opposite the All Season Motor Inn; then turn left onto West Dugway Road and follow signs to West Mountain Road. Pleasant Valley is open from dawn to dusk Tuesday through Sunday. Admission is $4.00 for adults and $3.00 for children age three through twelve and for seniors. Museum hours are from 9:00 A.M. to 5:00 P.M. Tuesday through Friday, 10:00 A.M. to 4:00 P.M. weekends and Mondays in the summer. The grounds are open until dusk. Call (413) 637–0320.

Hawthorne's new friend Melville lived not far north from him in a quiet country home outside Pittsfield called **Arrowhead.** From his piazza, Melville had a wide-open view of Mount Greylock, which he thought resembled a great white whale; the view inspired him to write most of *Moby-Dick* here in 1850 and 1851. In the Chimney Room, parts of the chimney are inscribed with words from Melville's short story "I and My Chimney." Upstairs, you can see his study, with some of his quill pens and his spectacles still on the table.

Behind this eighteenth-century yellow farmhouse stand stately trees, along with a red barn, a place where Melville was fond of chatting with Hawthorne. Arrowhead is at 780 Holmes Road off US 7 just south of Pittsfield, clearly marked by signs. Tours begin on the hour from 11:00 A.M. to 3:00 P.M. (the museum closes at 4:00 P.M.), Friday through Wednesday from Memorial Day weekend to Columbus Day. Admission is $12.00 for adults, $5.00 for students over fifteen with ID, and $3.00 for children age six to fourteen. Call (413) 442–1793.

The **Hancock Shaker Village,** 5 miles west of Pittsfield, is a major tourist attraction and often crowded. Still, this is the best place to learn about the unique chapter in New England history written by the Shakers. This unusual sect, founded in 1774, earned the derisive name of Shakers because of members' active style of singing and dancing at worship.

The Shaker community at Hancock reached its height in the 1840s with about 250 members. Women served alongside men as eldresses and deacons, and everyone worked together at dairying, furnituremaking, handweaving, and basketry. They became famous for the high quality of their products, particularly the furniture and oval-shaped wooden boxes.

Twenty of their original brick and wooden buildings stand scattered about the green landscape. A stroll among them on a sparkling sunny day is pleasant and in distinct contrast to the severity of their lives. In the **Brick Dwelling,** where the brethren and sisters lived, rising was at 4:30 A.M., but breakfast was not until 7:00. The sexes sat separately at plain wooden tables and ate in silence.

At the heart of the village, the **Round Stone Barn** is a thing of beauty, topped with a white cupola, and yet is eminently practical: It allowed one man standing alone in it to milk fifty-four cows. Other buildings show the work of everyday life: the washhouse, the tannery, the icehouse, and the poultry house.

Most days, there's a program: Shaker hymn music, baking or boxmaking demonstrations, or spinning and weaving. Occasionally, Shaker-style candlelight dinners are served.

Hancock Shaker Village is open daily. Hours are from 9:30 A.M. to 5:00 P.M. Memorial Day weekend to October 31 and from 10:00 A.M. to 4:00 P.M. the rest of the year. Admission costs $15 in high season, $12 in low season, and is free for children. Call (413) 443–0188; www.hancockshakervillage.org.

Also in Hancock is *Jiminy Peak Resort,* a four-season facility best known for its downhill skiing in the winter. The mountain has a vertical drop of about 1,000 feet and has more than 93 percent snowmaking coverage, a boon in Massachusetts. There is also a high-speed, six-passenger lift and a surprising number of black-diamond trails. Lift tickets are about $55 for weekends—cheaper on weekdays—rental packages about $32. In the summer the resort is a good place to stay while vacationing in the Berkshires or attending Tanglewood concerts. Facilities include the resort's new Mountain Coaster (think warm-weather bobsled on tracks), a rock-climbing wall, an alpine slide, an outdoor pool, tennis courts, hot tubs, and saunas. Jiminy Peak is at 37 Corey Road, Hancock; (800) 882–8855 (reservations), (413) 738–5500; www.jiminypeak.com.

Right in the middle of downtown **Pittsfield,** at 39 South Street, is the **Berkshire Museum,** a community museum with significant exhibits in subjects from fine art to natural history. Particularly outstanding in the art category

Round Stone Barn, Hancock Shaker Village

are collections of Hudson River School paintings, American primitives, silver, and ancient art—enough to put the fine art galleries right up there with the best art museums in New England. Local history is another strong area, with early tools and Native American artifacts. An aquarium joins more than 3,000 minerals and fossils in the natural-sciences section. This part of the museum is especially interesting to children, with lots of hands-on exhibits. They are open Monday through Saturday from 10:00 A.M. to 5:00 P.M., and Sunday from noon to 5:00 P.M. Regular programs, lectures, and musical events fill the calendar; (413) 443–7171; www.berkshiremuseum.org.

The entire area is well known for its many performing arts venues, one of which is the *Berkshire Opera Company,* at 297 North Street; (413) 528–4420; www.berkop.org. Two major operas are produced on a full opera stage in July and August (through Labor Day weekend), and a concert evening is offered earlier in the spring.

Outside the handsome brick downtown of Pittsfield are the large mills of Crane and Company, papermakers for almost 200 years. Just past the mills, 5 miles east of Pittsfield off Route 9, there's a sign for the *Crane Paper Museum* in Dalton.

Crane is the only company that makes paper for the U.S. government to print money on, a contract it has held since 1879. Paul Revere was the company's first banknote engraver. The seventh generation of Cranes is at work in the mills. The company has made nothing but fine rag papers ever since the first mill was built in 1801. Because of its consistently high quality, Crane paper was traditionally used in the nineteenth century for official documents, deeds, titles, and financial instruments and came to be known as bond paper. Until 1845, the paper was entirely made by hand, a single sheet at a time.

The museum is in an ivy-covered stone building with stair-stepped gables, a former rag room. On view are historic currency samples, exhibits on papermaking, and many samples of letterheads and invitations. It's open from 1:00 to 5:00 P.M. Monday through Friday from June through mid-October. Admission is free; (413) 684–6481.

There's no good way to get to *Becket.* And that's how townspeople like it. (You can get there by taking Route 8 south from Dalton.) The town of Becket is about as hinterland as it gets in the central Berkshires. Bypassed entirely by the Massachusetts Turnpike, Becket has kept itself in its own little time warp, remaining rural and undeveloped. Its population numbers only 1,600. The few buildings that constitute downtown Becket huddle together for encouragement along a short stretch of Route 8. As an intriguing counterpoint, one of the most prestigious dance festivals in the world is held here—*Jacob's Pillow* (413–243–0745; www.jacobspillow.org).

If you're a connoisseur of general stores, you'll find the **Becket General Store** the most idiosyncratically genuine of the many to be found in the central and southern Berkshires. Local men and women line up at the small counter in the morning in a steady and constant stream. Some sit down to sip coffee and munch doughnuts; others buy newspapers. The shelves hem one in so narrowly that two people cannot pass each other without do-si-do-ing down the aisles. Cramming the shelves is a hodgepodge of merchandise that would do a nineteenth-century general store proud: fishing lures next to birthday candles; toys such as crayons and Wiffle balls; shampoo and cough syrup; kitchen gadgets; and, in a nod to modernity, rental videos. Cardboard boxes full of potatoes, peaches, tomatoes, and bananas are stacked on the floor.

From Becket, you can take the Pittsfield Road right off Route 8, which eventually brings you back out to US 7 and US 20.

Northern Berkshires

Heading north on Route 7, you'll pass **Pontoosuc Lake** on the left. This is a nice place to sailboard or canoe, and there are rental outlets along the shore. For a scenic detour, take Peck's Road, a left turn that loops almost completely around the lake.

Mighty **Mount Greylock,** at 3,491 feet, is the state's highest peak. From its summit, you can see five states and up to 100 miles. The 10,000-acre reservation is popular for camping, hiking, and cross-country skiing along its 45 miles of trails, or for just plain seeking tranquillity from its rugged heights. A highlight of a visit here is the **War Veterans Memorial Tower,** built in 1932 at the summit and originally designed as a lighthouse. The **Williams College Outing Club** publishes a trail guide that describes all the local hiking trails; you can get a copy from the Outing Club, 1004 Baxter Hall, Williams College, Williamstown 02167; send a check for $14 made out to Williams Outing Club. You also can purchase the guide at great savings in the outing club's equipment room, open during the school year Monday through Thursday noon to 1:00 P.M. and Friday noon to 2:00 P.M. (413) 597–2317.

You can drive up the south side of the mountain from Lanesboro, and down the north side in North Adams. From US 7 north of Lanesboro, you'll see the entrance road. A short distance in, a visitor center holds displays on natural history. The season opens at Mount Greylock when "mountain spring" arrives, usually in mid-May, and closes in October. Call (413) 743–1591 for information. Those who love informality will welcome a stay at **Bascom Lodge** at the summit, a rustic stone-and-wood building constructed by the Civilian Conservation Corps in the 1930s. Bascom Lodge is run by the Appalachian Mountain Club, which offers private and dormitory-style rooms, plus family-style breakfast and dinner. For information about the park and its campgrounds or Bascom Lodge, write to the Mt. Greylock Visitors Center, Rockwell Road, Lanesboro 01237, or call (413) 743–1591 or (413) 499–4263.

Near the Massachusetts-Vermont border, Route 7 joins the Mohawk Trail (Route 2), formerly a Mohawk Indian footpath and now a migration path for tourists seeking scenic fall foliage. When you reach the junction, you'll be in **Williamstown,** the site of the pretty **Williams College campus.** A drive along Main Street through the campus shows off its smooth green lawns and ivied brick buildings.

On the Williams campus, the **Williams College Museum of Art** has over 10,000 works. Its collection is especially strong in ancient and modern arts, and features New England's finest collection of ancient Abyssinian sculpture. Extraordinary exhibits created and first shown here tour art museums throughout the country. This admission-free museum is an often-overlooked highlight in the Berkshires art scene. Open Tuesday through Saturday from 10:00 A.M. to 5:00 P.M., Sunday 1:00 to 5:00 P.M.; (413) 597–2429.

The Orchards is an upscale inn, its large guest rooms decorated in attractive furnishings with a tailored air. Many rooms overlook the courtyard that the inn completely encircles, a space filled with a well-manicured garden around a stone-lined pool. The plants are chosen for their year-round appearance so that the garden remains colorful and attractive even after the leaves have fallen. Afternoon tea is served to hotel guests daily, and other genteel details—goosedown pillows, fresh flowers, and a library—set The Orchards apart. Rooms begin at $175 in winter, $235 in summer, but some excellent packages make them quite a good value. The Orchards is at 222 Adams Road (Route 2), Williamstown; (413) 458–9611 or (800) 225–1517; www.orchardshotel.com.

The dining room at The Orchards is **Yasmin's Restaurant,** among the finest in the state. The service is an indefinable blend of very correct and very personal; the staff is made up of students from a top Swiss hotel school, so they are professionals working at their chosen career. The menu is creative and filled with interesting options as well as carefully prepared renditions of the classics. The rack of lamb is outstanding, cooked exactly as you request it. Not only is the wine selection one of the best in the east, but the cellar in which it is stored has been custom-designed and custom-crafted. If you are a wine aficionado and a guest at the inn, ask if the accommodating owner has a minute to take you on a tour to see the outstanding stonework and the fine wood-carving that cradles his collection of rare vintages.

Also on the edge of town, on US 7, is a lodging of an entirely different character. **Riverbend Farm** was owned by a friend of Ethan Allen's, before the Revolution, and Allen stayed there often. Fortunately for us, the house has been restored to as close to its colonial interior as possible, so guests can enjoy the historic atmosphere (although in a lot more peaceful surroundings than the house would have offered when rowdy Ethan and his friends were in town). Guests are invited to use the antiques and to sink into the wing chairs. Rooms characterized by fine paneling, homespun coverlets, braided rugs, and antique furnishings are around $120 and include a breakfast of homemade granola and breads, with honey from the innkeepers' hives. The inn is open mid-April through October. Write to Riverbend Farm at 643 Simonds Road (Route 7N), Williamstown 01267; (413) 458–3121.

A unique and welcoming place to stay outside of town is at the *Field Farm,* a Bauhaus-inspired house in the middle of 300 acres of valley wildland owned by the Trustees of Reservations, which also operates the B&B. Rooms are large and modern, with modernist furnishings of museum-quality. Some are private and others operate on a shared-lodging basis, designed for small groups or families. Two of the guest rooms have working fireplaces, and the building is wheelchair-accessible. The setting is idyllic, with gardens and birds and no other buildings in sight. The farm sponsors occasional weekend nature programs; 554 Sloan Road, Williamstown; (413) 458–3135.

At the *Western Gateway Heritage State Park* (413–663–6312) in *North Adams,* the railroad history of North Adams comes alive in a thoroughly entertaining way. Housed in six old wooden railroad buildings, the park also includes a cluster of shops and restaurants, linked by a cobblestoned courtyard and black iron streetlamps.

The visitor center tells the story of the building of the 4¾-mile Hoosac Tunnel through 2,500-foot-high Mount Hoosac—one of the greatest engineering feats of the nineteenth century. The project claimed the lives of almost 200 men and took twenty-four years to build. The ring of pickaxes, the shouts of men, and the dripping of water can be heard inside an old boxcar through an imaginative audiovisual presentation. Here in the eerie darkness, you experience the same working conditions the tunnelers did. The tunnel made North Adams "the western gateway" to commercial travel from the East, a long-sought goal. North Adams also became an important railroad town. Children can ride a miniature train around the freight yard in good weather.

The park is well marked by signs off Route 8. It's open daily from 10:00 A.M. to 5:00 P.M.

In a spot in North Adams, glacial melt rushing over limestone deposits carved out a deep chasm and left an arch above it—the only "natural bridge" of marble in North America. Now the centerpiece of a state park, the *Natural Bridge* is visible from a walkway high and narrow like a catwalk that lets you peer over and around the Natural Bridge from almost any angle. Chain-link fence ruins the photo opportunity; on the other hand, it keeps people from falling in and killing themselves. Despite the mighty forces that shaped it, the Natural Bridge itself is quite small—a span of some 20 feet—and so dark inside that it looks cavelike. Still, something about it mesmerizes. A few picnic tables spread about a grassy area in earshot of the water are a nice spot to lunch.

The park is open from 9:00 A.M. to 5:00 P.M. daily from Memorial Day to Columbus Day, and from 10:00 A.M. until 8:00 P.M. on weekends and holidays from May 15 to October 30. Call (413) 663–6392 or (413) 663–8469 off-season for information. There's an admission charge of $2.00 per car.

Just east of North Adams, a few miles past the junction of Route 8, Route 2 takes a giant bend, almost 180 degrees. The loop-the-loop in the road practically derails buses and gives cars plenty of pause. It's called the *Hairpin Turn,* and it's an inspiring place to stop. It just happens to be situated at one of the most fabulous vantage points for viewing the Hoosac Valley. You're up so high here that it looks as though you could hang glide right down into the valley. Few houses mar the pretty bowl of greenery below, and the blue sky and clouds reach up in front of you forever. In the elbow of the turn, there's a small parking lot with observation telescopes set up for a closer look, behind which are a nondescript restaurant and souvenir stand.

As you come back down Route 8 into the center of *Adams,* just past the McKinley Statue on Park Street you'll see the *Miss Adams Diner* on the left. This is an original diner built in 1949 by the Worcester Lunch Car Company that has been nicely restored, with a green-and-white tiled floor, plenty of chrome, and the original Worcester Diner clock. The diner offers blue plate specials, vegetarian burgers, and eggs Benedict, among other items. Call (413) 743–5303.

As a last stop in the northern Berkshires, an unusual political footnote awaits you in the town of *Cheshire.* A local pastor decided that a nice gift for President Jefferson would be a cheese made by Cheshire farmers. A big one. Molding it in a cider press, the farmers made a 1,235-pound cheese—one day's production of the town's dairies. The cheese was drawn by oxen to Albany and was then shipped by water to Washington, D.C., where, on January 1, 1802, it was presented to the third president amid great fanfare.

In commemoration of this moment of glory, the *Cheshire Cheese Press Monument* stands on a corner, a concrete replica of the cider press used to make the cheese. To get there, head south on Route 8 and turn left onto Church Street at the First Baptist Church. The monument is at Church and School Streets, just opposite the Cheshire Post Office. Slow down or you'll miss it; it's not very big, and it could be partly hidden by children climbing on it.

More Places to Stay in the Berkshires

Red Bird Inn,
Route 57,
New Marlborough;
(413) 229–2349.
A moderately priced bed-and-breakfast in an old stagecoach inn amid beautiful gardens.

Bow Wow Road Inn,
570 Bow Wow Road,
Sheffield;
(413) 229–3339.
A well-appointed four-room inn with rooms from $110 to $150.

More Places to Eat in the Berkshires

Church Street Cafe,
65 Church Street,
Lenox;
(413) 637–2745.
Healthy food needn't be dull, and it isn't at this "New American" stronghold where couscous and Japanese dishes share the menu.

La Bruschetta,
1 Harris Street,
West Stockbridge;
(413) 232–7141.
Picnics packed to travel, pizza, breads, and wines.

Hobson's Choice,
159 Water Street,
Williamstown;
(413) 458–9101.
Casual, with a long menu that includes several vegetarian entrees, and a good beer list. Salad bar is included with entrees.Dinner only.

Theresa's Stockbridge Cafe,
40 Main Street (back),
Stockbridge;
(413) 298–3915.
Nice design-your-own deli sandwiches, generous chef salads, quiche, in a bright cafe with a terrace. The apple pie is really homemade.

WORTH SEEING IN THE BERKSHIRES

Sterling and Francine Clark Art Institute,
225 South Street,
Williamstown;
(413) 458–2303;
Free off-season; Memorial Day weekend through October, admission is $10 for adults, free for students with ID or under eighteen.

The Mount,
Home of Edith Wharton,
US 7 at Plunkett Street,
Lenox;
(413) 637–1899

Mission House,
Main Street,
Stockbridge;
(413) 298–3239;
A 1739 home with gardens.

Tanglewood,
West Street/Route 183,
Lenox;
(413) 637–1600;
www.tanglewood.org

TO LEARN MORE ABOUT THE BERKSHIRES

Berkshire Visitors Bureau,
Berkshire Common,
Pittsfield 01201;
(413) 443–9186 or (800) 237–5747;
www.berkshires.org
Skiers should ask for the annual "Massachusetts Ski Guide" by calling
(800) 227–MASS (800–227–6277).

Indexes

Entries for Museums, Parks and Green Spaces, and Restaurants appear in the special indexes beginning on page 226.

GENERAL INDEX

PARKS AND GREEN SPACES

RESTAURANTS

About the Authors

After four years of college in Boston and Cambridge, respectively, Barbara and Stillman Rogers remained in the Boston area for several years and now live just over the line in the border town of Richmond, New Hampshire. They write about all of New England for magazines and in their newspaper and Web site travel columns, and they are authors of *New Hampshire Off the Beaten Path, The Rhode Island Guide, Secret Providence and Newport, Natural Wonders of Vermont, Vermont Off the Beaten Path,* and many other travel books. In this book, they have been joined by their daughter Juliette Rogers, a resident of Salem, who contributes her expert knowledge of the Boston restaurant scene and the North Shore. Juliette and Barbara have recently collaborated on *Eating New England,* a sourcebook of the best food in Massachusetts and the region.

Many of the descriptions of places in the book remain as written by its original author, Pat Mandell. Her words and observations on many of the state's attractions are as true today as they were when she visited them for the book's first edition. The Rogerses have revisited these and discovered many more of the state's hidden corners to update and add new attractions to this seventh edition.